Problems of Preschool Children

Problems of Preschool Children

Edited by

NAOMI RICHMAN

*Reader in Child Psychiatry, Institute of Child Health,
London. Honorary Child Psychiatrist,
The Hospital for Sick Children,
Great Ormond Street, London*

and

RICHARD LANSDOWN

*Chief Psychologist, The Hospital for Sick Children,
Great Ormond Street, London*

JOHN WILEY & SONS
Chichester · New York · Brisbane · Toronto · Singapore

Copyright © 1988 by John Wiley & Sons Ltd

Library of Congress Cataloging-in-Publication Data:

Problems of preschool children / edited by Naomi Richman and Richard
    Lansdown.
        p.   cm.
    Includes bibliographies and index.
    ISBN 0 471 91460 6 : ISBN 0 471 91932 2 (pbk.) :
    1. Preschool children.   2. Problem children.   3. Child development.
    I. Richman, N. (Naomi)   II. Lansdown, Richard.
    HQ774.5.P76   1988
    305.2′33—dc19
                                                                            87–36538
                                                                            CIP

British Library Cataloguing in Publication Data:

Richman, Naomi
    Problems of preschool children.
    1. Preschool children. Psychological problems
    I. Title   II. Lansdown, Richard
    155.4′23

    ISBN 0 471 91460 6
    ISBN 0 471 91932 2 Pbk.

Typeset by Inforum Ltd, Portsmouth.
Printed and bound in Great Britain by Biddles Ltd, Guildford.

Contents

List of Contributors

Arnon Bentovim Consultant Psychiatrist, The Hospital for Sick Children, Great Ormond Street, London.

Kathryn Bieber Psychiatric Social Worker, The Hospital for Sick Children, Great Ormond Street, London.

Helen Dawe Project Worker, National Children's Home, Harrogate. Formerly: Teacher, Department of Psychological Medicine, Day Centre, The Hospital for Sick Children, Great Ormond Street, London.

Jo Douglas Principal Clinical Psychologist, The Hospital for Sick Children, Great Ormond Street, London.

Philip Graham Professor of Child Psychiatry, Institute of Child Health, University of London.

Jennifer Jenkins Lecturer in Psychology, University of Stirling, Senior Clinical Psychologist, Forth Valley Health Authority. Formerly: Senior Clinical Psychologist, The Hospital for Sick Children, Great Ormond Street, London.

Richard Lansdown Chief Psychologist, The Hospital for Sick Children, Great Ormond Street, London.

Jacqueline McGuire Lecturer in Psychology, North East London Polytechnic. Formerly: Research Psychologist, Institute of Child Health, University of London.

Peter Milla Senior Lecturer in Child Health, Institute of Child Health, University of London. Honorary Consultant Paediatric Gastroenterologist, The Hospital for Sick Children, Great Ormond Street, London.

Naomi Richman Reader in Child Psychiatry, Institute of Child Health, London. Honorary Child Psychiatrist, The Hospital for Sick Children, Great Ormond Street, London.

Margot Taylor A Solicitor.

Marianne Tranter Psychiatric Social Worker, The Hospital for Sick Children, Great Ormond Street, London.

Marion Woodard Chief Speech Therapist, The Hospital for Sick Children, Great Ormond Street, London.

Introduction

NAOMI RICHMAN AND RICHARD LANSDOWN

This book is about problems of behaviour and development in preschool children. In a typical group of children at least 20 per cent are likely to have the kinds of problems described here; in some settings the number may be as high as 40 per cent.

Our aim is to link current knowledge about child behaviour and development with practical applications in day-to-day work.

No previous knowledge of child psychology is assumed. Where possible, case histories are used to illustrate the main points and in every example identifying details, such as sex or age, have been altered to preserve confidentiality.

There are two underlying themes to the book. One is that of adaptability and change. Families change over time in response to life experiences and the growth of family members. Early childhood in particular is a time of rapid development. This capacity for change makes it difficult to predict the future for most children because we cannot foretell the course of their development or the diverse family and community influences they will experience.

A further point is that in order to help children we must respond to their present stage of emotional and intellectual development, but also be aware of their potential for change.

The second theme is that of the interaction between a child and the environment. Children both influence their family and are influenced by it in turn. There is rarely a single cause of a child's problems, usually multiple influences are at work and throughout the book there is an emphasis on both family and social factors and how these relate to children's behaviour and development. It follows that a wide variety of interventions can help children. Often a combination of social, educational and therapeutic measures will be useful involving co-operation between several disciplines.

In keeping with this multidisciplinary approach the contributors are drawn from a variety of backgrounds. They are almost all members, past or present, of the Department of Psychological Medicine at the Hospital for Sick

Children, Great Ormond Street, where we have found this team approach is most useful in understanding and helping young children and their families.

The first two chapters on family and social influences provide a general introduction about the context in which children develop. Chapter 3, on early relationships, illustrates the interaction between the family and social context and the child's individuality in normal development and in the development of difficulties. The importance of the child's individual characteristics is further discussed in Chapter 4 on the brain and behaviour.

Chapters 5, 6 and 7 on language, clumsiness and learning focus on the development of specific abilities and emphasize that help for children with developmental delays must look both at children's capacities and the setting in which they are growing up.

Chapter 8 stands on its own to some extent. Child abuse is a topic that has received much attention recently; this chapter contains an up-to-date account of our knowledge of the subject.

There then follows an overview on assessment which looks at types of problems in young children and factors affecting how they cope with the various challenges and stresses of life. Various possibilities for help are discussed including social support, individual work with children, play therapy, family and marital work, and behavioural management. This last, one of the most valuable types of intervention for families with young children, is described in more detail in Chapter 10. The behavioural approach deserves a chapter to itself because the methods are being increasingly used in the primary health care setting and seem to be widely applicable to common behaviour problems.

This is not to say that behavioural methods are always successful or are appropriate for all problems. The topics of feeding problems and child abuse are evidence that for some children and families problems are complex and require very detailed assessment and a complex treatment approach.

Finally we return to issues which are of general interest when considering young children. Firstly there is a discussion on differences between boys and girls and how these could be explained. Here again it is necessary to consider children's individual characteristics as well as the way family and social attitudes to boys and girls might affect their behaviour. Boys show more defiance and aggression than girls and these problems tend to persist; they also have more learning difficulties.

Issues are raised related to the care of young children outside the home. Chapter 13 looks at the differences between various types of alternative care and their possible benefits and disadvantages both intellectually and emotionally.

Chapter 14 on play links with previous sections. The links between play and emotional and intellectual development, and with social learning are described.

Lastly there is a chapter on the law and young children. We are aware that legislation and judicial procedures are changing rapidly specific to a particular time and place. Nevertheless those working with young children are increasingly involved with issues related to child-care law, children's and parents' rights and disputes over parental custody and access, and it seemed essential to provide an overview of this area.

There is a list of further reading at the end of each chapter which will provide an entry into the literature for those who want to explore any topics in more depth.

We are grateful to our colleagues at the Hospital for Sick Children and the Institute of Child Health for agreeing to contribute to this book and for then completing their chapters so close to the deadlines we set.

Jackie Moore's help in typing, over and over again, was invaluable.

Problems of Preschool Children
Edited by N. Richman and R. Lansdown
© 1988 John Wiley & Sons Ltd

CHAPTER 1

The Family

NAOMI RICHMAN

INTRODUCTION

This chapter looks at how families function and how children are influenced by their families. By no means all families consist of a mother and father and one or more children. However for the sake of clarity, this chapter will deal mainly with the two-parent family.

In their earliest years young children's experience of the world is mediated almost entirely through the family, although as they get older wider social contacts gradually become more important. Through the family a child first learns about the physical world, about relationships and about social life. The way the family functions therefore has profound effects on development. Where there is quarrelling or strained relationships, neglect or lack of affection there is increased risk that the child will develop behavioural or learning difficulties.

Where there is affection and stimulation the child has more chance of optimal development. This is not to say that children are passive recipients, completely and predictably moulded by their life experiences. Children also influence the way their parents behave to them and each responds in an individual way to experience.

Nor does the influence of the family early in life completely determine a child's future. As discussed in Chapter 3, the effects of early difficulties may be overcome by later good experience and vice versa.

STAGES OF THE FAMILY

When thinking about a particular family it is helpful to consider the point in life they have reached and the challenges they may be facing. Families pass through various stages: a couple marry, have children; these grow up and leave home, and so on. Here we are concentrating on the time between birth and the next few years, before the children start school.

PREGNANCY

The family begins long before a child is born, with the relationship between the parents. For some couples pregnancy arises from a secure relationship, at the other extreme it can be an attempt to improve a poor relationship. For some young women pregnancy is an excuse to get away from home or a hope of finding some affection, at least from the baby.

Most parents will have some doubts and anxieties during pregnancy. 'Will the baby be all right?' 'Will I be able to cope?' 'How will it affect my life?' Pregnancy brings some couples even closer, but in others new tensions arise. Sexual feelings change during pregnancy and one or other partner may lose interest; perhaps the father feels pushed out by the coming baby, and resents the fact that the comfortable twosome will soon disappear.

Depression in the mother during pregnancy is not uncommon, occurring in about 16 out of 100 women. One study found that women who had a previous abortion were more likely to be depressed in pregnancy, perhaps because in some women guilt or regret about their past experiences are reawakened. Indeed sorrow about any previous bereavement may arise in pregnancy perhaps related to fear that this new baby may not survive.

AFTER THE BIRTH

The first weeks after the birth can be a stressful period for the family especially if the baby is in a Special Care Baby Unit, has a congenital deformity, developmental difficulties or other physical problems. Restless, irritable babies who are difficult to soothe and cry a lot can also be very trying.

Transient feelings of depression occur in many women in the first week or two postpartum, and about 10–20 per cent have more severe symptoms of depression which may last for one to two years. One per cent of births are followed by a severe mental illness (post-puerperal psychosis). The mother is often exhausted and depressed, especially if her partner is unsupportive or social conditions are poor. Pain following an episeotomy, worry over the baby and sleepless nights add to the strain. For some women, giving up work and economic independence are sources of further tension. Lack of the woman's earnings can have a marked effect on the whole family's way of life.

During these months parents have to make big adaptations in their lives in order to accommodate to the baby, and either parent may find it difficult to respond. Fathers particularly may not feel competent to do much with a young baby, and a pattern may emerge where they continue their carefree existence leaving the mother at home with the baby.

Grandparents are generally the major sources of practical and emotional help to new parents. But they can be unsympathetic or unsupportive. At the other extreme, some grandparents become over-involved in their grand-children, taking over most of the care and undermining the parents' confidence and independence. This is especially likely to happen with young parents and single mothers. Sadness about the loss of a grandparent may emerge when a baby is born, parents wishing that their parent could have seen the grandchild.

ADAPTING TO THE TODDLER AND PRESCHOOL CHILD

From the second year onwards parents face new challenges as their child develops mobility, language and increasing independence. At this stage, though, fathers may feel more comfortable with the child and become more involved.

Parents have to protect children from danger (accidents are the most common form of death in this age group), help them to learn family rules of behaviour, encourage their exploration of the world and of relationships. Difficulties arise if the child's growing competence is squashed or if no attempts are made to guide behaviour along social channels. Unrealistic demands to grow up and be extra competent easily lead to confrontation, for example over potty training or feeding, or to withdrawal and passivity in the child.

Toddlers want to try things out for themselves, and often will not accept help, and then become frustrated if they cannot manage. It is easy to become frustrated with their 'obstinacy'.

All too quickly children move into a separate world of nursery, with friends and experiences outside the family. This increasing separation is often more difficulty for the parent than for the child to manage; it means accepting the child as being no longer totally dependent on the parents.

FACTORS AFFECTING PARENTING

CURRENT STRESS

Many factors influence how parents manage these stages of family develop-ment. Social conditions are of major importance as discussed in Chapter 2. Poor housing, overcrowding, lack of money, ill-health, all cause great strain and are associated with maternal depression and marital tension.

THE PARENTS' RELATIONSHIP

When parents get on well they are usually positive in their interactions with the baby; when they quarrel or are unsupportive to each other the child is much more likely to show behaviour problems.

Many couples do not get on so well after the first baby is born. In part this is probably related to an increase in stress, for instance there is often less money because the mother has stopped working. In part it can be a failure to accommodate to a changed life, and to a lack of planning and discussion about the parents' new situation.

PREVIOUS EXPERIENCE

It is often said that parents repeat with their own children the way they were brought up themselves. This is particularly so with aggressive behaviour. There is a high likelihood that parents who were treated harshly in childhood will similarly inflict a harsh upbringing on their own children. Parents who had a cold or rejecting family have more difficulty themselves in expressing warmth.

For example, women coming from disrupted homes who in childhood were fostered or in a children's home have more difficulties with their young children than other women in comparable situations. They are less sensitive to their children's needs and have more difficulty in controlling them. However, it is important to note that many women who had early disruptions do not have parenting problems. It seems that later good experiences, especially having a supportive partner, can compensate for the early disadvantage.

FAMILY OF ORIGIN

The parents' own family or 'family of origin' continues to influence parents throughout life.

> Mr Sims was an only child who had been very indulged by his parents and not encouraged to take responsibility. Mrs Sims came from a large family where life had been tough and expressions of emotion not encouraged. The responsibility for bringing up the children was left to her, which she did very efficiently although in a cool manner. Mr Sims was warmer to the children but felt rejected by his wife who grew increasingly angry with him for not helping. In the end he returned to live with his own parents.

Sometimes feelings about their own brothers or sisters affect parents' behaviour to their children. Children may be particularly protected because they are a reminder of a dead sibling, or excessively criticized because they remind the parents of a more favoured sibling of whom they were jealous.

PARENTAL HEALTH

Mental distress or illness in parents is associated with emotional or behavioural difficulties in children. This is especially so if the children are young, or if the

parents' symptoms involve the child, for example if they are aggressive or
hostile towards the child.

Alcoholism, often leading to violence and neglect, can produce a chaotic and
uncertain life for young children. Drug addiction in parents similarly has
disastrous effects on many young children's lives.

An important research finding concerns the situation when one parent has a
mental illness or a poor relationship with a child. If the other parent (or another
adult) has a good relationship, this acts as a protection and the child is less likely
to suffer.

Much attention has been focused on the effects of depression and anxiety in
women, because it is so common, especially if they have a child under six and if
they also have other severe stresses in their lives and lack a supportive partner.
Rates of depression range from 30–40 per cent in women in these situations.

Depressed women are less effective in their discipline of young children;
they also involve their children less in extended conversations, and are less
responsive to them. Children of depressed women are more likely to have
accidents, perhaps reflecting a lack of supervision and awareness of their
activities.

Most of these depressions are mild, and a reaction to the strains of bringing
up young children. Generally they do not require drug treatment and it is more
useful to focus help on the family and social context which gives rise to
depression. Marital counselling, family work, or social support are possible
sources of help.

A MODEL OF FAMILY FUNCTIONING

All family members influence each other and are in turn influenced by the
outside world and by their own experiences. In trying to understand a family it
can be helpful to use a model like the one shown in Figure 1.1. This model
shows some of the interactions which influence families.

When considering how to help a child who presents with difficulties it is
essential to consider family interactions. One example is parents who them-

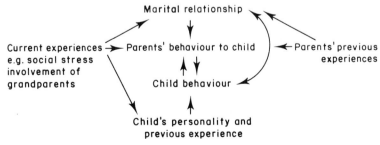

Figure 1.1   A model of family functioning.

selves were harshly treated as children, who are unable to give each other emotional support and find themselves repeating the pattern of severe punishment with their own children (see Chapter 8).

Often the current behaviour of grandparents plays a crucial role in family life.

One two-year-old with a severe eating problem and failure to thrive spent most of his time with the maternal grandmother. She was very controlling and fussed excessively at mealtimes and in fact prevented the child from eating lunch. The parents were afraid to tackle the grandmother about this because she had poor health and there was anxiety that she would break down if not allowed her own way.

Difficulties in particular areas of child rearing are often related not only to the parent's own childhood but also to their current relationship; it is common to find marital problems and childhood behaviour problems occurring together.

The capacity to exert control, take appropriate responsibility, communicate openly and express warmth to children are frequently affected in these cases and are a focus of treatment in therapy. The growing use of family therapy reflects the current belief that family interactions are extremely important in the genesis of childhood difficulties.

EXPRESSIONS OF POSITIVE FEELINGS AND WARMTH

Children need love and affection. They need to feel valued and wanted, to know that someone is interested in what they do and say, be encouraged to try new experiences and face challenges. Lack of parental warmth and constant criticism lead easily to childhood disturbance. When parents see nothing positive in their children and view everything they do in a negative light the children in turn develop a negative view of themselves and become apathetic and withdrawn or attention seeking and disobedient. A vicious cycle can start up: this difficult behaviour reinforces the parents' negative view and lack of warmth. Conversely parents who enjoy their children's company and praise their achievements, who do not criticize excessively, are more likely to have a confident, happy child.

SETTING LIMITS

Some parents are uncertain about how much they should control their child, worrying that discipline will make the child feel unloved. In practice this approach can leave children themselves anxious and uncertain. They continually test out how far they can go and usually seem relieved if parents begin to exert some control and do not place responsibilities on them which they are too young to cope with. Clear rules and routine help children feel secure that their own frightening impulses and fantasies will not overwhelm them.

Inconsistent or inappropriate control leads to confusion and exacerbates behaviour difficulties. When children are aggressive and disobedient it is often found that the whole family uses aggressive or coercive methods like shouting, teasing, or hitting to get each other to do what they want, or when they are angry. There is no attempt to be conciliatory or reach a compromise about difficulties. Often children continue their negative behaviour until the parent gives in, thus reinforcing the pattern which will be repeated at the next flare-up.

> Martin whines, screams and shouts because he wants to go out. His mother wants him to stay in because he has a cold. She also shouts at him and hits him, but when her patience gives out she lets him have his way.

Chapter 10 considers control issues in more detail.

DECISION MAKING

Some families are always in a state of crisis because they cannot come to any decisions about running their lives, even about simple matters like decorating the house, getting up in the morning, going out at the weekend. In some families this chaos reflects parents' unwillingness to take adult responsibility, anger with their own parents' strict discipline or a marital problem which they deflect on to arguments about organization.

> The Woods had three very lively boys aged 6, 5 and 3. There was no routine about mealtimes or bedtimes as both parents believed that children should have freedom to develop their personalities, and both resented their own parents' rigidity and conventionality. Neither parent wanted to impose a routine on the children. The result was three boys running wild and parents who ended each day exhausted and dispirited, often wishing they had never had any children in the first place.

COMMUNICATION

It is common for adults to think that children do not understand what is going on in the family, so nothing is said to them about important events like death, illness or adoption. This problem in communication is particularly keen in the case of children with severe health problems. It is very painful for parents to discuss what is wrong with their young child and again and again they will insist that the illness, handicap or unusual appearance does not worry the child. Without explanation the child's disorted understanding could be much worse than reality.

> One couple had reluctantly produced a 'life story book' (see Chapter 9) for their two adopted siblings. This book soon got 'lost' in the house. The parents denied that the 4- and 5-year-old needed to discuss in any way their traumatic early experiences.

There can, on the other hand, be excessive communication within a family, thus burdening children with problems inappropriately, for example they may think that they are to blame for their parents' ill-health.

At the right level discussing emotions of pleasure and pain helps children both to understand emotional states and how to cope with them. For instance, mothers who talk to an older brother or sister about the feelings and intentions of a newborn baby can help to promote positive feelings.

FAMILY ROLES

When children are young parents need to care for them and help them learn self-control. Sometimes these roles are reversed even with young children. The child will try to comfort and look after a depressed mother and the younger siblings. In some families decisions are left to the child quite inappropriately, about what to eat or wear for instance, or what it is safe to do.

> Billy, aged four years, used to wake early in the morning and go into the kitchen where he raided the fridge, or into the living room where he sometimes lit fires. His single mother would not take proper responsibility for his protection because she resented having the sole care of a young child.

Another distortion of family roles occurs when parents confide in children and treat them like an adult friend; this is likely to happen with a single parent or when parents do not get on together. In the latter case one child may become an ally of the father and one of the mother.

In all these cases too much responsibility is placed on the child who may react with anxiety or become controlling and manipulative of the parents.

Children find different roles in the family depending on their personality and the particular family.

> Colin was the family clown, always joking, rushing around and attracting attention. He seemed to keep the family going, providing the vitality lacking in his anxious father, and shy mother and brother.

It is common for parents to see one child as the 'bad one' of the family with all annoyance and criticism vented on to him or her, while similar misdeeds by brothers and sisters are passed over.

DEGREE OF INVOLVEMENT

In some families the degree of involvement between family members is excessive. Parents do not allow the children to speak for themselves, and it becomes impossible to separate out what each is really thinking or feeling. The children are not allowed to have their own thoughts but 'have' to do, feel and think exactly as the parents do. If they try to be independent the parents become anxious and angry.

Over-involvement also arises when a parent becomes preoccupied with the needs of a handicapped or chronically ill child, limiting the child's independence even further. Some children accept this situation passively, others react with exaggerated physical symptoms or difficult behaviours. In other cases parents become detached from an ill child, unable to respond to their needs or sympathize with them, as though it is too painful to be involved with a child who might die, or will never be normal.

DEALING WITH THE OUTSIDE WORLD

Families who are over-involved with each other may have difficulties in dealing with people outside the family. Suspicions or lack of confidence stop them making friends or seeking help from others. Thus when crises arise they have fewer resources for dealing with them.

Parents who abuse their children are particularly likely to be isolated and cut off from normal social contact. They then miss out on opportunities for learning about normal parenting and normal child behaviour through mixing with other families. Parents who have been in care or had unsatisfactory dealings with those in authority, for example, with schools, social services or the courts, are likely to view offers of help with suspicion. They may fear that any 'official' person is secretly planning to take their child away.

A HANDICAPPED OR ILL CHILD IN THE FAMILY

Some studies have suggested that rates of divorce increase in families who have a child with a severe mental or physical handicap, but other studies do not agree with this. Probably those families not coping well are balanced out by those who are. In many families the pressure of a handicapped child produces a sense of purpose and cohesion with positive effects. However, other children may suffer because of the demands made by the handicapped child. Parents may also expect more of the normal children, especially, it seems, from older girls who are expected to help out and be 'little mothers'. The frustration and worry about a handicapped child may become focused on other children rather than on the child with the handicap.

One mother was very distressed by the anger she felt towards her four-year-old daughter whom she found awkward and demanding. After talking things over she realized that her demands were too high; this little girl was expected to be extra good because her brother of seven, a severely retarded boy, required so much care.

Young children also need help in understanding and accepting the handicaps of their brother or sister. They may feel overlooked or not want friends to come round to play because the handicapped child is difficult or looks different.

Patterns of response to illness or handicap vary widely between families, ranging from parental over-involvement with the child to extreme detachment.

> Nat was a very overweight four-year-old with severe asthma. If he was thwarted in any way he had an extraordinarily severe temper tantrum. In the past he had held his breath occasionally during a temper. The parents were afraid to thwart him because they thought he might die in a temper. They took him everywhere in a pushchair and let him eat whatever he wanted.

At the other extreme parents may deny that a serious problem exists at all. They will not, for example, stick to a diet for a diabetic child or properly supervise a child with a bleeding disorder, almost as though by ignoring the problem it would go away. In extreme cases this behaviour becomes a type of child abuse (see Chapter 8). Parental responses to the birth of a handicapped child are discussed in Chapter 3.

DIVORCED AND RECONSTITUTED FAMILIES

Children from divorced families have higher rates of emotional and behavioural difficulties. This is related to many factors. First, the divorce is usually preceded by long periods of discord and unhappiness. Second, the single parent now looking after the child(ren), usually the mother, has to face considerable strain with perhaps difficulties over housing, money, work and child care. Third, family relationships may continue to be problematic. Relationships between divorced or separated parents are rarely amicable and the child may be the witness of continuous rows, or be the recipient of complaints from the parents about each other. Arguments over access are common; the father visits erratically, or wants more access than his wife wants. Access is a good weapon for parents to use against each other and a mother will complain that her child is too upset by the father's visits for these to continue. It usually helps the children to cope if they can keep in touch with both parents but often this proves difficult. Commonly fathers feel pushed out, and have nowhere to take the child when they visit. When the parent looking after the child is utterly opposed to the other parent and their visiting, it becomes very difficult for a young child not to take sides and turn against the parent. In this situation access will almost certainly break down.

> Mr and Mrs Norman had separated and were getting divorced. The wife was extremely bitter about her husband and could see no good in him. She criticized him frequently in front of their four-year-old daughter. This girl had enjoyed seeing her father but became increasingly reluctant to do so. Finally if he did visit she cried and screamed, and when seen on her own she said definitely that she no longer wanted to see him, although unable to give a reason.

Hopefully the development of conciliation services run by courts or from social service departments will help parents sort out their differences in a way which reduces bitterness and allows continuing contact with both parents.

Sometimes access is not in the best interest of the child. If there has been child abuse by one parent or one parent is very violent or behaves inappropriately towards the child access may be denied as in the following case.

The father had tried to keep both mother and three-year-old child virtual prisoners at home. He had not allowed the child to develop any independence, e.g. with potty training or self feeding and threatened the mother if she tried to live more normally.

A variety of responses to parental divorce have been described. These include misery and withdrawal or disobedience and tempers. Marked anxiety about the remaining parent going off, with fears about separation, nightmares, and sleeping and eating difficulties can appear. Boys remaining with their mothers are the most likely to present difficulties in management.

Children employ various devices to cope with the separation. Some deny that it has happened and insist that the absent parent is going to return or has not really gone. Some blame themselves and their bad behaviour for the break-up, or they invoke some unrelated external event like a parent's change of job. Great anger may be expressed, often to the remaining parent who is blamed for 'driving out' the father or mother. The absent parent may be missed a great deal and even if they are not talked about the child may be preoccupied with their whereabouts and fate.

Children vary in their capacity to cope. Young children are unlikely to discuss their worries unless encouraged to do so, and in fact may try to protect their parents by not raising awkward questions or anxieties. It helps all children to keep in contact with both parents, and to ensure that the contact with the non-custodial parent is regular and not associated with awkward arrangements or rows. Joint custody can work successfully but is not sought by many parents.

A secretive approach about separation adds to the child's anxiety and sense of responsibility about the break-up. Discussions appropriate to the child's understanding about what has happened and plans for the future help them to come to terms with the situation. Explanations are best if they avoid blaming either parents or children.

Further complications arise if new families are formed when people who already have children marry again. Children who have already been through the distressing experience of the break up of one family are then faced with a new one, which means new brothers or sisters as well as a new parent. As with all family interactions there is no certainty that children in these reconstituted families will be disturbed but the possibility must be considered. Once again, so much depends on how everything is handled.

FURTHER READING

P. Barker (1986) *Basic Family Therapy*. London: Collins.

G. Brown and T. Harris (1978) *Social Origins of Depression*. London: Tavistock Publications.

R. Patterson, (1982) *Coercive Family Process*. Eugene, Oregon: Castalia Press.

M. Rutter and L. Hersov (1985) *Child and Adolescent Psychiatry: Modern Approaches*. Oxford: Blackwell Scientific Publications. (There are several relevant chapters in this book.)

J. Wallerstein and J. Kelly (1980) *Surviving the Break-up: How Children and Parents Cope with Divorce*. London: Grant McIntyre.

CHAPTER 2

Social Factors

Naomi Richman

INTRODUCTION

Social factors affect children's lives in many ways; this chapter deals with social influences on the child and family. In the past there has been a tendency to concentrate on individual family problems and how the parents' behaviour affects their children. Whilst accepting the importance of family dynamics (see Chapter 1), it is essential not to overlook social influences on children even though these may act indirectly through their effect on the parents.

SOCIAL CHANGE

Striking changes have occurred in families over the past fifty years, for example:

(1) A fall in infant deaths; this was over 60 per 1000 births in the 1930s and fell to less than 16 per 1000 births in the 1980s.
(2) Parents in the West now expect all their children to live, this is one reason why they are prepared to limit the number of their children. The birth-rate has fallen steadily (although this fall now seems to be levelling off) and families are smaller.
(3) Freely available abortion and contraception means that parents can plan the number of births and space them more easily. It has also reduced the number of children available for adoption; in any case single women are now more likely to keep their babies.
(4) The divorce rate is rising; at the current rate two out of three recent marriages will end in divorce. Most divorced or separated people end up by remarrying or cohabiting with another partner, so that 'reconstituted' families are common.

(5) An increasing number of families are headed by a single parent, usually the mother.
(6) More women with young children are choosing to go out to work.

These bare facts imply changing attitudes and life patterns. The popular notion of a 'normal' family is one with two biological parents and two or more children, with the father working and the mother at home. People who do not conform to this pattern are sometimes criticized and yet it is clear that a decreasing number of families fit this norm. The preschool child may experience separation from one parent, then have to adapt to a new one, and possibly to step-siblings or half siblings as well.

One effect of these changes is that families with young children can be extremely isolated; this is especially so for single mothers with one child. In these situations the child's experience outside the immediate home is impoverished with possible ill-effects on social and emotional development.

CHILD-REARING PRACTICES

Together with the changes in family structure there have also been changes in child-rearing practices in Great Britain over the past fifty years. In the 1930s strictness about routine, sleeping and feeding habits was encouraged; whereas now more consideration is given to children's needs to express their feelings and be creative, and choices about food or bedtime are left more to the child.

There have always been marked social differences in child-rearing methods, for example one study carried out in the 1940s reported more physical punishment in working-class families than in middle-class families, and such differences probably still exist. There are also varied approaches to bringing up children depending on cultural background. Asian, Afro-Caribbean and indigenous British all have their own traditions of bringing up children, for instance in the amount children are involved in helping with household chores.

The degree of independence encouraged in different societies also varies. In Japan children are expected to be more quiet and obedient than Western children; in the former more dependency is encouraged and in the latter more independence. As an example, Western children are usually encouraged to sleep alone, whereas Japanese children are often used to sleeping with an adult right through early childhood.

It is not always easy to relate variations in child rearing to behavioural or emotional disturbance although it is possible, for instance, that lack of routine over meals and bedtime leads to greater rates of eating and sleeping problems. It used to be thought that particular events in childhood like time and method of weaning or potty training had long-lasting effects on personality and adjustment but there is no evidence to support this (see Chapter 3).

Differences in child rearing do affect children's social behaviour. Thus Israeli children brought up in kibbutzim in group homes are particularly responsive to their group's social rules; children with wider social experience are more likely to be confident and assertive. However, *within* each culture children always show a wide range of personality ranging between say timidity and assertiveness, or dependency and independence.

For example, North American children might on average be more outgoing than children from Great Britain but there are many shy youngsters in North America just as there are many talkative, confident ones in Britain. The differences *within* cultures are probably bigger than differences *between* cultures. As well as social expectations numerous other factors influence how a child behaves including family styles of interaction, children's experiences, and their own individual personality.

Traditionally it has been mothers who have looked after young children and remained at home involved with domestic chores, although some groups of women have always worked outside the home, for example the Lancashire mill workers. Now that more women have paid work, how does this affect the family and children's experience? It might be expected that the roles of men and women would change and possibly become more similar. However these changes are very slow, and women still have the main responsibility for child care and domestic work. Fathers tend to interact differently with their children compared with mothers, playing more boisterous games, especially with boys, and interacting more with their sons. When mothers and fathers are sharing the roles of parenting more equally, they do behave in more similar ways towards their children. It is interesting to speculate how changes in the behaviour of parents will affect boys' and girls' identifications of what is male and female behaviour, and whether this will lead to less aggressive behaviour in boys and more assertive behaviour in girls (see Chapter 12).

SOCIAL DISADVANTAGE

Children who come from disadvantaged backgrounds have an increased risk of behavioural or emotional problems, learning difficulties and poor health. Social disadvantage is usually defined using several different indicators. These include quality of housing, income, parents' level of education, whether adults in the household are employed and the type of work they do. A survey recently carried out in Britain concluded that approximately 10 per cent of five-year-olds fell into the disadvantaged group.

Social disadvantage produces an effect on children's lives in a number of ways, directly by limiting opportunities available to the child, and indirectly by its effect on parents. Parents stressed by their social circumstances are more likely to have physical and emotional problems and be less able to deal patiently, with their children's needs. Marital discord and maternal depression are more common in stressed families and, as mentioned in Chapter 1, both are associated with child behaviour problems.

Poverty and poor housing are most likely to occur in certain inner-city neighbourhoods and amongst recent immigrant groups who have not yet established themselves.

The quality of housing is particularly important to families' well-being, especially to women who are at home all day with young children. Overcrowded, damp, dilapidated buildings, and high-rise flats in large estates are often the only housing available for poor families. Behaviour problems in children and depression in their mothers are reported to be very common in some high-rise buildings, related to the difficulties encountered by a mother in getting out of the flat with her toddlers and the isolation experienced in these estates.

There are few studies looking specifically at young children from different ethnic backgrounds. Surveys of two- to four-year-olds do not find that any particular group stands out as having more behaviour problems in the home setting or in day nurseries, though more children of Asian or Caribbean origin are found in the latter.

A high percentage of children of Afro-Caribbean origin are in single parent families, nearly always with the mother, and it has already been mentioned that single parents are often in poor social circumstances. This applies particularly to very young mothers. Most under sixteens who become pregnant now choose to have abortions, but a small group of adolescents coming from unhappy homes have a baby as a source of comfort for themselves. These mothers are particularly likely to have financial and housing problems, to lack support from their families and to have difficulties in coping with their baby. They usually drop out of school before taking any examinations, and their chances of getting a job are consequently lowered. Disadvantage tends to be cumulative. For example, a poor education or racial discrimination reduces work opportunities, and in turn this leads to a lower income and therefore poorer quality housing.

Children from homeless families are particularly likely to suffer from physical ill health and disrupted family life. Often the families are housed in cramped conditions with no adequate play space or cooking facilities, and have to move frequently. In some cases fathers are not allowed to live with their family in the accommodation provided. Children in this situation miss out on health care and are also unlikely to attend a preschool group. All these problems may be exacerbated in families where a wife has to seek refuge because of violence from her husband.

Language delay and learning difficulties are also more likely to occur in situations of social disadvantage, the children affected tending to come from the largest and poorest families (see Chapter 7). These children receive less language stimulation at home because of the competing demands of their brothers and sisters; they are also least likely to attend any preschool facility.

WORKING MOTHERS

As mentioned already, one of the most striking changes in family life in recent years has been the increase in the number of women with young children who work. In the United Kingdom approximately 30 per cent of mothers of under five-year-olds work, mostly part-time. In other countries these figures are much higher, for example in Canada about 50 per cent of women with a child under three years work at least part-time. Many more women in the United Kingdom would like to work but are unable to find adequate day care.

For a considerable number of women, working outside the home provides an important source of satisfaction. Many women want to work: 'to get out of the house'; 'for company'; 'to break the monotony'. However the main reason for working is financial, this is especially so for women on their own, or where the father is on a low wage or unemployed.

In the UK, fathers are the most likely people to take over child care when mothers are working, this occurs in about 50 per cent of working mothers; often the couple alternate shifts. The next commonest source of care is a relative or childminder; only a small percentage of the children are in group day care (see Chapter 13).

The satisfaction a woman gets from her job, from meeting others, and earning money has to be balanced with the extra pressures on her of trying to do two jobs at once – working outside the home *and* looking after the house and family. In practice fathers usually do not help much with household chores; even when fathers are positive about being involved, working mothers still usually do the majority of housework and child care. For a single mother it is even more difficult to cope with the demands on her time.

Some studies show that going out to work prevents women from getting depressed or speeds recovery if they are depressed, other studies find no difference between working or non-working women, or even that some jobs increase depression. The effects of working probably depend on the kind of work and the amount of support for child care available. Women doing some low paid manual jobs may be more at risk of depression, whereas women with better paid jobs, e.g. teachers, may be less at risk.

A survey of a nationwide sample of five-year-olds in Britain looked at the work experience of their mothers and the association between work and mental health. They report that after taking into account other social factors which might affect mental health, women who had a non-manual job (such as teaching) were the least likely to be depressed. Those who had given up work or had a manual job (such as factory work) were most likely to be depressed, and women who had always been full time at home were in the middle. The most disadvantaged women were the most likely to be helped by working. These findings suggest that for some women work is beneficial and for others it is an added stress.

It could be that those depressed women who had given up work had done so because they were already depressed or that work had actually acted as a protective factor.

What is the effect on a child's adjustment of having a working mother? The effects will depend on circumstances but there is no evidence that by itself having a working mother is disadvantageous. Indeed there is some evidence that children benefit in terms of confidence and independence. The family might also benefit from the mother's earnings and from her improved mood and self-esteem. However, there are concerns that children in poor quality day care or with unsatisfactory childminders are suffering emotionally and from lack of stimulation (see Chapter 13). Children from the poorest homes are likely to have the poorest quality childminders because these will be the cheapest — there are of course exceptions to this rule — and therefore suffer further disadvantage. Descriptions of apathetic, withdrawn children with childminders, lacking adequate toys and attention have led to suggestions that mothers should not work. However, others argue it would be more sensible to put increased resources into day care and child minding so that disadvantaged children could have more social and educational opportunities.

SOCIAL POLICY

Social and government policy affects families through a variety of channels as listed in Table 2.1.

Government actions vary according to their policies. In Hungary for exam-

Table 2.1   Policy influences on families

General social measures	Preschool provision
Housing	Education
Health care	Day care
Services for the handicapped and physically ill	Play schemes
	'Family law'
Provision of benefits	Child-care law
Child allowance	Adoption and fostering
Maternity benefit	Abortion and contraception
Maternity leave	
Paternity leave	

ple, paid maternity leave for an extended period is provided to encourage women to have more children and also to go out to work. In France, créches and preschool facilities are extensive in order to boost the birth-rate.

In Scandinavia, changing ideas about men's and women's roles has led to innovations in parental leave. Parents have a certain amount of leave which they share between themselves as they want, to be taken in the child's first five years. They can use this leave for situations like taking a child to the dentist or looking after a sick child. In practice very few men take advantage of this leave.

However, there are moves in Great Britain and elsewhere for both men and women to work part-time to share child care. This is most likely to occur in professional families where it is easier for men to organize part-time work.

FOSTERING AND ADOPTION

Chapter 8 discusses the child who has been abused and Chapter 15 the law in relation to children. Recent changes in the law reflect new ideas about the needs of children whose parents are failing to care for them adequately.

Studies of children who have been 'in care', that is, either fostered or in a residential children's home, show that these children are very much at risk of showing disturbed behaviour. Such children often come from homes where there is much family discord and disorder. In addition, children's homes do not always provide continuity and there are many changes of staff. Finally, children often move around a great deal between home, foster parents and institutions producing a great deal of uncertainty for the children. A question often raised is whether being in a children's home has a permanent effect. One study examining this topic followed up children who were adopted after being in a children's home and found that they had a better outcome than those remaining in the home even though this was of good quality. The worst outcome, however, was in those children who returned home to their mothers. Often the mothers had a new partner, and perhaps a new baby and the older child rarely became a comfortable member of this new family.

A policy is now developing that is in the best interests of children to provide them with an alternative home as soon as it is apparent that the natural parents cannot care for them adequately, and that changes of placement and uncertainty about the future are disturbing to the child. It is recommended that after all efforts have failed to help the parent(s) provide adequate care, a permanent placement should be sought. Taking into account young children's needs to form stable relationships, a time limit should be set in which a decision must be made about whether the parents will be able to care for the child or not. These decisions are not easy and raise many questions about the rights of children and of parents.

Important issues in this field are:

(1) Whether parents should continue to see their child after long-term fostering or adoption has been agreed. This happens increasingly with older children but is uncommon with younger ones.
(2) Controversial decisions about children who have been living with foster parents for many months or even years and are then wanted back by their own parents.
(3) The adoption or fostering of children by foster parents who are different from the natural parents in social class, religion or ethnic group. In the past adopting and fostering families were usually white and in adoption

largely middle class. There are now pressures to take into account the child's ethnic origin when placing them. There have, however, been criticisms of this policy because it leads to children spending months in a temporary placement waiting for a suitable family.

There is particular concern about black children placed with white families, who have no chance to learn about black culture. White adoptive and foster parents vary in their awareness of these issues and may deny that colour is an issue for their black child. However by three to four years of age, children are well aware of colour differences and of the value given to different appearances. Black children in an all white environment may reject their appearance and want to look like the rest of the family.

PREVENTION AND PRIMARY HEALTH CARE

The high contact rate between children and primary health care workers provides a useful basis for preventive work even in the perinatal period. Prevention of physical disorder, for example by antenatal care and immunization, contributes to the prevention of childhood emotional disorder (see Chapter 4).

The majority of young children and their families have contacts in the primary health care setting with family doctors, health visitors, community nurses and doctors, and clinical medical officers. Many children also see paediatricians. About a third will have been admitted to hospital at least once by the age of three years. A high proportion of visits to both family doctors and paediatricians have an emotional or psychological component, for example stomach aches, sleeping and eating problems in the child, anxiety and depression in the mother. The mother's emotional distress is not always understood and she is often offered a sedative when social support and help in managing the children would be more appropriate. There are many ways in which support for families with young children can be provided.

IN THE NEONATAL PERIOD

It has been suggested that identifying families in the neonatal period at high risk of child abuse and offering them support then would prevent abuse from occurring but the evidence for this is not certain.

Support for some at risk groups does seem to be helpful, for example running support groups for parents with a baby in the special care baby unit, or for mothers at risk of depression.

BOOKS AND PAMPHLETS

These provide information on:

(1) Welfare rights and benefits, for example the attendance allowance, maternity leave.
(2) Local facilities like playgroups and play schemes.
(3) Lists of useful organizations, like support groups for children with specific handicaps, or for single parents.
(4) Books about development and behaviour.

SUPPORT GROUPS

These are usually for mothers rather than for both parents and are run by health visitors or other community workers to provide mutual support or deal with specific problems faced by parents with young children.

SELF-HELP GROUPS

An increasing range of voluntary national organizations offer support and practical help to families. Some organizations deal with specific areas, for example parents who have suffered a stillbirth, or who have a child with a particularly chronic illness, handicap or problem, like OPUS for parents who fear they are going to batter their child. Other organizations have wide activities. Initially the National Childbirth Trust concentrated on issues surrounding birth, but it is now involved in promoting breastfeeding and providing support throughout early childhood.

SPECIAL SUPPORT PROJECTS

Awareness of the plight of isolated women with young children has led to various initiatives combining the public and the voluntary sector. In one scheme (Homestart), volunteers, usually women who have had children, are put in touch with other women who have young children and are lacking support and practical help. In another scheme (Scope) volunteers receive training in running a group and then start one up in their own area, again for women with young children who are under stress, but also trying to involve fathers. Volunteers may receive a small payment.

In the Newpin scheme the volunteers, women with children, come from the same deprived background as the women they are befriending. After training, volunteers begin visiting families and there is a drop-in local centre where they can go for a chat or activities if they want to. Initial reports suggest that this support scheme is beneficial both to the volunteers and the women they befriend, boosting their confidence and helping them cope more positively with their children.

COMMUNITY AND FAMILY CENTRES

Another recent initiative is the development of local centres which offer various facilities to all young families in the community, and often to other groups as well. The centres may be new or arise from health centres or day nurseries. Services offered might include family planning, immunization, dentistry, day care and classes for adults ranging from psychology and child care, to whatever else the students organize.

The policy of these centres is:

(1) To provide a service for *everybody*, not just those who are disadvantaged or considered to be at risk.
(2) To involve families and community groups as much as possible in running and organizing the centres.
(3) To get rid of the fragmentation of services between health, education and social services which at the moment interferes with planning, and hinders parents who have to go to a different place for each service.

SUMMARY

This chapter has covered some of the social conditions which affect the lives of young children. It is true that individual children and adults vary in how they respond to social adversity, but in general disadvantaged parents or children are more likely to show evidence of stress than those in better-off families. In the parents this may or may not be shown by physical ill health, by maternal depression and by marital discord. In the children behaviour and language difficulties are more prevalent. Support for families could be increased in a number of ways. In particular, increased day care would help women who have to work for economic reasons and provide necessary social experience for isolated young children.

Current changes in family life affecting young children include increasing numbers of one-parent families, more divorce and remarriage, and more working mothers. New patterns of sharing responsibilities between couples are slowly emerging. However these changes are very limited and women still take the major role in child care and housework.

FURTHER READING

S. Dowling (1983) *Health for a Change*. London: CPAG.
A.F. Osborn, N.R. Butler, and A.C. Morris (1984) *The Social Life of Britain's Five Year Olds*. London: Routledge & Kegan Paul.

Problems of Preschool Children
Edited by N. Richman and R. Lansdown
© 1988 John Wiley & Sons Ltd

CHAPTER 3

Early Relationships

NAOMI RICHMAN

The family and social experiences of babies vary widely. Some babies live in a large family group where there are several adults and children of varying ages to relate to and play with. Others may be only children with just two adults at home or a single mother. One baby spends nearly all the time with the mother, another may be cared for at times by the father or by a child minder.

How do these early experiences affect infant development? Can we define common elements which are important for optimal development? How long lasting are the effects of less than optimal experience?

This chapter describes current knowledge on the development of social relationships and factors which influence them. Until recently interest has focused almost exclusively on mother–child interactions, other relationships were considered unimportant, at least for the first couple of years. The capacity of infants to form a variety of relationships has been underestimated but this attitude is now changing and the importance of fathers, brothers and sisters and other adults and children has been recognized.

WHAT CAN NEW BABIES DO?

Babies are born with predispositions to act and respond in certain ways. These predispositions derive from biological factors influencing how the brain functions and right from the start of life the baby is a very active participant in the family. Babies interact with and learn from what goes on around them and in turn affect the behaviour of the adults and children they meet.

Take sleep patterns as an example of how babies' behaviour is modified according to their experiences and stage of development. As the brain matures babies are able to stay awake for longer and longer periods, and also sustain a longer period of sleep at one time. Usually the long periods of sleep become concentrated in the night-time, and wakefulness occurs most frequently in the daytime. However the development of this diurnal or daily rhythm depends on living in a social environment which encourages peace and quiet at night and stimulation during the day. It would not be too difficult to reverse the sleep rhythm so that a baby slept mostly during the day; and babies who receive very little stimulation are often passive and spend a great deal of time sleeping.

The interplay between development and social experience is very obvious in the flowering of social relations. Babies have inborn characteristics which make them especially interested in other human beings and which form the building blocks of social behaviour. Video-films played in slow motion show that almost from birth they respond with facial expressions and body movements which exactly follow those of someone who is speaking to them. By the age of a few months this will develop into a 'dance' of interactions, when they and an adult talk and play together and mirror the sensitive to and fro interactions which occur when adults talk.

Babies have an in-built tendency to respond selectively to human voices and faces. They respond to the voice especially and by four months have themselves developed the particular intonation of the language they hear most.

Newborns are also selectively attentive to patterns of visual contrast which are more face-like, such as two dark blobs on a white card rather than, say, a pattern of stripes. This means that they will look attentively at the human face especially at the eyes.

So from birth, human beings are the most interesting objects in the baby's environment. Very soon they recognize the particular characteristics of their mother, her smell, her voice, her appearance. Other familiar people are also recognized. Over the months mother and baby get to know each other and build up a familiar routine of feeding, nappy changing, talking and playing. Initially mothers have to adapt their behaviour to the babies' and follow their lead, trying to decide whether they want to feed or play or sleep. Soon babies learn that *their* responses influence the mother, that turning away can stop tickling if it is getting too exciting, that looking and smiling can start a game going again. These mutual exchanges form the basis of social interaction, they become more elaborate as the child grows older, and require sensitivity from both partners in order to respond smoothly and appropriately. The playing together of Mrs Thorn and her five-month-old daugther Rita illustrate this.

Mrs Thorn hears Rita crying and decides that she is not hungry because she was fed two hours ago, but that as she has just woken from a nap she is probably bored. She holds Rita quietly on her lap for about five minutes giving her a chance to quieten down. When Rita looks at her attentively, Mrs Thorn slowly starts to play a game, bringing her face close to Rita's making a blowing noise, then drawing her face away. She gradually increases the pace and noise of the game. Rita smiles, and then laughs, and then looks serious and turns her face away.

Every time she turns away her mother also pulls away, gives Rita time to quieten down, and the game starts up again. Mrs Thorn allows Rita to decide the pace and intensity of the game and follows her cues so that she does not get over-excited or upset.

THE DEVELOPMENT OF SPECIAL BONDS OR ATTACHMENTS

Babies soon learn to recognize familiar people and show differential responses to them, for example, more smiling, but up to the age of about six months they do not seem to have a specific *preference* for particular people. Before this time they do not show marked distress about being separated from parents and can find comfort from most sympathetic adults.

By about six months, infants have formed special bonds or 'attachments'. The presence of attachment is assumed if the baby shows certain behaviours towards someone. These behaviours include seeking to be close to them; distress if they go away; going to them for comfort; showing confidence in their presence, like exploring a new place or toy without fear.

This stage is thought to be an important landmark in social relations in that the baby has now developed a distinct awareness that certain people are significant. Soon after the development of specific attachments most children develop a wariness of strangers and are less easily comforted by them. This, too, seems to be evidence that infants are highly sensitive to unaccustomed appearance and behaviour and the difference between familiar and unfamiliar people.

Attachment has been studied in laboratory situations in which infants (usually under eighteen months) and their mothers and fathers enter a strange room with toys. The baby is observed with the parent, then with a stranger, and finally when the parent leaves the room and returns. The most common reaction in this situation is that shown by eighteen-month-old Richard in the health clinic he visits with his mother. He explores the room and unfamiliar toys with great gusto, but keeps his eye on his mother who is chatting to an acquaintance, occasionally going back to her for a confirmatory pat. He even goes up to a stranger and pokes her, running back to his mother excitedly. When his mother leaves the room for a brief period his behaviour changes. He stays near his mother's acquaintance but does not look at her and stops playing. When his mother returns he smiles at her, runs for a cuddle and soon starts playing again.

In the laboratory situation some infants show extreme distress when their mothers return after a brief separation, and cling to the mother but cannot be comforted. These infants are said to show 'anxious or insecure attachment'. Other infants ignore the mother on her return and respond to her no differently than to the stranger; these children are said to show 'avoidant attachment' behaviour. Some studies have followed children with 'anxious' or 'avoidant' attachment to later childhood, and found that they are more likely to have emotional or behavioural difficulties. This has led to the suggestion that the mother–child relationship is in some way impaired if 'avoidant' or 'anxious' attachment behaviour is seen. However, these particular patterns of behaviour do not *necessarily* persist or indicate that there is something seriously wrong with the parent–child relationship and much more research is required before one can be confident about the meaning of these behaviours.

HOW DO SPECIAL ATTACHMENTS ARISE?

It used to be thought that babies automatically became attached to their mother and only to her because she was present most of the time and was the provider of food and of daily care. In fact attachments occur to a variety of people, some of whom are not involved in daily physical care at all. For example, children who were cared for in a group setting on an Israeli kibbutz by a child care worker still formed their primary attachment to parents whom they saw only for short periods daily. One study found that when initial attachments began, 29 per cent of a sample of infants formed several attachments at the same time; 10 per cent of these infants had at least five people they were attached to. At eighteen months, 57 per cent of the sample had multiple attachments. Babies become attached to relatives, particularly fathers, and other caretakers, and about a third of them form their major attachment to the father rather than the mother.

Infants also develop strong bonds with other children such as their siblings and can be comforted by their presence if parents are absent. Twins are especially likely to be strongly attached to each other. An oft-quoted story is of a group of six children who were together from early infancy in a concentration camp, cared for by an everchanging group of adults who were under great stress. When the children reached safety at the age of three years they were strongly bonded to each other but had no such links with adults.

It has been suggested that the development of attachment depends not so much on the quantity of time spent together, although presumably there must be a minimal amount of contact, but on the quality of interactions. Infants are most likely to become attached to adults who are sensitive to their needs and promote satisfying reciprocal social interactions.

Adults who interact very little, who overwhelm the infant with stimulation, or whose responses are determined by their own inner needs rather than the infant's needs, are thought to be less likely to promote attachment, and to produce 'anxious' or 'avoidant' attachment behaviour.

ADULTS' ATTACHMENT TO INFANTS

Just as the infant's attachment to adults develops gradually so usually does that of parents and other adults to babies. It is common for parents to feel detached from their babies at first, and to worry that they are never going to love them. Other parents feel very close from the moment of birth. Variations in feelings may seem irrational to the parents themselves.

> Rita was very special to her parents right from birth because she was born after many years of infertility when they had given up hope of every having a baby. On the other hand Patrick was born after a difficult pregnancy and painful labour to a mother who was very stressed and not getting on with his father. She found it extremely difficult to feel positive towards her son.

Recently there has been a great deal of emphasis on the importance of early contact between mothers and babies as essential for promoting a good relationship. Instead of whisking the newborn into the nursery, early skin contact is promoted between mother and baby or father and baby and women are encouraged to put the baby to the breast as soon as possible. Other changes in obstetric practice include encouraging fathers to be present at birth and faciliating as much contact as possible between parents and babies in special care baby units. Parents are encouraged to visit frequently, hold or touch their babies and do as much as possible for them. These changes are all to the good. Childbirth is a family affair and the 'medicalization' of birth and putting babies in separate nurseries has made it an unpleasant and soulless experience for many mothers and fathers.

However, the emphasis on the importance of early contact has probably been exaggerated. The differences between mothers and fathers who had early contact and those who had not are negligible when families are followed up some months later. There is no evidence that what happens in the first few hours or even days after birth is crucial for later adjustment. Parent–child relationships develop over time at varying paces, and good relationships can develop throughout childhood. Children who are adopted later in childhood, after the age of four years, can still form close and loving relationships with their new parents and vice versa.

There are many reasons why people find it difficult to become attached to their children. Although parents often come to accept an unplanned or unwanted child, such children are at risk of rejection. Children born to mothers who sought but were refused an abortion have a high chance of ending up in someone else's care or if remaining at home being poorly adjusted. Parents may remain detached from a child who has been very ill or nearly died or one who is severely handicapped. It seems that emotional investment in these babies is too painful for them. Mourning by parents for a lost child or a dead parent can also make it difficult for parents to relate to a new baby. Parents who for some reason wanted a boy or girl may be unable to accept their baby if it is the 'wrong' sex.

Severe stress of any sort such as poverty and poor housing, unemployment or ill health can affect parents' capacity to devote sufficient energy and attention to their baby to promote their relationship. Women who suffer from depression following the birth are particularly likely to have difficulties in relating to their babies.

THE HANDICAPPED CHILD

There is always an interplay between parents' and infants' behaviour and the infants' characteristics also influence the parents' attitudes and acceptance of them. A baby's behaviour is never completely independent of how it is treated, but some babies are particularly irritable, fussy, difficult to soothe and require extra patience and tolerance which stressed parents do not always possess.

Certain handicaps make it less easy for infants to establish relationships. Those with brain damage may be irritable and irregular in their habits and less rewarding to care for. It requires considerable persistence from parents to continue stimulating a retarded child who is passive and unresponsive and takes longer than normal to develop smiling or cooing.

Children with hearing or visual impairment are also challenging and special techniques are needed to communicate with them and use the channels they do possess whether it be sight, hearing or touch. Physical contact and movement are more important to them than to other children. Smiling or babbling will be later in infants with sensory impairment. Visually impaired babies are more at risk and commonly develop habits of self-stimulation like rocking or, if they have some vision, flicking their fingers in front of their eyes, and are generally slower in developing social play.

Children with infantile autism can be particularly difficult for parents to relate to (see Chapter 5). Some of these children are reported to have developed normally in the first few months or first couple of years of life. Many present difficulties of communication in babyhood which are not recognized at the time. They are often described as 'good' babies, not demanding attention, not responding with excitement to the sight of a familiar person, never putting out their hands to be picked up. Vocalizations are delayed and the normal reciprocal play between parent and child does not develop.

Although autistic children may not form specific attachments in their early years, they often become very anxious when separated from familiar people and a familiar environment where responses and situations are predictable.

In spite of the enormous barriers to communication presented by autistic children, and those with other handicapping conditions, most parents become attached and work hard to promote their development. Each type of handicap presents specific problems of management and adjustment to parents. For example, children with severe spina bifida or cerebral palsy require a great deal of physical attention; children with severe retardation often have marked behaviour difficulties with poor sleep and extreme restlessness. Nevertheless, all parents have to go through a similar painful process of adjustment to having a handicapped child. Their first response is likely to be one of numbness, shock, and disbelief. This is followed by a time of sadness and mourning for the healthy child who might have been. Anger is common, often expressed towards the doctors or nurses for not preventing the handicap. Guilt and self-blame are also frequent, with preoccupations about how they, the parents, might have contributed to the handicap or avoided it. Feelings of embarrassment or disgust about the child's appearance add to the parents' guilt, as does the anger which they often have towards the child. Finally, resignation and acceptance appear with energies devoted to helping the child, and perhaps involvement in a local or national support group. Some parents find this last stage hard to reach and remain angry or depressed. Others continue in a state of disbelief and spend much effort in trying to find a cure. However, parents who do not accept everything they are told by professionals about their child and who continue to fight for extra resources should not be criticized. This approach is often productive and evidence of coping well.

Perhaps surprisingly, parents' responses are not clearly related to the severity of the handicap or illness. A severe handicap is just as likely to be coped with as a mild one and conversely some parents become very upset by relatively minor handicaps. Social attitudes towards handicap and the behaviour of others, especially relatives, can either help or hinder parents' adjustment. Thoughtless remarks, or insensitive staring, stop some parents from going out in public with their baby at all. Some relatives, especially grandparents, refuse to accept the handicap, either denying that it is a problem, or withdrawing from contact. Parents need support, not only in coping with their own feelings, but in knowing how to explain the situation to others. Many families with a young handicapped child become quite isolated, unwilling or unable to find support. The presence of local support groups of parents with the same problem can be invaluable.

ARE THERE LONG-TERM EFFECTS OF EARLY EXPERIENCE?

Relationships are not static and even when there is a stormy beginning parents and children can often readjust and become close.

What of the child who continues to have long periods of unsatisfactory care because of neglect or rejection? A prolonged and difficult time with an uncaring or harsh adult will make it more difficult to trust adults and to form satisfactory relationships with them or with other children. However, it seems that the effects of even very poor early experiences can be compensated for by later good relationships and this process of compensation can continue even into adult life. For example, a group of women who had been brought up in care, that is away from normal family life, experienced a caring relationship in adolescence or in some cases adulthood. Their self-esteem and self-confidence improved and they had better relations with their own children compared with a similar group of women who had also been in care but who had not experienced a caring relationship.

Unfortunately many people who have a bad start in life with neglectful or harsh parents or many changes of caretaker may not have any compensating experiences. They may remain in an unsatisfactory situation and because their social opportunities are restricted they may also continue to be disadvantaged as adults. It is this lack of compensating experience and continued disadvantage which can lead to unhappiness and emotional difficulties in adulthood rather than the initial unsatisfactory experience by itself. This possibility of compensation also applies to a greater or lesser degree to intellectual deprivation (see Chapter 7).

EXPERIENCE OF SEPARATION

One type of early experience which has attracted much attention is separation from the mother or father. As mentioned previously, even brief separations from a parent in an unfamiliar situation can cause distress in young children. More extreme reactions have been observed in children admitted to hospital without a parent or familiar person. Depending on the length of separation, they show first a period of protest, then one of despair and apathy, followed by detachment when they play and relate indiscriminately to others tending to ignore their parents. On return home from hospital, children often show clinging, upset behaviour, are less amenable, and may revert to more baby ways like wetting and wanting a bottle. These reactions are less likely if a familiar person is with the child in hospital and also if they are prepared for the admission. There is some evidence that two or more admissions to hospital in the preschool period predispose to the development of later behaviour problems. It is not clear whether this is related to separation, being in hospital, or to other factors which increase the likelihood of being hospitalized.

Two points to remember about any separation are first that the age of the child is important. Children under six months seem to be little upset by separation because they have not yet formed any specific attachments. Children over three to four years are able to hold in their minds memories of their family and to understand that they will return. It is between six months and two years that separation is hardest for children.

The second point is that the presence of another familiar person apart from the mother counteracts a child's distress. If they are with someone else to whom they are strongly attached they will not be upset by the mother's absence.

The point needs stressing because there is a lot of pressure for mothers to stay with their children *all* the time, and women have come to feel very guilty about leaving them at all, particularly to go out to work. All the evidence available shows that if alternative care is consistent and good, children do not suffer. Indeed they have much to gain in developing a variety of relationships and in learning to adjust to separation gradually.

What of the child who is separated for long periods or even permanently through death, parents separating, or being taken away from home into care? Many factors will affect adjustment including the child's age and sex, the relationship with their parents and the subsequent care arrangements. Repeated or long separations are most likely to have an effect on a child if they are associated with discord at home or a poor parent–child relationship. The presence of a good relationship with at least one parent appears to act as a protective factor. Boys cope less well with adverse experiences like discord at home or separation, and are more likely to show problem behaviour than girls.

SOCIAL AND INTELLECTUAL DEVELOPMENT

Intellectual and social skills are closely linked and develop together. Delayed development and especially delayed language development often occur in children who have been understimulated and neglected. To make maximum use of potential an infant has to be in an environment which stimulates interaction; social interaction provides the most powerful learning situation.

Take language development as an example. Young babies gurgle and coo and play with the sound of their own voices. The extent and complexity of these early sounds depend on how much the infant is talked to and their noises responded to playfully by an adult. In order to elaborate these first noises into the sounds and rhythms of everyday speech and then into recognizable words and phrases, the infant requires social 'conversations'. The interplay of games and vocalizing which parent and baby do over and over again is a necessary stage in the development of language. At every stage of language, conversation in a social context is a necessary stimulus to optimal development (see Chapter 5).

It has been suggested that infants get great pleasure from learning how they affect things around them. For instance they will smile when they solve a problem. Very young babies will learn to turn their heads in one direction or kick their feet to make something interesting happen like a mobile move. As soon as the solution is found the infant smiles and coo's and then stops trying to make the mobile move. It seems as though it is the *intellectual* satisfaction of finding how to cause the movement, rather than the movement itself which gives them such delight.

Learning requires opportunities to influence the environment at a level where efforts are bound to be successful. Social interactions are a good source of these opportunities. Infants learn that when they smile or coo, so does the other person in response. Parents can sensitively grade their responses, so that the baby is always encouraged to try out new and more difficult skills.

If babies become passive and lacking in spontaneity because of lack of stimulation, they will stop making overtures to their parents who will in turn respond to them even less. A vicious cycle can easily be established in which there is less and less interaction between parent and child and the child becomes increasingly passive.

RELATIONS WITH PEERS

It used to be thought that young children did not really notice each other, and that they were interested only in adults. Observations of babies have shown that they do interact with each other and enjoy each other's company. Throughout early childhood children learn a lot from each other about sharing and social relations.

When very young babies are put together in a playpen they tend to treat each other as objects, poking and crawling over each other like kittens. Gradually they begin to respond socially to each other by smiling, cooing, offering toys. By one year there can be considerable pleasure and interaction between infant pairs who know each other well. Even more social interaction appears if children are brought up together. Twins in particular play together a great deal and may develop their own secret language at an early age. As children grow older their interactions become elaborated into conversations, games, imaginative play. They learn social skills from each other which cannot develop with older children or adults. With peers there has to be mutual adaptation, turn taking, consideration of the other's feelings, attempts at conciliation after a squabble over a toy. This is less likely to happen with adults who, in play, usually adapt to the young child and do what they want. Observations of young children show how skilled they become in negotiation and compromise; in modulating their own behaviour in order to make social life smooth.

Children also learn a lot from playing with children of different ages, particularly siblings. Both boys and girls are often protective and caring with younger children, involving them in their more grown-up games. In this way the younger child has a chance to try out games and ideas, practise new skills and develop imaginative play.

Although in a preschool setting children choose to mix with others of the same age there are advantages in mixed age groupings. However, staff in day-care centres often feel that in a mixed age or family group the younger children get left out. On the other hand, younger children require more physical care and there may be less time to spend on teaching and occupying the older group.

DEVELOPMENT OF SYMPATHY AND EMOTIONAL UNDERSTANDING

An important aspect of developing social relations is the capacity to sympathize with others' distress, understand or empathize with how other people are feeling, and try to comfort them.

Part of the baby's inbuilt behaviour is a sensitivity to *signs* of emotion in others and to changes in their behaviour. Early on a crying baby will start other babies in the nursery crying. Smiles from others elicit smiles in the baby.

Babies are also sensitive to *incongruous* signals. They will be puzzled if a strange voice seems to come from their mother's familiar face shown on a TV screen, or if she looks at them blankly instead of with her customary smile and interest.

It seems likely that babies soon become aware of the subtle changes which occur in the faces and behaviour of their mothers and other familiar people according to their mood.

From these simple responses an awareness of the feelings *underneath* these emotional signals gradually emerges.

The development of this awareness is shown by the way in which children try to comfort others in distress. At first the babies will look upset or perhaps cry. By around a year they will try to comfort a distressed child or adult by offering a toy, or even their own favourite blanket. It will be some time before they realize that adults are comforted by different forms of comfort from themselves.

This understanding of other people's feelings is most likely to develop and be shown within the family and with brother and sisters.

RELATIONS BETWEEN BROTHERS AND SISTERS

Although attention is usually paid to the negative aspects of these relationships as shown by fighting and jealousy, there is much positive feeling as well. Young siblings show affection to each other, enjoy playing together and comfort and care for each other.

By the second half of the first year many babies show particular pleasure in the presence of an older brother or sister. By eighteen months they are clearly attached to them, miss them when they are away, and go to them for comfort, or for security in strange situations.

Older children enjoy their baby brothers and sisters too. They act like parents to them and make allowances for their understanding by adjusting their behaviour. For instance they will talk to them in simple short phrases in a high voice, using diminutives and repeating words.

'Bicky Jo-Jo. Nice Bicky', says four-year-old Andrea offering a biscuit to eleven-month-old Jo.

Most young brothers and sisters spend a lot of time playing together and the youngest gain a great deal by copying them and becoming involved in their games. The familiarity and closeness of the relationship provides exceptional opportunities for developing social understanding for both older and younger sibs. This sophistication is well shown by the way children in their second year tease and provoke an older child. This shows the capacity even at this young age to understand what is important to someone else and what will upset them.

Eighteen-month-old Nicholas knocks down Liza's elaborate house of bricks because Liza will not allow him to touch it. He then runs to his mother for protection, obviously aware that Liza will be upset and angry.

What influences whether brothers and sisters get on well or badly? Many factors affect the relationship and unfortunately parents cannot ensure their children will get on well, however hard they try to encourage this.

The majority of young children react quite strongly to the birth of a baby. At first most of these reactions are directed towards the mother, and seem to a large extent, a response to her decreased attention. There has been little study of how the arrival of a new baby affects a young child's behaviour towards the father, but it seems that children do become more attention seeking.

On the arrival of his sister, Harry, aged three years, became negative and defiant to his mother, he was also whiney and miserable, and started wetting in the day again. On the other hand he also became more independent and wanted to do more for himself, for instance dressing himself.

The children with the most marked reactions are not necessarily the ones who are most hostile to the baby; even though showing signs of upset, they can be affectionate and interested in the baby. Children with difficult temperaments who are negative and intense in their moods react more adversely to the birth as do those who previously had a lot of confrontations with their mothers. Interestingly, first born girls who had a very close relationship with their mothers may find it particularly hard to adjust to a new baby.

Mothers can help the older child by being as positive as they can to them, involving them as much as possible in the care of the newborn and talking to them about the baby. Most of the adverse reactions towards the mother or baby have cleared up after a few months. However, children who become withdrawn after the birth are most likely to have persisting difficulties with their young brother and sister, and once a negative relationship towards the new baby is set up in the early months it is likely to persist, perhaps because the younger child also begins to react with hostility in response to the older one's negativism, and the pattern becomes perpetuated.

There are many variations in the development of these relationships because all family members affect each other in complex ways. For example, where the firstborn has a good relationship with the father this lessens negative behaviour to the mother, and firstborn girls whose mothers are depressed after the birth are more likely to form a close relationship with the younger sibling and to some extent take on the mothering role.

CONCLUSION

First, babies have the capacity from birth to interact socially and their social and intellectual development depends on having a rich and varied human environment which is responsive to their needs.

Second, they have the capacity to form strong emotional ties to a varied range of people, not just to the person who has prime responsibility for their care. There is no evidence that by having many bonds these are necessarily shallow. Through experiencing a variety of relationships the child's social repertoire and understanding is enriched and this provides a good foundation as social horizons expand. Neither parents nor children live in a vacuum and the social context of their lives has enormous impact; their other relationships cannot be ignored. With many children now living in small families, often a single child with a single parent, it is particularly important that more varied social experience is available for both parents and children. Good quality day care would seem to play an essential part in this as well as the kind of self-help schemes described in Chapter 9.

The third point is that continuity of care is necessary but that good parenting does not require the *continuous* presence of the parent since it is the *quality* of interactions which are important, not just the mere quantity. The emphasis on an exclusive mother–child relationship is unnecessary.

Finally, early adverse experiences are not of themselves bound to have lasting ill-effects on intellectual or emotional development. If a separation is the beginning of a train of adverse events such as lack of adequate care and frequent moves, then this first separation might be linked to a poor outcome. But the intervening process of adversity would be mainly responsible rather than the initial separation. Throughout childhood (and adulthood) it seems that positive events can often set going a process of compensation for previous adversity.

Most children have a mixture of positive and negative events in their lives and it is the balance of these combined with the individual child's vulnerability which determines their outcome.

FURTHER READING

R.D. Ross (1981) *Fathering*. London: Fontana.
M. Rutter (1981) *Maternal Deprivation Reassessed, 2nd edn*. Harmondsworth: Penguin Books.
D. Stern (1980) *The First Relationship*. London: Fontana.
B. Tizard (1977) *Adoption: a Second Chance*. London: Open Books.

Problems of Preschool Children
Edited by N. Richman and R. Lansdown
© 1988 John Wiley & Sons Ltd

CHAPTER 4

Physical Influences: the Brain, Genetics and Behaviour

PHILIP GRAHAM

PHYSICAL DEVELOPMENT OF THE BRAIN

The brain goes through its most rapid period of growth from about the third month of pregnancy up to about eighteen months to two years after birth. After that time, the brain continues to grow more slowly until it reaches adult size. Almost incredibly, about five months into the pregnancy, nearly all the nerve cells in the brain are already present. Although the cells continue to grow in size, and their connections with each other become more complex during the pregnancy and after birth, the number of cells remains relatively unchanged. Many cells migrate to different parts of the brain and others die in early life, but there continues to be a certain amount of cell division, so the numbers remain relatively constant.

The physical development of the brain is probably largely 'programmed' and under genetic control, but there is evidence that it may be modified by the child's experience. For example, experiments on the cat's visual cortex (that part of the brain concerned with receiving visual stimulation) has shown that its development is affected by the visual experience with which the cat is provided. It is quite possible, then, that the physical development of a child's brain is also affected by that child's experience.

LOCALIZATION OF BRAIN FUNCTIONS

As the child matures, so different parts of the brain become specialized in their function. The two sides of the brain are known as the right and left hemispheres. By the time the child is born, the left side of the brain (the left hemisphere) has become important in the control of movements on the right side of the body and vice versa. In right-handed people, speech and language functions become more and more localized to the left side of the brain, and the perception of the way in which objects in space are related to each other (visuo-spatial perception) becomes localized to the right hemisphere. In left-handed people localization is more variable.

This localization of function is accompanied by increasing lateralization — the tendency to prefer to use one side of the body when both sides are capable of performing the task in question. About 90 per cent of the population becomes right-handed, and lateralization can also be detected in eye, foot and ear preference. It can be noted very soon after birth: even newborn babies usually prefer to turn their heads to the right in response to a sound stimulus. Hand preference in drawing, hitting, picking up objects, etc. is usually quite firmly established by the age of five years, and it can often be detected by the age of two years. Neither left-handed children, nor children who show mixed laterality (e.g. right-eyedness and left-handedness) have particular tendencies to learning difficulties. However, children who are generally slow to mature and have learning difficulties are also slower than others to develop clear laterality.

BRAIN DAMAGE AND RECOVERY

The fact that the brain is growing at its fastest rate in pregnancy and during the early years of life, makes it more vulnerable to damage if this occurs at the time of birth or later in life, for example, as a result of a traffic accident. On the other hand, in some ways, the fact that parts of the brain have not become so specialized means that when one part of the brain is damaged, another part can take over its function. This means that when brain damage occurs it is quite difficult to predict how this will ultimately affect the child's performance. Occasionally, quite severe and widespread brain damage may be recoverable, but also, unfortunately, localized damage, especially to the motor areas, may result in permanent impairment.

PHYSICAL INFLUENCES AND BEHAVIOUR

GENETIC INFLUENCES

All child development occurs, at least to some degree, as a result of an interaction between genetic (inherited) factors, and experience (what happens to the child in the womb or after the birth). Some characteristics, such as the colour of the eyes, are entirely inherited: some influences on development, such as what a child eats, are entirely determined by experience. Many characteristics, such as height and intelligence, are heavily influenced by both genetic factors and experience. In most of the chapters in this book attention is given particularly to the child's experiences in explaining behaviour and learning. This is appropriate, because it is this aspect that is most open to change. It is important however, not to omit a description of genetic influences because these do sometimes limit the degree to which intervention can produce change in a child. Further, on occasions, understanding a child's genetic constitution may act as a guide to the sort of experiences it is most helpful to provide.

Genes and chromosomes

Inherited characteristics are transmitted by genes, which are strips of a chemical called deoxyribonucleic acid (DNA for short). These genes carry a code that 'instructs' each cell in the way it develops. So, indirectly, the genes determine how our bodies, including our brain cells, are built, and the way we are made up (especially the way our brains are constituted) determines to some degree how we learn and behave.

The genes are carried on chromosomes — short, thick structures, each of which carries tens of thousands of genes. Humans have 23 pairs of chromosomes. One pair, the so-called sex chromosomes, determine the sex of the child. Females have two X chromosomes (XX), and males an X and a Y chromosome (XY).

Children may be born with abnormalities of the chromosomes. A single chromosome or part of a chromosome may be missing, duplicated, or have moved out of place. In any event, a large number of genes may be affected, so it is not surprising that most chromosome abnormalities are not compatible with survival of the fetus to birth. Some children with chromosome abnormalities do, however, survive to birth, and indeed, some such children may experience a reasonably normal quality of life.

The most common example of a chromosome abnormality is Down's syndrome (mongolism) which is caused by an extra chromosome at position 21. The chromosome abnormality in Down's syndrome affects the development of the brain as well as the physical appearance of the child. So, in addition to the slanting eyes, broad nose, large tongue, incurved little fingers and short stature, the child also shows impaired learning ability. Children with Down's syndrome do, however, vary quite considerably in their intelligence. This is partly because there is so much variation in the way children are treated at home and at school.

Other, rarer chromosome abnormalities, include Turner's syndrome, Klinefelter's syndrome, and the fragile X syndrome, all of which occur because of an abnormality of the sex chromosomes.

Abnormalities of single genes

When an important single gene is deficient in some way, the child may or may not be affected — it depends whether the deficient or abnormal gene is 'dominant' or not. Dominant conditions are inherited from one parent only, and this parent will show the condition himself or herself, unless the condition has arisen as a result of a mutation (see below). An example of a disorder inherited because of a dominant gene abnormality is achondroplasia — a cause of short stature with a characteristic facial appearance, often seen in circus dwarfs.

A deficient or abnormal gene that is not dominant, which is inherited from one parent, will not normally affect the child's development or health. If, however, the corresponding gene inherited from the other parent is also abnormal, then the child will be affected. This type of inheritance is called 'recessive'. A number of rather rare disorders, such as cystic fibrosis (a condition mainly affecting the lungs) are inherited in this 'recessive' way.

Some single gene disorders are due to gene deficiencies on the X chromosome. Only boys are affected by these conditions (an example is haemophilia) because in girls, the gene on the other, normal X chromosome makes up for the deficiency.

Polygenic inheritance

This form of inheritance arises as a result of the influence of numerous genes, and is of much greater importance to those dealing with children with behaviour, learning and developmental problems than are chromosomal or single-gene abnormalities. Characteristics such as height and intelligence are probably influenced by large numbers of genes, each of which has a small effect. We may assume, say, that there are a hundred genes affecting the height of a child. If 70 of them are tending to promote height above the average, and 30 tending to make the child below average height, the child will turn out rather above average height. Naturally tall parents pass on more genes tending towards tallness and vice versa.

Most of the variation between children's development that is genetic is inherited in this way. Thus, the age at which children learn to stand, walk, speak their first words and are toilet trained is determined to some degree by polygenic inheritance — the influence of numerous genes of small effect. In some of these aspects of development, inheritance (and therefore polygenic inheritance) is the most important cause of variation between children. In other facets of development the experience of the child is of far greater importance, and polygenic inheritance of little significance. Genetic factors are, however, almost always significant in the *pattern* of development. Thus, while experience is probably the major factor in when and how children express themselves in language, genetic factors determine the fact that understanding of language is nearly always in advance of expression, and single words come before sentences.

Further, there is often a complex interaction between polygenic factors and experience. Thus, for example, a child may be heavily disadvantaged genetically for becoming dry by day and night. However, if the parents are relaxed and child-centred in the way they cope with toilet-training, the child may be dry at night at about the same time as other children. A child with rather poor genetic potential for intelligence may achieve at least average level if the parents are especially good at stimulating the child's abilities. By contrast, even children with very good intellectual potential may do only moderately well or even poorly if brought up in disadvantaged circumstances.

Studies of inheritance

The fact that a problem does or does not run in families, usually tells us very little about how far genes and how far experience are contributing. For example, bed-wetting runs in families — if one child has this problem, then the brothers and sisters are likely to show it too. But this might be because the parents have difficulties in helping their children become dry, or it may be because all the children have inherited the problem. Even when there is no one else in a child's family suffering from the particular disease or delay in development, this does not mean that genetic factors are unimportant. Sometimes, in the process of cell division and multiplication, new variations ('mutations') may occur affecting the child in a way the parents have not themselves suffered.

At the present time, we are dependent on the findings of studies carried out on twins and adoptive children for our knowledge of the relative importance of genes and experience. If identical twins, who share all their genetic pattern, are more similar in a particular skill than non-identical twins who share only half their genetic pattern, then probably that skill is quite heavily genetically determined. If identical twins are no more alike than non-identical as far as a particular characteristic is concerned, then it is probably mainly environmentally determined. In studies of adopted children, the investigators try to find out whether the child's problems are present more often in the adoptive parents' family or in the family of the biological parents. If, for example, a child adopted shortly after birth is delayed in language development, and the biological parents, but not the adoptive parents, showed the same problem, this suggests genetic factors are more likely to be responsible.

Unfortunately, in the individual child, it is only rarely possible to draw definite conclusions about the relative importance of inherited factors. Scientific advances may make this more possible in the future, but where polygenic factors are concerned, we are always likely to be somewhat uncertain about the precise part inheritance plays. (See also Chapter 7 on children with learning difficulties for a further discussion of this topic).

PHYSICAL INFLUENCES IN PREGNANCY AND BIRTH

Fortunately, in our society, most pregnant women enjoy the conditions necessary for a good outcome for their baby. Such conditions include an adequate, well-balanced diet in pregnancy, a life not over-taxed by severe stress, and the availability of competent nursing and medical care.

When a baby or young child shows a developmental, learning or behaviour problem, the question is often raised whether something occurring during the pregnancy or at the time of the delivery could have been responsible. Except in occasional cases, it is usually impossible to be sure about this, but studies of babies whose mothers experienced problems in pregnancy and at birth have helped to provide information about the probability of risks to the baby following particular complications.

One of the most important causes of pregnancy complications is an abnormality in the fetus itself. Thus, many early miscarriages occur because the fetus has a chromosome abnormality (see above) that is not compatible with life. The miscarriage is nature's way of preventing an abnormal child being born.

A further important cause of problems lies in the placenta. This is the organ that grows during pregnancy on the inside of the womb to provide nourishment for the baby, and is expelled after pregnancy as the afterbirth. If the placenta fails to develop properly, then the baby will not receive sufficient nutrition, and will not grow at the expected rate. When a baby is born at the expected time, but is low birthweight, the reason usually lies in a placental abnormality of this type producing 'intrauterine growth retardation'. If the baby is still a reasonable weight, over five-and-a-half-pounds, then no adverse effects may be expected. With babies smaller than this, born at the expected time, there is a slight increase in subsequent learning and behaviour problems. Most, however, will be normal from this point of view (see also Chapter 7).

Other pregnancy problems known to affect the baby include heavy smoking and alcohol intake. Babies born to heavy smokers are, on average, about half-a-pound lighter at birth than those born to non-smokers and do not develop so well subsequently. Regular, heavy alcohol consumption, especially in the early stages of pregnancy, may result in a baby born with the fetal alcohol syndrome, showing a particular appearance and slow to develop and learn. Lesser degrees of smoking in pregnancy affect the fetus to a smaller degree, but it is, as yet, unclear whether moderate or light alcohol consumption has a similar effect. It is also uncertain at this stage whether marijuana smoking in pregnancy has an adverse effect. Babies born to pregnant women who are addicted to heroin, cocaine, barbiturates and other hard drugs develop withdrawal symptoms at birth and require special care. It is uncertain whether exposure to these drugs in the womb harms the baby in any permanent way. Medically prescribed drugs, especially if taken early in pregnancy, may affect the fetus, sometimes, as was the case with thalidomide, to a very marked degree. Although as far as most prescribed drugs are concerned, the evidence suggests an absence of harmful effects in pregnancy, it is often difficult to rule out such effects in an individual case with any certainty.

Many mothers suffer infectious diseases in early pregnancy and there is often a concern that these have harmed the baby. It is well known that German measles (rubella), contracted in the first few months of pregnancy can result in a baby born with some degree of deafness and/or visual impairment, as well as general developmental delay and behavioural difficulties. A small number of other infections can also have an adverse effect. However, it is not likely that common flu and flu-like illnesses in the pregnant mother harm the developing baby.

Other common complications of pregnancy are unlikely to have affected the baby. For example, one or two episodes of early bleeding, the development of a mild degree of high blood pressure (toxaemia) in late pregnancy, a stressful experience, a fall that is not followed by bleeding — all these are very common events in pregnancy, and there is no evidence that they are, in general, likely to result in the baby being harmed.

Common complications at the time of delivery are also not usually followed by harmful effects. The fact that a baby was born following induction, with the use of forceps or by caesarean section does not, in itself, have any adverse effect. Babies who are in very poor condition after birth, take a long time to take their first cry, and subsequently develop distressed breathing or convulsions, are however at greater risk for slow development later on. Such post-natal complications may arise because the baby has been born with some abnormality that has been present from the time of conception, or early in the pregnancy, or because the baby has been damaged in the process of birth. In general, one can gauge the seriousness of the baby's condition after birth by the length of time the baby was thought to require special care. Babies kept in a special care baby unit for more than three or four days may have had something fairly serious wrong with them, although most will develop normally.

One exception to this rule is the baby that has developed normally in the womb, but is born earlier, sometimes much earlier than expected. Such premature babies are usually provided with special care and not discharged until they weigh about five-and-a-half-pounds (2.5 kilograms). Providing such babies do not develop respiratory distress or convulsions, and do not show disorders of vision, hearing or movement in the first year of life, they are likely to develop normally. This remains the case even for babies born at very low birthweight (two to two-and-a-half-pounds) only just compatible with survival.

PHYSICAL INFLUENCES ACTING IN EARLY CHILDHOOD

Malnutrition

Fortunately, most children in Western society receive adequate nutrition, and indeed obesity is a much more common problem than under-nutrition. When malnutrition does occur, it is almost always accompanied by severe poverty, frequent chronic infections and lack of environmental stimulation. This means it is extraordinarily difficult to establish whether malnutrition alone produces adverse effects on brain function. From a number of studies carried out in developing countries, it seems possible that the brain does indeed suffer when a child does not receive enough to eat, but that appropriate stimulation can, to some degree, make up for the deficit. In one sense, of course, the question whether malnutrition alone produces harmful effects is not a very important one. Children living in poverty-stricken circumstances and not getting enough to eat, obviously need all the help they can get to improve their dietary intake as well as to enhance their living conditions and the quality of stimulation available to them.

The possibility that inappropriate diets can cause hyperactivity is discussed later in this chapter.

Infectious diseases

Infections can affect the way the brain works by directly damaging the brain or its linings.

Infection directly affecting the brain may be congenital or acquired after death.

(1) Congenital. The fetus may be infected as a result of the pregnant mother transmitting an infection. Congenital rubella (German measles) is probably the most common condition in which this occurs, and the way the baby is affected is described above. In this and other congenital infections such as AIDS (Acquired Immune Deficiency Syndrome), the baby may appear normal at birth, and shows abnormalities of development only after several months of life.

(2) Postnatal infections (contracted after birth). Infections of the brain tissue (encephalitis), or the brain linings (meningitis) are uncommon in babies and young children, but they do happen. Very occasionally they occur as a complication of common infectious diseases such as measles and whooping cough. More commonly, they occur as a result of infection from other viruses and bacteria. Usually children make a full recovery, but, very infrequently, the child is left with major or minor disability. Paralysis, sensory deficits and learning problems may occur. However, when a learning problem occurs in a child without physical disabilities, living in

poor circumstances, who has also suffered encephalitis or meningitis, it is more likely that the learning difficulty is due to the poor circumstances than to the infection.

Lead

It is known that children who have very high levels of lead in their bodies (usually because they chew bits of lead containing old paint still found in dilapidated buildings) may develop brain damage, since lead has a direct toxic effect on the functioning of brain cells. It is uncertain whether exposure to the lower levels of lead found in the atmosphere in big cities harms children, and this controversial subject is discussed in more detail below in the section on hyperactivity.

It is important to remember that the most common toxins affecting children's brains are nicotine and alcohol, inhaled or ingested by pregnant women, and the various forms of medication (especially anticonvulsant medication) prescribed to children themselves, perhaps sometimes unnecessarily, by doctors.

CHRONIC BRAIN DISORDERS AND BEHAVIOUR

Children may be affected by a number of chronic disorders affecting the brain, including cerebral palsy and epilepsy. These are briefly described below. When children suffer from a chronic brain disorder they are particularly likely to show emotional and behaviour problems. In one survey carried out on the Isle of Wight, children with physical disorders not involving the brain were found to have emotional and behaviour problems about twice as frequently as healthy children. But children with brain (cerebral) disorders, such as cerebral palsy and epilepsy, were found to show disturbed behaviour four to six times more commonly than children in the general population. So it seems as if brain damage 'sensitizes' the child and makes him or her more vulnerable to the development of psychological and psychiatric disorders.

CONGENITAL MALFORMATIONS

Some children are born with cysts, tumours (swellings) and other physical abnormalities of the brain that interfere with brain function and thus with development. These abnormalities may also give rise to epileptic attacks (see below). Sometimes such malformations are inherited, sometimes they occur because of a disorder of development while the baby is growing in the womb (intrauterine). Neurofibromatosis is an example of an inherited condition. In children with this disorder, there is an overgrowth of the cells that usually line the nerves. This results in the development of swellings (tumours) that may grow in the brain and interfere with nerve function.

Spina bifida is an example of a disorder of intrauterine development. There is a failure of fusion of the vertebrae, so that the spinal cord protrudes into the skin and, in severe form, this produces paralysis and loss of function below the point at which the vertebrae fail to close. Sometimes, in addition, there is a blocking of the drainage of the cerebrospinal fluid that normally fills the small (cavities) ventricles in the brain. The cavities then become distended (hydrocephalus) and when this occurs pressure is put on nervous tissue that may affect its functions.

CEREBRAL PALSY

Brain (cerebral) damage may occur producing weakness or paralysis (palsy) of the arms or legs as a result of an inherited disorder, a failure of development in the womb, or trauma during the birth. Such cerebral palsy may be associated with abnormal spontaneous movements, speech and language problems, epilepsy (see below), and perceptual difficulties (i.e. problems on making sense of what is seen or heard). Children with cerebral palsy also have an increased tendency to show general learning difficulties, although some are of at least average ability.

A difficult birth, or complications immediately after birth, have often suggested the child is at risk. During the first year, the child may be noted to be unusually stiff or floppy, either on one side of the body or on both sides. The 'motor milestones' (sitting up, standing, walking, etc.) are usually delayed.

As the child develops, it becomes clear just how much or how little the child is disabled. Some children with cerebral palsy have very mild clumsiness and weakness of one arm or leg that may improve as they get older — others have gross paralysis of all four limbs with associated severe mental retardation. Clearly therefore the label 'cerebral palsy' tells us little about the degree to which the child will be handicapped.

The degree to which the child is disabled will also depend, to some degree, on the quality of care he or she receives from the family, as well as from teachers, physiotherapists, occupational and speech therapists. Many of the complications of cerebral palsy can be limited, at least to some degree, if the child receives appropriate care from therapists, and if parents and others can work out ways of helping their child to become as independent as possible despite some inevitable disability.

FEBRILE CONVULSIONS AND EPILEPSY

An epileptic fit occurs when there is a rapid discharge of electrical activity affecting all or part of the brain. If the entire brain is affected, then the child will usually have a major (grand mal) attack in which there will be a fall to the ground and a period of unconsciousness with spasmodic twitching of the arms and legs. Sometimes, even though the whole brain is affected, a less severe attack occurs (petit mal) with a brief lapse of consciousness and twitching of the eyelids. If only part of the brain is affected, then the child will briefly show movements, or experience paralyses or unusual sensations depending on the part of the brain affected (minor fits).

Febrile convulsions

When epileptic fits occur in preschool children, they are commonly isolated events, that happen when the child has a fever. These 'febrile convulsions' occur in about one in thirty children. The child, usually aged between nine months and two years, but sometimes up to four or five years, has often been unwell and feverish for a few hours. The cause may be an ear infection, a sore throat, or some other infectious illness. Suddenly the child is noted to be unresponsive with all four limbs twitching. This usually lasts anything from a few seconds to about five minutes. The sight of a fit is very frightening to those around, especially to parents who are naturally terrified the child will die in the attack. Fortunately, this almost never occurs, and the child can be expected to recover completely.

Although a proportion (about one in five) of children will go on to have one or more further febrile convulsions, only about one in twenty go on to develop epilepsy (see below). Further, unless the febrile convulsions are frequent, severe and prolonged, there is no evidence that the child's brain is damaged by them in any permanent way. The great majority of children with febrile convulsions do not have any significant learning problems later in their school lives.

Febrile convulsions and other epileptic attacks are frightening to witness, and it is helpful if those around the child have a clear idea what to do if they occur. In fact, apart from laying the child on his side, no particular action is necessary — the fit will nearly always stop of its own accord. If it goes on for more than about ten minutes, or the child's face goes blue, then a doctor should be called or the child taken at once to the local accident or emergency department. Here an injection can be given to stop the fit.

Most doctors believe that in some children, especially those who have several febrile convulsions, it is wise to try to prevent further attacks by putting the child on regular anticonvulsants or medication for two or three years. It is important to realize that such medication may alter the child's behaviour or learning ability in some way, for example, by making the child irritable or affecting concentration.

Epilepsy

Major or minor epileptic fits occurring in the absence of fever, although more worrying than febrile convulsions, may disable the child only to a minor extent.

In some cases of epilepsy there is evidence of brain damage, such as paralysis (cerebral palsy) or very poor learning ability (mental retardation), but usually the child is otherwise normal. Investigations, such as a brain wave test (EEG) or brain scan may be necessary to discover whether the epilepsy has a cause that can be treated. Often no cause is found, and it appears the child has inherited a tendency to epilepsy. Occasionally this will be suggested by the fact that a close relative has epilepsy.

The form that epileptic fits take can sometimes be puzzling. The grand mal fit (see above) is characteristic and easy to recognize, but some children have fits in which they just have vacant spells, occasionally accompanied by sucking in of the cheeks and twitching of the eyelids, or sudden nodding or bending of the neck. It may take some time before these attacks are recognized to be epileptic.

Usually fits come out of the blue, but occasionally they are triggered by stress or by eating certain foods. In these circumstances it may be possible to take avoiding action. Children who have recurrent epileptic attacks are usually, though not always, put on regular medication until they have had two or three fit-free years. Again such medication may affect their behaviour and learning, and if this happens the doctor prescribing the medication should know so that, if possible, other forms of medication can be considered. Like febrile convulsions, epileptic fits are very frightening, and it is important that those dealing with a child suffering from them feel confident what to do when one occurs (see above) and understand that they are not dealing with a form of madness or a sign of serious illness. As the child gets older, he or she will also need an explanation, and an opportunity to discuss the strange experiences and feeling of being out of control that may accompany the attacks.

Breath-holding attacks

These may be mistaken for epilepsy. The child, usually aged between one and three years, will hold his or her breath after being frustrated or experiencing pain. The child may go blue, and even briefly lose consciousness and twitch before starting to breathe again. Such attacks are of no particular significance. Occasionally children will use breath-holding attacks as a means to get their own way, and behavioural methods (see Chapter 10) can provide effective means of dealing with this problem.

HYPERACTIVITY

Normal young children vary considerably in their level of activity. Some are generally rather slow and cautious in their movements, while others are more active and tend to rush around a good deal. Although there is no clear, sharp dividing line between normal and abnormal levels of activity, most doctors and psychologists agree that a minority of children do show abnormal overactivity. They are described as being overactive or hyperactive (the words mean the same thing) and if, in addition, a cluster of other problems is present, then one refers to such children as showing the 'hyperkinetic syndrome'. These other problems are likely to be a short attention span, poor concentration, lack of persistence, a tendency to impulsive and reckless behaviour, and lack of normal social restraints, such as absence of normal shyness with strangers.

HOW ACTIVE IS HYPERACTIVE?

As already stated, there is no clear line between normal and abnormal levels of activity. All the same, a three-year-old who cannot sit at table for a meal for more than a minute or two, or settle to quiet play or a puzzle or listen to a story for more than three or four minutes at a time, without getting up and wandering around, must be considered to be unusually active.

There are considerable problems in establishing just how active a child is. Some parents, perhaps those who have already had a particularly quiet child, call their children overactive because they have unreasonably high expectations about how long a young child can sit in one place. Some tolerant parents do not notice that their children are quite unusually active. When teachers complain about their children, parents may underplay the difficulties that are present. Some playgroup leaders and nursery teachers who, quite rightly, are worried about children being labelled hyperactive or abnormal, may deny that children in their care are 'different' when, in point of fact, quite serious problems are present.

Such difficulties in assessing activity levels are increased because many young children are very overactive in one situation (for example at home) while showing normal levels of activity elsewhere (for example in the more structured setting of a nursery school or playgroup). This can result in parents and teachers or playgroup leaders not really believing each other when they discuss a child's behaviour.

John, aged four years, was brought by his mother to the general practitioner because of hyperactivity. He had been difficult from birth, a restless feeder who often regurgitated his food. This problem improved, but when he started to walk his mother found him very difficult to control. He started at a playgroup at three years, but the playgroup leader asked if he could be removed because he was so restless and aggressive to the other children.

CAUSES OF HYPERACTIVITY

Hyperactivity is probably rather rarely due to one cause. More commonly a variety of factors contribute.

Brain dysfunction

Although this section on hyperactivity comes in the section of disorders arising from brain dysfunction, it is probably only in a minority of cases of hyperactivity that this is the major factor. Some children, who show other evidence of brain damage or dysfunction (for example, epilepsy, cerebral palsy, or severe mental retardation) are also hyperactive. Clearly, in these cases, the activity level is also likely to be, at least partly, a result of brain damage. This is probably the case with children who show severe levels of overactivity in all situations, and in whom evidence for other causes is clearly lacking.

Incidentally, the term 'minimal brain dysfunction' is sometimes used to describe a cluster of behaviour and learning problems similar to or identical with the 'hyperkinetic syndrome' described above. Those using the term assume that the syndrome must have a physical cause. As we shall see, there are many other possible reasons why children are hyperactive, so this term has now largely gone out of fashion.

Temperament and genetic factors

Normal children differ in many aspects of their everyday behaviour, not just because of their upbringing (though clearly this is an important factor) but also because of their temperament, the constellation of tendencies to behave in particular ways with which they were born. Thus some children inherit a more active nature than others. If this level of activity meets with parental disapproval, the level may reduce. But if one way in which the child reacts to being told off is to become more restless, then a vicious cycle can be set up in which the parents' punitive reactions can lead to worse behaviour by the child.

Inappropriate parental handling

Sometimes the way parents behave towards overactivity can make the overactivity worse. There are other mechanisms by which parents can, unintentionally, increase their child's level of activity. Some rather passive parents may only respond to their child's need for stimulation if their child rushes around to attract their attention. Other parents are rather inconsistent in the messages they communicate to their children, or provide a chaotic, disorganized environment, and their children may become restless in response. Children who are neglected in their early years, or who are brought up in an institution with dozens of different people taking care of them may react in the same way.

Diet

Much attention has been given in the press and on the television to the notion that artificial colourings and food additives may make children hyperactive. It is certainly possible that food could have this effect — the child might be showing an allergic reaction, or the food might actually be having a toxic (poisonous) effect on brain function. Numerous parents have reported that their children's behaviour has improved when they have withdrawn these substances from their children's diet. Unfortunately, such parental reports cannot necessarily be taken at face value. When a child is being overactive and disobedient, and the parents decide to change the child's diet, other aspects of their handling may also change. For example when parents start being firm about the food the child eats, this may be the first time that they have shown they really mean business, and are determined to get the child to do what they want. This display of firmness may be as important as the alteration in the child's food intake in producing a change in behaviour.

A number of studies have been carried out to see whether dietary factors in themselves do produce hyperactivity. Usually these studies involve giving the child on separate occasions foods indistinguishable in taste and appearance, some containing additives etc. and others without, to see whether the child's behaviour worsens when the artificial substances are added. In these experiments it is obviously important for neither the parents nor the child to know which food the child is getting. In general, the results of such studies have been negative, suggesting that diet is a relatively unimportant factor. However, a small number of studies have suggested that some children at least, may indeed respond badly, not just to artificial foods, but also to ordinary foods such as wheat, eggs, milk and chocolate.

Lead

The possibility that lead, especially lead in petrol, affects children adversely has also been much studied. The difficulty is that children living in big cities, who are most exposed to high levels of petrol fumes, are also those who are likely to be socially deprived, living in poor housing and overcrowded circumstances. Such children may be overactive and have learning difficulties for a whole range of other reasons. The results of studies of the effects of lead which have taken account of social factors, suggest that lead is, at the most, only of minor importance in producing children's behaviour and learning problems. Of course this does not mean that children should be exposed to lead in the environment any more than is absolutely necessary. No one has claimed that lead does children any good, and it is conceivable that, in some vulnerable children, it does indeed do harm.

REDUCING HYPERACTIVITY

Just as there are various causes of hyperactivity, so one can take different approaches to improving the behaviour associated with it.

Fitting the environment to the child

People dealing with overactive children may sometimes find it helpful to remember that overactive children may be different in personality, but usually do not have a disease or psychological disorder. They need to be treated as individuals. If children are unusually active, they may well benefit from being given plenty of space and opportunities to run around. They may need more visits to the local park, fewer breakable objects on the mantelpiece, sturdier toys to play with. They may also need a more structured approach to their care. Thus, while some children can be more or less left to work out their own boundaries of acceptable and unacceptable behaviour, the overactive child may benefit from the parent or playgroup leader making it much clearer what is permitted and what is not. Overactive children are also easily over-stimulated and distractable, so that it is usually a good idea to bring one toy or puzzle out at a time.

Behavioural management

Techniques for removing undesirable behaviour and replacing it with more adaptive behaviour are described in Chapter 10, and will not be discussed in detail here. Clearly, if children are given more attention for overactive, difficult behaviour, this is likely to worsen the problem. If, by contrast, it is possible to ignore such behaviour and to reward the child for sitting still at table or concentrating on a puzzle for just a little longer than usual, then the child's behaviour is slowly going to change for the better.

Diet

The overactive child does sometimes improve when colourings and additives are removed from the diet, though, as already stated, why this is so is not always clear. An additive-free diet is more expensive than an ordinary diet however and it is sometimes not at all easy to get a child to stick to it. It is necessary to exclude:

(1) Processed ham, bacon, salami, sausages, ready cooked and frozen meat, frozen fish.
(2) Ice-cream, ice-lollies and all forms of confectionery. Flavoured crisps, sauces etc.
(3) Fizzy drinks and fruit squash (except those specially labelled additive and colouring free).
(4) Most types of wrapped bread and breakfast cereals.
(5) Shop-bought cakes, biscuits, desserts, jellies.
(6) Margarine, processed or coloured cheese.

No harm will come to children if they are put on a diet excluding these items, and they may benefit. A sensible approach will first involve the parents noting if the child's behaviour does indeed seem worse after any particular food or drink — chocolate or orange squash, for example. If the child's behaviour is better when one or two items are excluded, then clearly it is sensible to try to avoid them. If the child's behaviour remains difficult, then a diet excluding all colourings, additives and preservatives (see above) can be tried, but this will only be justified if the child is really showing a definite problem. If improvement occurs, then the parents can gradually reintroduce food items to see whether any particular food is responsible. If the child remains very seriously overactive, it may be worthwhile considering the effect of a further trial of dietary restriction with limitation of ordinary foods. This is perhaps most likely to be effective if the child has a history of allergic disorders such as eczema or asthma, or a close relative suffering from such a condition. However, even in these cases, the treatment should not be undertaken lightly, for the child's social life may be badly affected by his not being able to go to parties, eat school lunches, etc. Further, such treatment should only be done with the help of a dietitian, who may well also feel that a paediatrician should be involved.

Drug treatment

In children who are severely overactive, both at home, and in a nursery or play-group setting, and in whom other measures have failed, the use of stimulant drugs has been found to be effective in producing improvement. It might well be thought that stimulant drugs are the last treatment that overactive children need, but, paradoxically, when used in appropriate circumstances, they do seem to calm children down and improve their concentration and attention span. They are often given in the morning and at lunchtime, so as not to keep the child awake at night. They never make a severely overactive child normal, and may have side effects, like poor appetite, but just occasionally, the benefit they produce is very worthwhile.

WHAT HAPPENS TO HYPERACTIVE CHILDREN?

This mainly depends on how severe the problem is in the first place. The child who is somewhat more exuberant than most will do very well. The child with severe overactivity, present in all situations, who is behindhand in other aspects of development, and showing other problems such as aggression, may well turn out to show learning problems and other behaviour difficulties later on. The overactivity may improve, but a very short span of attention and concentration may then handicap the child in learning situations. If those around the child can retain a positive attitude towards the child, showing acceptance, though providing firm limits, and praising, even for small improvements, then the child is more likely to show a favourite outcome.

FURTHER READING

C. Carter (1977) *Human Heredity*. Harmondsworth: Penguin Books.
D. Scott (1973) *About Epilepsy*. London: Duckworth.
E. Taylor (1985) *The Hyperactive Child: a Parents' Guide*. London: Martin Dunitz.

Problems of Preschool Children
Edited by N. Richman and R. Lansdown
© 1988 John Wiley & Sons Ltd

CHAPTER 5

Language and Communication

MARION WOODARD AND RICHARD LANSDOWN

INTRODUCTION

Three parents discussing their children:

'Kevin is five, he can't talk but he's not daft.'

'Elaine chatters away nineteen to the dozen. The trouble is I am the only person who can understand a word she says.'

'My twins are as different as chalk and cheese. Alan never stops talking but Sharon's like a little mouse. I sometimes wonder if she is deaf.'

These three parents are describing different ways that language difficulty can show itself:

Kevin has an expressive disorder, he can understand what is said but cannot get words out. In other ways he shows that he is intelligent but at five he is now quite a serious worry.

Elaine is only three. She enjoys the act of talking and her family at least can understand what she says. There is no cause for anxiety in her case at the moment.

Sharon may be deaf; if she is she will be at a serious disadvantage and the sooner her hearing is assessed the better.

A couple of basic points emerge from these children.

(1) Language is essentially a form of communication which has to be learnt. Learning starts from the earliest moment that a baby has an interchange with someone else: the hugs and smiles and 'goo goo goo' and the gurgles of pleasure from the baby are the first steps that lead eventually to a highly developed skill enabling one to read this page.
(2) It is helpful to divide language into two categories:

Expressive language, i.e. that which is spoken.

Comprehension, that which is understood.

(3) *Speech* is a more specific term than language and refers to the act of talking.

THE COMPONENTS OF LANGUAGE

Children need first to be aware of another person in order to communicate. This means that it is easier for them to develop language skills if they can see, hear and touch, with hearing being especially important. It is also necessary that communication brings some reward, a point that is probably built into their system.

To obtain an illustration of the importance of an adult in developing language, watch a young baby and a mother, or whoever is the person mainly responsible for the baby's care. Observe them carefully and watch to see how even a very young child will take turns with the other person, picking up cues on when to start and when to stop. The 'conversation' may not seem to be very close to what we call talking, but you will be able to see that it is the foundation for what comes later.

As they move from babbling to the use of words, children need a degree of understanding in order to realize that a sound made with the voice can stand for an object or an idea. For example, the sound of the word *car* has nothing to do with the way a car looks or sounds but children learn that the noise they make when they say the word signifies the vehicle that mummy uses to take them to play school. This symbolic use of sound is quite a sophisticated concept and its need may explain why so many attempts at teaching animals to talk have been unsuccessful.

RECEPTIVE LANGUAGE

Before infants can link the abstract symbol of a word to an object or action they must first be able to understand something of the world around them. For example, they must know about feeding before they can link a spoon with the act and before they can link the word 'spoon' with the actual object. They also learn that objects retain their shape regardless of their position in space and whether they are in view or not.

Babies start to understand spoken language between the ages of six and ten months. At this stage they respond to whole phrases used in particular situations combined with non-verbal cues such as the speaker's tone of voice, facial expression and gestures. Then they respond to particular words within a phrase, but again only in context. For example, they might look at a cup when asked, 'Where's your milk?' during a mealtime but will not be able to link the word and object if it is not mealtime and the cup is not in view. True verbal understanding comes only when the child relates a particular object or event with a spoken word and there are no additional clues of context or gestures to help.

Often the first word the infant understands is 'no' because of the amount of repetition of that word, the strong tone of voice and facial expression of the speaker and, perhaps the accompanying physical restraint. Other early words are the child's name and familiar objects or actions such as 'ball', 'drink' and 'gone'.

It is important to remember that, at this stage, although the children appear to be understanding the full sentence they are often responding only to the key word. For example, in the phrases 'Where's your sock?', 'Find me the car', the child is only really responding to 'sock' and 'car'.

The next stage (approximately two years) is when children relate two concepts within one sentence: for example 'Put the brick in the box', 'Where's mummy's hair?'. By three to four years of age they learn to understand more abstract concepts such as size, shape and colour. They understand more complex grammar and can cope with more information-carrying words in a sentence. In a request such as 'Put the *blue* spoon *under* the cup', a two-year-old will probably just put *any* spoon *in* the cup, having picked out these two words and related them to previous experience, i.e. spoons go in cups. A four-year-old will be able to analyse the key words and meaning of the total sentence, i.e. that the spoon should be blue and go under not in the cup as is customary.

Children continue to learn the meaning of grammatical structure until their teens and the development of vocabulary continues through life.

EXPRESSIVE LANGUAGE

Comprehension precedes expressive language by several months; this balance continues through development into adulthood. The first words an infant says are not necessarily those which are understood first but those which have the most value in meeting communication needs. The pattern of development of expressive language is similar to that of comprehension.

For young children single words have to do many jobs, but as language skills develop, communication becomes easier. Two-word phrases reflect the child's level of understanding: objects are related together such as: 'teddy bed' (put teddy in the bed), 'dolly drink' (I am giving dolly a drink).

By two-and-a-half-years the child should be using simple sentence structures with verbs ('Mummy go shops') and by three years using words to express abstract concepts. At this age they will also use plural forms, simple adjectives such as 'naughty', 'big', 'dirty' and simple past tenses. Children go on to learn how to ask indirect questions 'Can we have chocolate ice-cream?' and imply meanings by language and tone of voice 'Wouldn't it be nice if I had someone to read me a story?'

Table 5.1   Early language norms

Comprehension	Expressive language
3 months	
Turns eyes/head to sound	Uses different cries
Quietens to mother's voice	Coos for pleasure
6 months	
Responds appropriately to angry or friendly voices	Enjoys babbling with single and double syllables, e.g. ahdah, oogoo
Turns to parent's voice across a room	Directs vocalizations to people or objects
Is interested in human voice	
9 months	
Understands 'no' and 'bye-bye'	Babbling becomes more complex with different vowels and consonants, e.g. bama, meedee
Understands whole phrases when used in context, e.g. arms up, come here	
Enjoys turn-taking games of peek-a-boo, clap hands	Uses many intonation patterns of adult speech
	Initiates babble sequences
	Reaches towards desired objects
	Uses body movements and noise to get adult to repeat actions

Table 5.2   Language development

Comprehension	Expressive language
12 months	
Understands own name	Uses specific pointing with finger to indicate wants. Pointing often accompanied by vocalization
Understands familiar names in context, e.g. go and get your coat, give it to mummy	
	Echoes some adult words
Demonstrates use of common objects, e.g. brush, spoon	Shakes head for no
	Says one or two proper words
18 months	
Understands at least fifty words	Repeats words heard in conversation
Can point to some body parts with names, e.g. nose, eyes, hair	Uses 10–20+ words

Table 5.1 (*contd.*)

Understands the key words in a familiar command, e.g. mummy's shoe, put the cup on the table	Great use of 'jargon' with wide range of pitch and sounds

24 months

Selects one common object from a group of five	Echoes great deal of adult's speech
Listens to conversation and responds with more conversation	Constantly asks names of objects
	Uses simple two-word phrases, e.g. daddy gone, more milk
Carries out simple instructions without cues of context or gestures	Talks to self while playing
	50–70 per cent of speech may be unintelligible

36 months

Understands action picture, e.g. who's reading	Uses large vocabulary and three- to four-word phrases
Understands in/on/under	Uses personal pronouns, plurals and prepositions
Identifies objects by use or function	
Carries out two related commands, e.g. 'pick up the big shoe' and 'put it in the box'	Uses who, what, where and simple past tense
	Relates own experience
Understands big/little in relation to objects	Enjoys repetitions of rhymes and stories
	Gives own name and gender when asked

48 months

Increase in understanding of abstract concepts such as size and shape, colour	Listens to and tells long stories
	Uses long sentences of six to eight words
Enjoys simple jokes	Grammar mainly correct but uses wrong forms, e.g. wented, sheeps
Understands incorrect sentences	
Understands imaginary situations such as 'Let's pretend'	Speech intelligible to strangers although may still have some errors, e.g. poon for spoon, wed for red
	Speech may be non-fluent at times

LANGUAGE DISORDERS

DEFINITIONS

A language disorder can take the form of difficulty in understanding language, either spoken or written or of expressing oneself in language.

Communication disorder is a much wider term including problems with non-verbal behaviours such as gestures and body language.

Delayed and deviant development

Delayed development arises when the child is able to learn but does so at a slower rate than most.

In *deviant development* the child is unable to learn language by the usual processes and so the pattern of development is different from normal.

NUMBERS OF CHILDREN WITH LANGUAGE DISORDERS

It is very difficult to give accurate figures of language disorders as studies in the past have used different criteria. Surveys carried out in Great Britain give totals ranging from 3.1 to 17 per cent of the child population while a US study of 1970 gave between 5 and 10 per cent.

Language disorders can be primary or secondary, the latter being associated with more major handicaps such as hearing loss, mental handicap and physical handicap.

Causes

There are seven key causes of language disorder.

(1) Hearing loss.
(2) Mental handicap.
(3) Neurological impairment.
(4) Autism.
(5) Emotional problems.
(6) Environmental deprivation.
(7) Developmental language disorders.

In children most language disorders are related to problems arising from congenital or developmental factors, with relatively few resulting from trauma or acquired problems.

Hearing loss

The type of language problems resulting from hearing loss depends on the nature and severity of that loss. Children with a severe loss will, at best, hear muffled, distorted speech patterns and will have extreme difficulty in analysing and interpreting what is heard. They are impaired in the development of both receptive and expressive language; abstract vocabulary and underlying meanings which are inferred from word order will be hard to grasp, for example, the passive verb tense: 'The man was bitten'. They will not be able to analyse meaning and grammar from information contained within a word, e.g. to distinguish between mummy/mummy's, miss/missed, because they cannot hear the speech sound combinations.

Children with a mild loss, particularly an intermittent one, may have some difficulty with comprehension development in the early years as the messages heard will be distorted and erratic. They may find it easier to 'cut out' speakers and so will not develop good attention and listening skills: two prerequisites for good language development. They may have problems on the expressive side, for example, ignoring the difference between take/takes, look/looked.

Children with hearing loss are likely to be limited in their uses of language for communication. They will not participate in babble or jargon as there is little pleasurable reinforcement of hearing their own speech sounds. They may not use language to comment on and direct their play activities (as young children) if this serves no purpose. If verbal language is difficult for them to hear and formulate they may prefer to rely for communication on the non-verbal meanings of gestures and signs.

Mental handicap

Language comes later in these children but the course of development is similar to that in children without mental handicap. It is important to remember that language must be viewed in relation to overall development. For example, if a child with a chronological age of six years is functioning at a three-year level in all areas of development, then it is appropriate for language skills also to be at a three-year level — the 'developmental' rather than the 'chronological' age. If this child has a language age of eighteen months, i.e. far below the general development level, then there is said to be a particular problem with language development.

There can be problems in the development of both receptive and expressive language in children with mental handicap. They may not be able to understand non-verbal language and fail to comprehend cues of pointing and gestures. They are slower to understand abstract concepts such as those of function, colour and spatial relationships.

Expressive language shows many differences. Sentences are shorter and more simple; complex tenses ('would have been') and conjunction words (but, also, however) may not be used. A reduced vocabulary is used, one word representing many things and there is difficulty in associating words with abstract concepts. The use of language may be inappropriate to the social setting and children may appear to be rude if they do not understand the conventions of what can be said and where. They generally have difficulty in conversational skills — not using the cues of the speaker to join in the turn-taking routine correctly, failing to follow the drift of the conversation and not providing opportunities for a two-way exchange of ideas. The use of language is likely to be affected more if the child is in an institution rather than a home-like setting, as there the needs and opportunities to use and develop language are more limited.

Does language delay mean mental retardation?

Unfortunately, it is a common fallacy that children with speech and/or language problems are always mentally handicapped. This is most definitely *not* the case. The first question that many parents ask a speech therapist is 'Is my child backward?' because this is the first reason that comes to mind.

Children who have specific problems in speech and/or language are average or above average in other areas of development. It is essential that adequate assessments are carried out by relevant professionals to determine the strengths and weaknesses of a child's abilities and potential.

Neurological impairment

Damage to the brain can be caused by injury, illness or congenital abnormalities (see Chapter 4). If the damage affects the areas of the brain where the language processes are centred then problems with language may result. The extent and severity of the damage will affect both the nature of the language disorder and the child's response to therapy. There may be a general delay in receptive and/or expressive language. There may be specific problems involving the correct selection of specific words and the formulation of sentences.

Impairment of speech as in cerebral palsy can affect the length and complexity of sentences. If the child has to make enormous efforts to co-ordinate the movements of the throat, lips and tongue to produce voice and speech sounds then sentences may be reduced to key words only: correct grammar is put aside to make communication more effective.

Severe traumatic neurological damage can sometimes result in the complete loss of language in a child who had normally developing skills. Fortunately cases like this are relatively uncommon in children and if they do occur the degree of recovery is usually good. The term 'aphasia' is used to mean a total loss of language and 'dysphasia' a partial loss. Brain damage is the responsible factor in only a very small proportion of children with language delay or deviance.

Autism

All autistic children have difficulties in some aspects of communication and some never develop a linguistic system. They may lack normal pre-linguistic skills such as eye-pointing, gestures or finger pointing or use these in a very limited way. They have great difficulty in understanding that a sequence of sounds represent an object or action, however about 50 per cent of autistic children develop some meaningful language. In the initial stages, adult speech is often echoed (echolalia) many times without real understanding and no relation to what is going on at the moment. Understanding of complex parts of speech is slow to develop, e.g. of pronouns, and phrases like 'Do you want a biscuit' will be used instead of 'I want a biscuit'. Some children use only these set phrases and are never able to initiate or create their own language. Those who do find the rules for conversation hard to interpret so that their uses of language are limited: they may be able to ask for objects or reply to questions but their conversation remains monotonous and stilted and they are unable to use language creatively in conversation or make believe play (see Chapter 14).

> Christine (four years) had problems relating to others, did not look at speakers, and rarely smiled, laughed or showed emotion, gave endless monologues during her play, describing what the toys were doing, but the content of her speech did not match her actions. If an adult commented on her play she echoed features of their grammar and vocabulary in her narrative but she could not answer simple questions about things around her or her actions.

Emotional problems

The exact nature of the presenting language disorder will depend on the underlying disturbance. Children who are emotionally disturbed may have good skills in the form and content of language but have deviant patterns of use. They may use language only to particular people as in elective mutism; may answer questions but not ask anything or join in conversations; may listen to what is being said but not respond and continue with their own monologue that does not reflect the social setting around them. Their language may not match up with what they do or with what they say.

Environmental deprivation

The evidence is not conclusive about the effects of cultural, social and material deprivation on language development in young children. In early studies it was implied that different social or cultural backgrounds resulted in poor linguistic skills. However, this issue is not a simple one as the vocabulary and dialects of certain social groups should not be viewed as automatically inferior or deviant; rather the total linguistic structure and content may be different. Material poverty does not necessarily mean a poor environment for a developing child; the quality of social interaction and the responsiveness of caregivers to the children's needs are the important factors. However, it is accepted that social deprivation puts the child at risk in language development. If the environment is unresponsive and unstimulating, early attempts at communication will not be encouraged, and there will be few opportunities later to hear and develop new vocabulary and sentences.

The onset of language may be delayed in children raised for a large part of their early lives in inadequate institutional settings, with poor staff–child ratios, or in homes with unresponsive parents. Such children will have limited expressive language if they are not exposed to new sights, experiences and conversation. They are likely to be reluctant to initiate language, preferring to use gestures or let others talk for them. Grammar will be limited if they have little opportunity to participate in conversation and imaginative games. When asked to describe a picture, 'What's the lady doing?', Jane replied 'Doing that'. She knew that she had to reply with a verb (do) and used the right tense (-ing) but was unable to use higher skills of descriptive vocabulary.

> Mark (three years) was the youngest in a family with three boys. The home setting was good in material terms and Mark had lots of toys to play with while his older brothers were at school. Although his understanding was at an age-appropriate level his expressive language was limited to some single words with a few two-word phrases. His attempts at words had often been ignored by his mother as they were not clear, so he had given up trying to use new words. His mother gave him few chances to participate in conversation — as he was a 'quiet' child she was happy to let him play alone with his toys while she worked around the house. As a result he did not have the opportunities to develop turn-taking and conversational skills in play and social games.

Developmental language disorders

Often the cause of a language disorder cannot be pinpointed. Many children who are assessed as having language problems show no evidence of neurological damage, hearing loss, mental handicap or marked psychological problems. They have good home backgrounds with caring, responsive parents who give them appropriate play and linguistic stimulation. Yet, in spite of the lack of adverse history they fail to develop language in the normal ways. These children have specific problems in the acquisition and development of language. Children with a severe disorder are unable to relate meanings to sounds or words and so receptive and expressive language will be impaired. They may be unable to analyse and integrate the various components of language and so do not have the basic principles which allow them to create new sentences. Sometimes the term 'developmental dysphasia' is used to describe a language disorder of this nature and severity.

In mild disorders, children have difficulties only in some specific components of language. They may have good understanding and use a wide range of single words appropriately but be unable to apply rules to produce phrases and sentences. They may be able to understand simple everyday commands and conversation but not long sentences with abstract word meanings and complex grammar.

Bilingualism in itself is not necessarily a cause of language disorder. If a child is exposed to two languages equally then it is likely that there will be normal development in both. There may be some confusion in the early stages, for example, a combination of the two vocabularies might be used in the same sentence, but gradually the different systems will be differentiated. Often the two languages are not given equal emphasis. Perhaps one is used more in the home and another in a different setting such as nursery or playgroup. In these instances there may be some differences between the levels of the language: the child may understand both languages equally well but use one more than the other and so have better linguistic skills in the favoured language. If a child from a bilingual background is not developing language along normal lines then it is likely that there is a specific problem, and assessments must be carried out to determine the cause of the difficulties.

The diagnosis of the cause(s) of a language disorder is often a difficult process. Sometimes there are several factors which may have effects at different stages in the child's development.

SPEECH DISORDERS

ARTICULATION

The term articulation is used to describe the process of producing speech sounds. Speech sounds fall into two main groups — consonants, such as m, p, s, sh and vowels, such as oo, ee, ay. Many chldren have difficulty with speech sounds at some point in the development of their speech. Some of these 'errors' are acceptable features of developing speech patterns but when a child is unintelligible or has many 'errors' there may be a speech disorder, i.e. a specific difficulty with the discrimination, production and use of speech sounds.

Examples of normal errors in speech development can be seen in the types of omissions and substitutions of consonants that children make. Children up to two-and-a-half-years of age may omit final consonants in words: 'bus' becomes 'bu', 'coat' becomes 'coa'. Words with two or three consonants can be hard for young children and so they often reduce the number: 'spoon' becomes 'poon', 'blue' becomes 'bue'. Some consonants are hard for children to say and so they use another instead: 'fish' becomes 'bish', 'shoe' becomes 'doe' and 'chips' become 'tips'. Sometimes children add an extra syllable to a word — 'chimney' becomes 'chiminey', or sequence syllables incorrectly — 'animal' becomes 'aminal'. Sometimes they make the physical production of a word simpler by making consonants in the same place, 'tat' is easier to say than 'cat' and 'goggy' is easier to say than 'doggy'.

Children with specific difficulties may have problems in using consonants in a systematic way. For example, they may be able to imitate a 'k' sound when asked to do so, but use 't' in its place when they talk: 'car' is said as 'tar' and 'cake' is said 'tate'.

Children with hearing loss will be unable to hear vowels and consonants clearly and so may not be able to produce them in their own speech. Also they have difficulty in hearing their own speech to know whether attempts at the word or sound are correct.

Children with cerebral palsy have difficulty controlling and co-ordinating the many subtle, rapid movements of lips, tongue and jaw that speech require: their speech may be slow and slurred.

Children with abnormal dentition may have problems with the clear articulation of consonants, particularly 's', 'sh', 'ch' and 'j', but this is not necessarily the case. Tongue-tie, where tongue movement is restricted by a short frenum (tissue going from the underside of the tongue to the floor of the mouth) is often thought to be the cause of a speech problems but this is not usually so.

RESONANCE, VOICE AND FLUENCY

Children with repaired cleft palate may have difficulty with articulation and/or another feature of speech — that of resonance. In English speech sounds are produced on air breathed out through the mouth: the exception being the 'm', 'n' and 'ng' sounds when air escapes down the nose too. If there is inadequate closure between the soft palate and the back of the throat some air may escape inappropriately through the nose, making the speech sound distorted. Listeners may describe this as the child 'talking down his nose' — the speech of children with severe nasal obstruction can also sound distorted in resonance but usually the problem resolves itself when the nasal obstruction improves: for example, children with severe catarrh and colds.

Sometimes children have persistently hoarse or croaky voices. They should be referred to an ear, nose and throat consultant in the first instance and then for assessment by a speech therapist.

Children may 'trip up' over words, stammering, e.g. b-b-bus or have difficulty in starting to say something. Such stammering or stuttering is common. Young children are not fluent all the time — no more than adults are, but when hesitations become more noticeable and cause concern for the child or parent then speech therapy advice should be sought.

EFFECTS OF SPEECH AND LANGUAGE DISORDERS

Young children unable to understand the language of those around them easily become angry and frustrated with themselves and others, or withdrawn and isolated as they fail to cope with the demands of the social world. If they cannot communicate their needs, feelings and wishes they may turn to other unacceptable ways of self-expression. There is a strong association between behaviour problems (temper tantrums, aggression, etc.) and language disorders in pre-school children and these problems often continue into school age.

Children who cannot communicate easily miss out on chances to mix with others and to learn social and conversation skills. They also miss opportunities for creative language: if they cannot talk to others they cannot take part in make-believe games. They easily develop poor self-esteem — it is very hard to be confident in yourself when no one responds to your attempts at language and interaction.

Children are also at risk in the development of reading and writing; if they have difficulty with the analysis and organization of speech sounds, word meanings and grammatical rules then it is understandable why they may later have problems with another symbolic code — that of written language.

WHAT TO DO

It is essential that any problems in the development of language and communication are detected as soon as possible; it is most important that problems at an early age are not ignored or minimized. In discussing developmental disorders, Martin Bax, a British paediatrician, comments 'It is rarely safe for a doctor to say "he will grow out of it". While it is true that the child who at three has a delay in speech and language will probably be talking by five, that is not the end of his troubles; he is highly likely to be in difficulties with reading at school within two or three years and is more likely to be a child with a behaviour disorder'.

In Great Britain the routine developmental screening of all preschool children by community paediatricians and health visitors helps, although some problems are still not picked up. The child with a suspected language problem should be referred for a full hearing test and to the speech therapy services for detailed assessment of the communication problem. Referrals to other disciplines will depend on the child's presenting problems and diagnosis. This may involve a psychologist, teacher of the deaf or occupational therapist and particular medical departments such as neurology, and ear, nose and throat.

In Great Britain speech therapists generally accept referrals from any source: health visitors, parents, doctors, nursery and playgroup staff and teachers. In urban areas it is not uncommon for therapists to provide a screening service in day nurseries and nursery schools.

Professionals who work with preschool children should be aware of the danger signs in children who are failing to develop language in the normally accepted ways. The points given below (page 68) are symptoms or behaviours of children with potential or current problems in hearing, speech and language. Regular intervention may not be required: the therapist may consider that the child is showing good potential and does not require specific help. However, it is important for these children to be seen: the therapist will be able to give the parents practical advice and information about language development and ways in which they can help their child: preventative counselling and intervention is as important as direct therapeutic treatment.

Table 5.3   Indicators for referral

If by six months they:

1. Show no interest in sounds (speech or environment).
2. Do not try to follow sounds with their head or eyes.
3. Show little interest in people or toys. (NB refer for audiological assessment).

If by one year they:

1. Show no consistent responses to sound (speech or environment).
2. Have stopped babbling or have not started. (NB refer for audiological assessment).

If by eighteen months they:

1. Do not understand simple commands, e.g. pick it up, give it to me.
2. Do not point to familiar objects or people when they are named, e.g. daddy, car, ball, shoe.
3. Show no interest in communicating by pointing, gestures or sounds.
4. Are not attempting to copy or say words or do not use jargon.
5. Use less than ten words.

If by two years they:

1. Do not understand simple commands, e.g. go and get your coat.
2. Do not relate two nouns in a request, e.g. put the *cup* on the *table*, show me *Daddy's sock*.
3. Do not have a vocabulary of fifty words.
4. Do not use simple two-word phrases, e.g. 'shoe gone', 'here teddy' which express two ideas.
5. Are still echoing most of what is said to them.
6. Are not using any consonants in their speech, e.g. p, b, t, d, m, n.

If by three years they:

1. Are not able to select pictures by verb only, e.g. 'who's eating?'.
2. Are not able to select pictures or objects by function, use or verb, e.g. 'which one do we eat?', 'which one do we wash with?'.
3. Do not understand simple prepositions, e.g. in, on, under, behind.
4. Are not using three to four word sentences with some past tenses and plurals.
5. Are not using, who, what or where questions.
6. Have speech which is intelligible to strangers *less* than 80 per cent of the time.

If by four years they:

1. Are unable to follow stories.
2. Show signs of not understanding everyday conversation.
3. Are not understanding more abstract concepts of colour and size.
4. Are not using full sentences. (Errors on irregular verb tenses and plurals are accepted.)
5. Show difficulties in correct word order in a sequence.
6. Are unable to relate simple events.
7. Have speech that is difficult to understand.
8. Show inappropriate use of language in social contexts or in relation to the speaker's conversation.
9. Have noticeable non-fluencies in their speech.

If by five years they:

1. Have difficulty following commands of two to three parts, e.g. go and get your coat and give your book to Jane.
2. Are unable to follow and relate events in a simple sequence.
3. Have any non-fluency of speech.
4. Show incorrect grammar in speech, e.g. omit verb tenses, confuse pronouns or auxiliary verbs. (NB some features are acceptable depending on adult dialect, e.g. she done it.)

General

1. If a child's voice is constantly too loud or too soft, of poor quality, or too monotone.
2. If a child sounds as though he or she is talking through their nose.
3. If a child shows irregularities in the rhythm of speech or intonation patterns.
4. If after five years there is any difficulty in producing or using speech sounds.

ASSESSMENT

A child referred for a speech therapy assessment may be seen for several diagnostic sessions. The therapist will carry out observations and assessment of play, attention and language skills by informal games and conversation and formal measurement on standardized tests. Information will be obtained from the mother or caregiver about the history of the problem, the nature of the child's problem and how the child communicates.

The therapist will recommend appropriate management: this may range from periodic reviews to check progress to regular therapy sessions. The facilities for the frequency and type of therapy offered vary greatly depending on the needs of the child and the local resources available. Some children are seen in intensive language groups in health centres and nurseries, others receive individual therapy in weekly sessions. Some children receive therapy at special playgroups or assessment centres where there are other professionals such as physiotherapists, teachers and psychologists. Whenever possible the treatment programmes are carried out in conjunction with the mother or main caregiver.

HOW OTHERS CAN HELP

The teaching of language is not an easy subject as there are many skills that have to be used in the assessment and treatment programmes. Many books are now available which give practical ideas (see the further reading list).

Any activities and materials used should be within the child's developmental level and be interesting and fun. Tasks should be presented in small stages so that the children succeed and progress. There must be a lot of repetition and opportunities for the skill to be applied in different situations: for example the concepts of 'big' and 'more' can be applied to many objects in many settings — not just one toy in the therapy room.

ATTENTION

A child must attend in order to learn. Children with poor concentration are helped if they are not expected to attend to more than one thing at a time. Sometimes it helps physically to turn them to face the person talking to them, or to put adults' hands over theirs during play to gain their attention. This must not be done too often as children become cross if their games are constantly interrupted.

PLAY AND INTELLECTUAL DEVELOPMENT

The development of play is described in Chapter 14. Play and language go hand-in-hand in a young child. Children with language problems, particularly delayed receptive language, often show limited imagination and creativity in their play. The improvement of play skills is an integral part of language work and therapeutic approaches are often carried out through play. Ideas on how to promote and stimulate play are also given in Chapter 14.

RECEPTIVE LANGUAGE

The type of activities to encourage the development of understanding will depend on the level that the child has reached.

Children at a pre-verbal language level need activities directed towards mixing with others and the understanding of gestures, phrases and key words. They need to develop joint attention, when they and the adult show mutual interest in objects, activities and events. Anticipation and turn-taking routines will develop listening and attention skills and help children learn a principle of conversation: the sequence from one person to another. This later extends into the child initiating actions or noises which the adult responds to. All the familiar, traditional baby rhymes and games are suitable for developing these skills. Routines of combining phrases with actions encourage association of the two and lead into understanding phrases and words, e.g. 'ready-steady-go' for cars moving, 'all fall down' for bricks falling down, 'in there' and 'all gone' for games of putting away, 'here I come' for games of chase/catch and tickling. Nursery rhymes and finger games also combine repetitive phrases with actions and provide changes for matching body parts with names (e.g. 'heads, shoulders, knees and toes'). The concepts of 'gone', 'hidden', 'find', and repetition of simple names of objects are used in hide-and-seek games.

The understanding of phrases and single words can be encouraged in numerous ways. Adults should speak in short, clear, simple sentences that relate to the objects or situations presented. In this way children can attend to language at their own level rather than becoming confused and distracted by unnecessary words in long sentences. Natural gestures should also be used to give information to help understanding. For example, saying, 'Here's your car, put it in the box' accompanied by appropriate pointing is much better than an excessive commentary of 'Here's your car under your chair, let's put it away over here and then it's time for dinner'.

Daily routines of mealtimes, washing and changing provide many opportunities for simple repetitive input, e.g. asking children to find their socks when they are being dressed, rather than automatically dressing them without comment. If they cannot link the word 'sock' with the actual item then the following sequence can be adopted. The question 'Where's your sock?', a wait for them to respond, and then gently guiding their hand towards the sock and getting them to hand it over, or selecting the sock with 'Here's your sock, it goes on your foot'. In this way they are hearing language, linking a word with an object and being provided with extra information to develop an awareness of objects.

Similar routines can occur in bathing and general care such as finding body parts during washing, drying and cleaning teeth.

A box of everyday objects that can be sorted through, explored and tipped in and out of the box provides chances for developing vocabulary and concepts of use and function. Cups can be drunk from, brushes used for brushing hair and teeth, toy food can be eaten. A teddy or doll can act as a model for demonstrating everyday actions to develop representative play. Even a simple game of blowing bubbles, used well, can encourage the concepts of pointing, 'look', 'gone', and 'move'; building towers with bricks encourages turn-taking and concepts of 'up', 'down' and 'again'.

The presentation of similar objects offers chances for concepts to be generalized, e.g. the child learns that things can be called the same even though they do not look exactly the same. Cars can be matched with others of different size and colour, toy apples can be 'matched' with toy cakes as they can both be eaten. Simple picture books provide excellent material where children can follow and use pointing and pretend actions as they hear the names of objects and actions and link one form of symbols — pictures to another — words. They will learn to link representations with real life objects as they point to the picture of a shoe and then show their own.

EXPRESSIVE LANGUAGE

Imitation is used a great deal to encourage early expressive language. The adult must be sensitive to how, when and why the child is communicating so that correct interpretations of sounds and actions are made and appropriate reinforcement given. For example, it is a good idea to copy the babbling patterns that a child makes so that there is a 'conversation' during play and care activities. The 'conversations' encourage listening, social interaction and turn-taking. At first it helps to imitate the sounds children make so that they become familiar with the copying routine. Later it is possible to introduce new sequences with different consonants and vowels or intonation patterns (going up and down in pitch) which children can learn to copy. It is useful to make symbolic noises for the appropriate toys or pictures — all children love to listen to noises for cars, trains and animals and often use the noise to 'name' the object before saying the proper word.

If a child makes some gesture or attempt at reaching for an object, that attempt should be rewarded, if possible by giving the object to the child. For example, at twelve months Harry was not using specific gestures — if he wanted to be picked up he would wave his arms and wriggle. Initially this was accepted by the adult to reinforce the idea that his action had meaning. Then the adult held up Harry's arms before picking him up — showing him that a specific action on his part was required before something happened. At first Harry just continued to wave vaguely and wriggle but when this was not accepted (i.e. he was not picked up), he started to make the specific movement of arms up — which was reinforced. Within a week the routine of a specific gesture for a specific request was established: the use of an accepted symbol for communication had been achieved.

If simple commentary for play activities is provided, children will learn to link names with objects and actions. Later they will use language to direct their actions and control their environment. For example when looking at picture books ask the question 'What's this?', wait for a response and then provide the answer if necessary. Gradually children will provide the name when the picture is pointed to, they learn basic conversation routines in this game too. This routine can be extended to more complex questions — 'Find me x', 'Where's the x?', 'What's x eating?', as a progression from the very simple 'What's this?' question.

If children point at something, wait for them to use words. If they do not or cannot name it, provide the name, wait for a response and then give them what they want. Of course some children do not respond to this tactic to encourage them to talk — they simply walk away or go and get what they want without speaking. It can be very difficult knowing how long to hold out for a child to say something — if you are too demanding the child may opt out of asking altogether. It is important to try to work with situations or objects where the child really wants something so that they are motivated to respond.

When children see that language has an effect on people, they are more inclined to use it. The technique of role reversal can be used in this way, particularly in small group work. Give a child a command that has to be carried out. Then the child must give the same command to another child, or the adult or perhaps a doll or teddy. This approach reinforces the notion that language can be used to gain objects or actions in situations when pointing or looking are inadequate.

To encourage particular vocabulary or forms of language the technique known as forced alternatives can be used. If a child is uncertain of vocabulary or can say the words but is reluctant to do so, provide a choice: 'Do you want the cars or the lego?' The child must recognize and select the right word. This approach can sometimes be used to develop forms of grammar. When a child is describing pictures, an attempt at a two-word phrase can be assisted by asking 'is the dog walking or sleeping?'. The right vocabulary and form have been provided and the child has a model to use. This technique has to be used with care and discretion as it is not always appropriate. A child who cannot cope with alternatives will respond by saying both; a child with echolalia simply repeats the last word and may give the impression of responding correctly.

Reinforcing and expanding what children say provide simple additional vocabulary, grammar and meaning for them to understand and assimilate. For a young child at the naming stage, reinforce attempts by confirming: 'Yes, that's a car isn't it, here's another one'. For an older child provide more information, e.g. 'Yes, you've got a little blue car, the doors open don't they?' Reinforce the correct content and meaning of the child's statement but *do not try to correct the grammar*, for often children are not at a stage where they are able and ready to do so. In a classic example of the futility of correction a mother tried nine times to change a child's statement of 'Nobody don't like me' to 'Nobody likes me'. Finally the child's exasperated last attempt came out as 'Nobody don't likes me'.

If children have specific problems in learning linguistic rules they will be unable to produce correct sentences by imitation alone: highly specialized therapeutic techniques will be required.

Language teaching should be enjoyable, meaningful and involve children in activities where language provides commentary and structure for their own actions and needs and where language is used for social interaction. Children themselves must play an active role in learning, for communication is a two-way process. Language work can be fun and rewarding for adults too: when the child progresses the combined sense of achievement from child and adult is worth all the efforts that are made.

AUGMENTATIVE AND ALTERNATIVE COMMUNICATION

Children who have difficulty coping with spoken language are sometimes taught other systems of communication. Children with severe hearing loss or severe developmental dysphasia may be taught a signing system such as British Sign Language or Paget-Gorman, where words are represented by finger and hand movements. Children who cannot cope with these complex systems may be taught a more simple one such as that of Makaton. The Makaton system is often used for children with mental handicap.

Children with cerebral palsy who can neither speak nor use their hands to form signs can still communicate using symbols or pictures to which they point.

If their hand control is too poor for pointing or pressing switches they can still communicate thanks to recent developments in microcomputers that can be controlled by switches operated by the mouth or by eye or head movements.

The systems can be used either to replace spoken language or to supplement it. For example, in the manual signing systems of Paget-Gorman and Makaton, the children are encouraged to attempt to say the 'words' they are signing.

The introduction and teaching of signing or visual symbol language systems is a complex matter. The speech therapist recommends such a system only after careful assessment of the child's language levels, needs and motivation and the family environment and support. A system must be used and understood by all the immediate family members or care-givers so that the children receive language input in that system, as happens with verbal language. Also they must have sufficient cognitive skills to be able to cope with a symbolic code.

FURTHER READING

D. Cox and J. Pearson *Material for Language Stimulation*. London: The College of Speech Therapists.

P. Hastings and B. Hayes (1981) *Encourage Language Development*. London: Croom Helm.

D. Jeffree and R. McConkey (1976) *Let Me Speak*. London: Souvenir Press.

M.B. Karnes (1982) *You and Your Small Wonder*. Books 1 and 2. Circle Pines: American Guidance Service.

A. Manolson (1983) *It Takes Two To Talk*. Toronto: Hanen Early Language Resource Centre.

G. Shiach (1972) *Teach Them To Speak*. London: Ward Lock Educational.

Problems of Preschool Children
Edited by N. Richman and R. Lansdown
© 1988 John Wiley & Sons Ltd

CHAPTER 6

The Clumsy Child

RICHARD LANSDOWN

INTRODUCTION

Mark was four-and-a-half when his mother took him to her doctor. He has always seemed a bright little boy he spoke earlier than his sister and was reading quite well already. But he was a big disappointment to his father who was a professional footballer. Mark was just not interested in kicking a ball and he had butter fingers. He was not very keen on his tricycle either. His mother reflected anxiously that he had been slow to walk, his father dismissed him as lazy or wilfully disobedient. Mark, realizing how he was not meeting his father's expectations, became alternately sad and frantic.

DEFINITION AND FREQUENCY

There is no generally accepted definition of a clumsy child. One that is used quite often is:

> Children whose motor co-ordination is poor, disproportionate to their general developmental level.

This emphasizes the fact that we are not concerned so much with children who are generally retarded, more with those whose development is uneven. But we are left with the rather vague word 'poor' to determine whether or not a child is called clumsy. One authority has suggested that any child whose poor co-ordination causes anxiety to adults should be included in the group. This is a partial answer but adults vary so much in their expectations that it is far from satisfactory.

There is, indeed, no universal agreement on the use of the word 'clumsy'.

Some authorities see it as having too many negative associations, children so called are automatically put into a substandard category. The preferred phrase is — children with perceptual motor difficulties.

There is agreement on two points, though: we should exclude from this group those children who are constantly getting in the way and bumping into things because they are overactive or excitable, and we should exclude also those who have a clearly observed neurological deficit.

Partly because of the lack of an accepted definition and partly because of the difficulties of measuring motor development in preschool children (discussed below) it is not possible to say exactly how many clumsy children of different ages there are. It is suggested that 5–7 per cent of seven-year-olds will fall into this category with more boys than girls, perhaps in a ratio of 2 : 1.

RECOGNIZING CLUMSY CHILDREN

In one sense, all preschool children are clumsy some of the time. Even a future ballerina will stumble when taking her first few steps. This observation can have two consequences. One is that it may stop some people from worrying unnecessarily: we should not expect young children to be perfectly controlled in their movements any more than we expect them to speak correctly from the outset. The other is that adults may dismiss clumsiness as 'something they all grow out of'. In a minority of cases they do no such thing; this minority is the subject of the present chapter.

A further difficulty in this area is that there is no typical pattern of behaviour. Some therapists are reluctant to use any blanket terms and prefer to describe specific areas of weakness. It may help, for example, to discriminate between:

(1) Difficulties with large muscle movements involving running, walking and climbing (gross motor problems).
(2) Poor finger co-ordination, involving individual finger movements (fine motor problems).
(3) Deficient visuo-motor skills, producing difficulties with catching a ball, drawing and writing (visuo-motor problems).

On the other hand, there are some ways in which these children are similar to each other.

(1) Developmentally the skills are present but their quality is poor. It is similar to the child who has learnt to swim but not got beyond the dog paddle to more refined strokes. Perhaps most importantly of all is a common problem of organization and planning: children seem to know what they want to do but cannot plan how to do it.

Peter was doing a puzzle with pegs to be put into a board. He accidentally dropped a peg onto the floor. He could see it and his arms were long enough to allow him to pick it up without moving from his chair. But his lack of organization led him to getting off his chair, then walking round three sides of the table, picking up the peg and returning to his seat.

(2) Children can often see that their planning is wrong but they do not know how to correct it. This leads them to starting something but not completing it, the result being an infuriated, frustrated child and an unfinished task.
(3) There are notable weaknesses in rhythm and the judgement of force or power. An example of a problem of judging force is the child bouncing a ball against a wall to be caught on the rebound. The clumsy child invariably throws it far too hard and it comes back like a rocket. Rhythm and force are involved in writing: the child with problems will write jerkily, pressing far too hard on the page.
(4) Dealing with anything in a sequence is a fearsome obstacle. Dressing is an example of a motor sequence that can bring humiliation to children and anger to adults. When a boy seems unable to realize that jeans have to be put on before shoes his parents may be forgiven for wondering about his intelligence.
(5) So much that they do is much slower than expected. It is tempting to try to hurry children, but the more this is done the more flustered the child is likely to become.
(6) Children are unable to comprehend some organization related words. For them it is no use saying 'Wash behind your ears' because they do not know what 'behind' means.

The examples given above show why it is that parents are often the first to recognize clumsiness, since it is made evident in everyday living activities. Sometimes though, it is not noted until children are expected to write. It is by no means uncommon to find that clumsy children have language disorders as well, see Chapter 5.

The assessment of children can take three forms. The first is what most parents do: to compare a child with other children to see if there are any developmental differences. Sometimes comparisons are made informally: 'My Johnny is not as good at throwing snowballs as her Darren'. At other times a chart or check-list is used, see Table 6.1.

The problems surrounding the use of such charts are discussed further in Chapter 7. They can be useful but can also be misleading. It is of the utmost importance to remember that children develop unevenly: they may lag in one area while forging ahead in another.

The second approach to assessment is the formal test. First a group of tasks is devised, all of which involve some aspect of motor skills. These tasks may include walking along a straight line, putting bricks or buttons into a box,

Table 6.1   Motor development by age

Gross motor

1 month	Large, jerky limb movements with arms more active than legs.
3 months	When on tummy child can lift head and upper chest.
6 months	May sit unsupported for a few moments. Feet bounce up and down when child is held appropriately on a hard surface.
9 months	Moves around by some means or another.
12 months	May stand alone for a few moments; moves about the floor rapidly.
15 months	Walks, but unsteadily; goes upstairs by one means or another.
18 months	Walks well on level surface, walks upstairs with help.
2 years	Runs safely but not smoothly; throws a ball.
3 years	May climb on apparatus; rides a tricycle.
4 years	Walks alone, one step at a time, up and down stairs.
5 years	Runs lightly, is active on apparatus.

Vision and fine motor

1 month	Notices dangling object 6–8 inches away.
3 months	Visually alert; watches own hands.
6 months	Uses whole hand to grasp; reaches for objects.
9 months	Passes objects from hand to hand.
12 months	Picks up objects with thumb and first finger.
15 months	Scribbles with pencil in imitation; can put one brick into another.
18 months	Scribbles spontaneously and can build tower of three bricks.
2 years	Scribbles circular patterns; one hand may be preferred by now; can use spoon quite well.
3 years	Copies a circle; eats with spoon and fork.
4 years	Draws recognizable person with head, legs and trunk, and possibly features.
5 years	Copies a square and triangle.

Note: The above table is no more than a rough guide. It is based on that given in *Child Development Made Simple* by Richard Lansdown, published by Heinemann in 1984.

copying shapes with a pencil or putting pegs into a board with holes in it. These tests are then given to several hundred children from the general population in order to obtain some idea of an average level of skill. Then, when an individual child does the tests, his or her performance can be compared with the average. The basic approach is similar to that used in devising intelligence tests and has both the same advantages and some of the same disadvantages (see Chapter 7).

Some general developmental tests, for example, the Bayley Scales, and some intelligence tests, for example the McCarthy Scale, have a motor component, allowing some estimate to be made of how disproportionate the child's motor development is. This is especially useful when considering whether a child is generally backward.

The third approach is that used by the trained therapist who observes children carefully, giving certain tasks to help the observation, but coming to a conclusion based on the *quality* of the child's performance rather than any total score. To give an example: two children may have difficulty in using a posting box, but their difficulties could come from different causes. Mary may constantly try to put the square shape in the round hole (a problem of shape recognition) while Darren may select the correct hole but fail to push the shape in (a problem of motor control).

CAUSES OF CLUMSINESS

The first point to make is that there is rarely anything wrong with the child's hands, arms, legs or feet. The root of the problem is generally the brain, the way it functions and its organization (see Chapter 4). It seems likely that messages to the brain from the outside world, or messages from the brain to hands and feet, are not processed as efficiently by clumsy children as they are by others. This is really an assumption since the indications of clumsiness are found not by a direct examination of the brain but by observations of children's behaviour. It must be emphasized again that children called clumsy in the sense in which we are using it are not suffering from cerebral palsy (although cerebral palsy undoubtedly brings clumsiness), nor is it appropriate to use phrases like 'brain damage' or 'minimal cerebral dysfunction', since both make assumptions about the brain that are not warranted.

One vital area to check is vision. Children who cannot see properly often go undetected in their preschool years, some go undetected for much longer, since to them the blurred world they experience is normal and so they do not complain.

Clumsiness and poor visual perception are often linked. Perception in this sense means making sense of what is seen. The two children playing with a posting box are an example: Mary's problem was primarily one of visual perception since she could not make sense of what she saw to allow her to recognize that a square shape is associated with a square hole. What is more, perception extends to more than just the recognition of a shape, it includes the ability to deal with information about objects in time and in space. As an exercise to underline the complexity of all this, try to analyse the skills involved in catching a ball. (Then look at the analysis on page 81).

Perceptual skills are learned, experience being crucial, and so once again general brain function is involved. Most of the skills discussed in this chapter involve a combination of perceptual and motor skills and it is likely that visual perception is often a very large component in explaining motor difficulties.

A distressing consequence is the difficulty that many of these children have in keeping friends, their awkwardness annoys at all levels.

CONSEQUENCES OF CLUMSINESS

Some consequences have been touched on already. Children may be labelled as lazy, they may see themselves as generally inferior becaue they fail so frequently at tasks that are so clearly valued by adults. The tasks concerned have special power because they are, by definition, visible. Children can hide some deficiencies but they cannot easily hide clumsiness.

What is more, the child who finds motor skills difficult is likely to give up trying. Since practice is such an important component in the development of this area, one consequence of clumsiness is likely to be more clumsiness.

As children reach school age so more is demanded of them in terms of visuo-motor skills. They are expected to move about a room without knocking things over, to copy shapes, to write, to begin rudimentary mathematics in some cases. All of these may present problems for the clumsy child.

HELPING THE CLUMSY CHILD

The first step is recognizing that help may be needed. This may sound so obvious that it does not need saying but, as has been mentioned above, it is easy to fall into the trap of labelling children stupid or lazy when in fact they are neither.

The second is to try to establish both the nature and the cause of the clumsiness. This will probably involve a medical examination and an assessment by a physiotherapist and/or an occupational therapist. It may be useful to have a psychologist's opinion as well.

The value of establishing the nature of the problem can be seen when a programme of activities is devised. Some children need much more practice than others in order to build up a pattern of movements necessary for a smooth performance. But for other children simply practising a movement is likely to do more harm than good since, if they cannot properly perceive what they are supposed to be doing in the first place, practice will get them nowhere and usually leads to frustration rather than success.

Once the nature of the problem has been established there are several ground rules to be observed.

(1) It is essential to spend some time on what children can do in order to maintain their confidence and self-respect.
(2) Training or practice sessions should be short rather than long.
(3) Tasks should be broken into small, manageable steps.
(4) Children should never be hurried; they have their own rate.
(5) Strategies should be taught to overcome specific problems, dressing is a good example of this need.

Perhaps most important of all: children should not be asked to do what adults know they are not capable of. This may sound obvious but many adults seem ignorant of the obvious and try to force children to achieve a skill, using humiliation as a weapon. The only lessons of humiliation are negative and no one gains.

THE OUTLOOK FOR THE CLUMSY CHILD

If not detected and treated, clumsy children are more likely than their peers to be at risk of both learning and behavioural difficulties. If helped there is no certainty that they will not remain in the lower reaches at games for example, but at least there is a chance that the more extreme difficulties will be avoided and in mild cases normal performance may be expected. Come what may, if the notion that they are lazy or stupid is dispelled, much good will have been done.

CATCHING A BALL

The discussion given below is based on Judith Laszlo and Philip Bairstow's *Perceptual-Motor Behavior* published in 1985 by Holt, Rinehart and Winston.

There is a long developmental lead in to the skill of catching, starting with reaching and grasping stationary objects in the first year of life.

A crucial aspect is that the environment is constantly changing: the ball moves and the catcher must move both body and hands. Movements of eyes, head, arms and hands have to be co-ordinated and synchronized with the movement of the ball.

The catcher must be aware of body and hand movements, through the sense of kinaesthesis, the sense which enables people to analyse their own movements and be aware of where limbs fingers and toes are.

Preparation for catching, based on experience, is essential. The skilled catcher will adopt an anticipatory position for both body and hands to save time once the ball has been thrown.

The ball has to be followed by eye, with accurate predictions made about its speed and trajectory, i.e. an understanding of time and space.

Prediction comes into the grasping action as well, for this begins well before the ball makes contact with the hands (young children make errors here, grasping when it is too late).

Acknowledgement

The author would like to thank Alison Wisbeach, Head Occupational Therapist, The Wolfson Centre, University of London, for her kind advice on this chapter.

FURTHER READING

N. Gordon and I. McInlay (1980) *Helping Clumsy Children*. Edinburgh: Churchill Livingstone.

Problems of Preschool Children
Edited by N. Richman and R. Lansdown
© 1988 John Wiley & Sons Ltd

CHAPTER 7

Children with Learning Difficulties

RICHARD LANSDOWN

INTRODUCTION

Mary's mother is watching some children playing in the park. She notices, not for the first time, that Mary is apart from the others. Sometimes another girl or boy approaches but, seeming to get no response, drifts away to play with someone else. Her mother reflects that Mary is different from her other children and, again not for the first time, she worries about her development. She thinks of John, one of Mary's brothers, who was so lively and friendly when he was the same age. She has read somewhere that one in five children in Britain will need some sort of special educational help at some time in their career and she worries a bit more.

Comparing one child with another is understandable, even inevitable, but it can be a dangerous pursuit. Children vary widely in their abilities and in the rate at which they develop, as Table 7.1 indicates. From this table it can be seen that the attainment of some skills stretches over many months. Mary's mother might have been worried, for example, about her daughter's ability to scribble. While about a quarter of children will, according to the information in Table 7.1, have learnt to do this by the age of about twelve months, another quarter will not have done so by sixteen months and even at two-and-a-quarter years about 10 per cent will still not have reached this stage. (The ages given in Table 7.1 are based on American children and should not be seen as more than a rough guide for others.)

There can be dangers in comparing skills in the same child, for some develop very unevenly. One mother brought her eighteen-month-old to the clinic saying she thought he was backward because he was walking so badly. When he was examined it was found that his walking was slow but within normal limits and his language was very advanced. His mother was reassured and in his case he grew up to be academically highly successful but always a little clumsy. There have, of course, been many other children who are initially a little slow in

Table 7.1   The range of ages at which children attain certain milestones (Adapted, with permission, from W.K. Frankenburg, A. Fandal, W. Sciarillo and D. Burgess (1981). The newly abbreviated and revised Denver Developmental Screening Test. *Journal of Pediatrics*, **90**, 995–999.)

	25%	50%	75%	90%
Laughs	6 weeks	8 weeks	10 weeks	14 weeks
Smiles spontaneously	6	8	13	20
Rolls over	10	12	16	20
Grasps rattle	10	14	16	18
Turns to voice	16	$5\frac{1}{2}$ months	$7\frac{1}{2}$ months	$8\frac{1}{2}$ months
Thumb–finger grasp	7 months	$8\frac{1}{2}$	9	$10\frac{1}{2}$
Stands well alone	10	$11\frac{1}{2}$	13	14
Scribbles spontaneously	12	$13\frac{1}{2}$	16	27
Uses spoon, spilling some	$13\frac{1}{2}$	$14\frac{1}{2}$	18	$23\frac{1}{2}$
Combines two different words	14	$19\frac{1}{2}$	22	27
Washes and dries hands	19	23	$2\frac{1}{2}$ years	3 years

walking or talking who grow up to be quite normal in both.

Nevertheless, as was mentioned above, some comparisons are inevitable if we are to think about children constructively, since we have to see them in some form of context. What is crucial when we are thinking about children who have learning difficulties is that we are aware of the possible pitfalls.

CATEGORIES OF LEARNING DIFFICULTY

Some authorities argue that we should not put children into any kind of category because to do so means that we automatically label them and labelling is harmful. They point to the fact that labels change at regular intervals: people in our grandparents' generation might have been called 'idiots', or even 'cretins', depending on the severity of their disability. Our parents might have called such people 'mentally deficient', possibly 'educationally subnormal' or just plain 'backward'. A little later the phrase 'slow learner' might have been used. It seems that labels gradually develop unpleasant associations so that sooner or later a new set has to be employed. What is more, putting children into categories can lead to adults having unduly lowered expectations of them; 'Oh, she's only a retarded child, we can't expect any more of her'.

A further, powerful argument, based on the observation of many children, is that we cannot simply divide people into watertight groups. It is true that we can distinguish between the high fliers and the very slow, but between these extremes there is much overlapping. Rather than just assigning children to categories it is better to say something about a child's level of ability and what he or she can or cannot do. This is far more helpful than a crude label. On the other hand, just as there is some justification for using descriptive terms, for example 'profoundly deaf', when we are referring to certain groups of children, so the use of categories can at times be helpful in allowing us to communicate about children without needing to write cumbersome descriptions of each individual child.

CHILDREN WITH SEVERE LEARNING DIFFICULTIES

DEFINITION AND FREQUENCY

There are two ways of defining children with severe learning difficulty (sometimes referred to as mentally handicapped), one based on test results, the other on the abilities that the children are expected to attain when they reach adulthood. Neither is perfect.

Testing children is discussed below (page 92). Many of the tests used give results in the form of a quotient, that is a score which is based on the child's ability to manage certain tests, with allowances made for the child's age. For example, two children aged four and five may be given the same set of ten tests. The four-year-old can manage six of them and the five-year-old manages seven. But when the children's ages are taken into account the four-year-old will have the higher quotient. A quotient of 100 is average; a score of approximately below 50 is associated with severe learning difficulty. The lower the score the greater the assumed problems.

The second way is to look at what the child is doing now and to make an estimate of the level that will be reached in childhood. A crucial criterion is whether or not the person is likely to be able to function independently. These estimates are based on previous experience of children who have been followed up into adulthood. They are often no more than a rough guide, and can be misleading, for it is now realized that people with mental handicap can do far more than was imagined in the past. However, some expectations are fairly certain. For example, if a child of four is unable to walk or to utter intelligible words and also seems unable to understand what is said, there is a reasonable chance that this child will continue to need supervision for the rest of his or her life.

Surveys in several developed countries give a rate of between three and four children per 1000 falling into the category of severe learning difficulty.

INDICATIONS

Children with severe difficulties will generally do everything later than most.

This is true of skills such as sitting and walking but it is particularly so of anything to do with communication. So an early sign may be a delay in recognizing a familiar face, or responding to a smile. Severely retarded children seem less curious than one would expect and seem to have less desire to join in with others in communication at any level. This becomes especially noticeable at the time when children are expected to talk: babbling and imitation are delayed and clear words come very much later, if at all. Other skills, like the use of a spoon, also come very much later.

There are two further points that sometimes cause confusion. One is that some children have what are known as islets of ability, that is they are well behind others in almost everything but seem able to keep up in one area. Often parents comment on how good a child's memory is, particularly so in cases of infantile autism. The presence of one isolated skill does not, unfortunately, mean that there is an expectation that other skills will come into line with the one that is quite good.

The second point is that children with learning difficulties of the severe to moderate kind are often referred to as 'slow learners'. This is, in some ways, an accurate description, since they do learn much more slowly than others, but it is misleading in that it gives the impression that they will eventually catch up and be normal. We certainly know that all children *can* learn up to a point and no child should be abandoned educationally, but to imagine that all children can catch up if only they and their teachers try hard enough is to put an intolerable strain on everyone concerned, not least the children themselves. Indeed, it is sad but often observed that the gap between the attainments of some children and their peers widens with age, a point that is hard for parents to cope with but one that has to be faced.

CAUSES OF SEVERE LEARNING DIFFICULTIES

Recent advances in the understanding of disability has enabled us to make an accurate diagnosis in about 80 per cent of cases. This is a great and welcome improvement on the position as it was only a few years ago, welcome especially for parents who are often enormously relieved when a cause is found.

As a general rule, the more severe the problem the more likely the cause is to be organic, that is physical, in origin. A paediatric examination is, then, a crucially important part of the work in the early stages of diagnosis (see below, page 92 for a discussion of the assessment of children).

PRENATAL CAUSES

About 55 per cent of severe learning difficulties can be traced to causes occurring before birth. Down's syndrome, an abnormality of the chromosomes, is the most common of these, with approximately one child in every 660 live births being affected. It must be noted that not all children with Down's syndrome are severely retarded; here is a good example of the danger of easy labelling. Children with inborn errors of metabolism form another group affected before birth. They are children whose bodies do not process food in the normal way, leading often to a reduction in brain weight and to retardation. One example of a condition that can now be detected very early in a child's life is phenylketonuria, or PKU for short. Tests done just after birth can indicate the presence of this condition and dietary management can lead to a reasonable chance that the child will grow up to be within the normal range. Other parental factors are sometimes less certain. The health of the mother is a good example of this uncertainty. It is known that mothers who are heavily addicted to drugs are likely to have damaged babies and both smoking and drinking have been implicated as possible causes of retardation. While neither is to be advocated in excess it would be most unwise to say that *any* indulgence during pregnancy inevitably harms the baby.

PERINATAL CAUSES

'Perinatal' causes are those arising between the 28th week of pregnancy and the end of the first week after birth. They account for about 20 per cent of cases of severe learning difficulty. Causes in this area are often associated with prematurity. There have been enormous strides in perinatal care in the last ten years or so and many more premature babies survive than before. It is now acknowledged that the term 'premature' is too general to be helpful in this context, it is better to be precise. Babies born weighing less than four-and-a-half pounds (2000 grammes) are known as *low birthweight* infants. Those born prematurely, i.e. after a short prenatal period are called *short gestation period* infants and those who are small considering the length of their gestation are called *small for dates*.

Generally it is the last group, the small for dates babies, who give rise to most concern, but all who are born premature are likely to have some developmental delay compared with others, at least in the first year or so. Providing they receive adequate care and as long as there are no other complications most catch up well by the age they are due to go to school. The management of prematurity is a good example of the need to consider the interaction between children and their environment: two children may be born with identical problems physically but their development will depend on how well they are treated, both physically and psychologically.

Injury at birth can lead to a range of difficulties, including those affecting learning. The phrase 'brain damage' conjures up all sorts of often misleading pictures and is usually best avoided. Nevertheless, there are occasions when a baby is damaged at birth, sometimes for example, through a lack of oxygen. Once again, recent advances in medical care have helped to reduce the numbers of children affected.

POSTNATAL CAUSES

In developed countries about 10 per cent of severe learning difficulties can be traced to events occurring after the child's birth, most often the cause is an accident, especially a road accident, leading to damage to the brain. One authority, reflecting on the fact that many if not most accidents can be prevented, has described accidents involving head injury as 'One of the disgraces of the 20th century'.

MILD LEARNING DIFFICULTIES

DEFINITION AND FREQUENCY OF CHILDREN WITH MILD LEARNING DIFFICULTIES

This is much harder to estimate, since there is much less agreement on the definition of a mild learning difficulty. To a large extent it depends on the provisions that are available. There is little point, it is sometimes argued, in assessing children and categorizing children, if nothing can be offered to help them, so the counting exercise is not carried out. As a rough guide one might talk of about 1 per cent of all children having mild learning difficulties, but if one broadens the category to consider all children who have *any* problems in learning then the Warnock Committee's estimate of 20 per cent can be quoted.

INDICATIONS

Because children with mild learning difficulties vary so much there are no clear cut, universal indicators. Some children are generally a little slow in development, others are uneven, in some ways reaching normally expected levels. One common factor is that the suspicion of any problem usually comes very much later, often not until the child has been in school for a year or so.

CAUSES OF MILD LEARNING DIFFICULTY

Some causes are organic and have been mentioned above. A child with Down's syndrome, for example, may have only a mild learning difficulty, a road traffic accident may lead to damage that causes no more than mild problems.

UNDETECTED SENSORY DEFECTS

Whenever a child is suspected of having a learning difficulty it is always worthwhile asking questions about possible problems with vision or hearing. Mild hearing loss is a particularly important cause to investigate since it is so easy to overlook. Children are perceived as lazy, or more commonly dreamy when frequently they cannot hear properly. The intermittent nature of much mild hearing loss causes even more problems, one day everything is fine, the next there is a loss in performance. If there is any suspicion of language delay, or of any other learning difficulty come to that, it is of the utmost importance that the child's hearing be properly assessed, and 'properly' in this context means in a fully equipped clinic.

Vision is a rather different matter, the association between learning difficulties and mild visual problems being less clear cut. Children who are just a little impaired may not differ significantly from others; they may be less good at tasks requiring hand–eye co-ordination, although this is not always the case. There is even some evidence to suggest that children who are congenitally shortsighted learn to read more quickly than their peers. However, the lack of certainty does not mean that visual defects are of no importance and a careful examination of children's visual acuity should always be made if there are grounds for suspecting that a defect is present.

ENVIRONMENTAL CAUSES

It is John's third birthday. He wakes up in his own bedroom and he finds his mother and father standing by the bedside, wishing him a happy birthday. A few minutes later he has breakfast of cereal, milk and fruit with his parents and his older sister and together they talk about the plans for the day. As it is a Saturday John's father will be at home and there will be a ceremony of opening presents. The first is a book, which John's sister reads aloud while John eagerly follows the text. Later in the afternoon there is a small party with some of John's friends, several of whom join in games in the garden, helped by the adults. Just before he goes to bed John has an extra story as it is his birthday.

Peter is also three. He also lives with his older sister and his mother but they are in a single parent family and Peter cannot remember what his father looks like. His sister is sick and her coughing has kept him awake a lot of the night since her bed is very close to his in the same room. His mother also sleeps in the same room and she, too, had been kept awake. She is short tempered partly because she has gone without sleep and partly because she is worried about money to pay the bills that are due. She has forgotten that it is Peter's birthday and even if she had remembered she would not have done anything about it since she cannot see that a child of that age understands birthdays. Peter is given a cup of sweet tea and some bread and butter for his breakfast by his sister and they go off to eat in front of the television. Their mother tries to do some housework but she is unable to find the energy to do much and wonders whether the pills that her doctor has given her for depression are doing her any good. But she takes another one and manages to get everyone dressed ready to go out. She is to visit her father who lives about an hour's train journey away. She likes seeing her father but dreads the journey because the children play up so much. No matter how much she tells them to sit still and be good they just wriggle about and ask questions and start squabbling. Often she wishes she had never had children and sometimes she tells them so. But somehow she gets through the day and the grizzling kids are put to bed.

These two accounts are not exaggerated in their differences, they indicate the enormous power that environmental factors can and do play in influencing children's development (see Chapters 1, 2 and 3). John is given the message that he is wanted, he is treated as an individual by parents and a sister who have time to do so and his learning needs are met in a variety of ways. Peter, on the other hand, has little opportunity to learn much more than the facts that he is not really wanted and that the best way to obtain his mother's approval is not to be curious but to sit quietly doing nothing. One could say that he is learning to be stupid.

The relationship between social disadvantage and learning has been studied extensively. One of the best known sources of evidence is the National Child Development Study which noted that a very wide range of factors related to health and education were related to social conditions. Three main factors emerged from this work.

(1) *Family composition*. The story of John and Peter above illustrates how important it is that parents have time to give sufficient attention to children. Those in one-parent families with many brothers and sisters will almost certainly miss out on this most vital commodity.

(2) *Low income*. Not only will there be less time, there will also be less money the larger the family and that in itself can bring extra worry to the parent. Low income in itself is a contributory cause to the kind of environmental pattern that hinders children's development, not only because there are worries about bills but also because there is little left over for what are perceived as luxuries like books.

(3) *Poor housing* is the third factor, clearly related to the other two, illustrated in the story of the two boys.

At this point it must be made clear that social disadvantage is not an automatic passport to learning problems. There are many children from homes where there is only one parent, who are poor, living in cramped conditions, yet who develop normally as happy individuals, able to cope with everything that is asked of them. The essential point to make is that the child from a disadvantaged home is more likely to have learning difficulties.

GENETICS VERSUS ENVIRONMENT

There have been fierce arguments about the relative contributions of genes and the environment. Some say that the social factors just mentioned are of little importance since children inherit so much of their intelligence that the environment really has only a negligible effect. Others assert the exact opposite, saying that there is no evidence whatsoever to support the 'genes are everything' view. Now the controversy has virtually passed for the consensus opinion is that children do inherit certain capacities but there is an interaction between those capacities and the environment in which they are brought up, and it is the interaction which determines the final level of achievement that is reached.

SPECIFIC LEARNING DIFFICULTIES

It is easy to regard children with specific difficulties as a subset of those with more mild problems; in fact they are quite different. They are hard to detect, especially in the preschool years, they are often very hard to teach and they may continue to puzzle their peers and themselves even into adulthood.

DEFINITION AND FREQUENCY OF CHILDREN WITH SPECIFIC LEARNING DIFFICULTIES

This term refers to children who have generally average or good abilities in most areas but have specific weaknesses. Some have a specific language delay: good at walking, jumping and catching, they are unable to process the spoken word. Others may be clumsy, never catching a ball, never learning to ride a bicycle. Some cannot master mathematics and others remain stumped by reading or spelling, the latter group are, sometimes, referred to as suffering from dyslexia. Because there are no agreed criteria to define precisely different types of specific difficulties it is not possible to say how many children can be described in this way.

> Pat was outwardly normal in every way. She had been a little slow to talk but no one was worried by this and she was a lively, friendly toddler. She went to nursery school at three and showed promise at drawing and making models. But even when her best friends were starting to read simple words she showed no interest in reading, although she loved listening to stories. She grew up to be articulate, good at science and nature study, but she was a slow reader and an appalling speller.

> Steven, on the other hand, began scribbling in books at the age of three, in imitation of his parents and he could read at four. But he was always more interested in pretend games than in puzzles and he showed no interest in number work. He grew up able to take a degree in English but was incapable of getting past a twelve-year level in maths.

INDICATIONS

Clumsiness and specific language delay are usually detected during the pre-school years but problems with more academic tasks like mathematics and spelling are rarely suspected in most children before the age of four, frequently not until very much later. However, it is of the utmost importance for those dealing with young children to be aware that such problems can arise, since it is very easy otherwise to fall into the trap of thinking that a child who is poor at one skill is poor at all others. Careful observation of each child's strengths as well as weaknesses is the key to the detection of specific difficulties.

THE ASSESSMENT OF CHILDREN

THE PEOPLE INVOLVED

It is customary good practice to involve four or more groups of people in the assessment of children thought to have learning difficulties.

Parents are, in many ways, the most important group. It is often they who first notice that there is something wrong; they are in an excellent position to give a full medical and social history; they can fill in details of behaviour at home when one is observing a child in clinic or nursery.

A medical opinion should always be sought, with particular reference to hearing and vision. Tests of these two functions, plus those related to general development, are often given as a matter of routine when a child is taken to a clinic for a regular check up, but there may be occasions when more sophisticated tests than are available in most clinics are required.

Teachers are a third group, in the case of the preschool child this can mean anyone professionally concerned with children's care. They can bring everyday experience of other children to bear; they can observe a child over a long period, watching to see how different challenges are met.

Psychologists, occupational therapists, speech therapists and physiotherapists are the fourth group. Trained in child observation and formal assessment they can augment the opinion of others partly by giving tests themselves, partly by collating the observations of others.

TESTS USED WITH PRESCHOOL CHILDREN

Some tests are specific in their area of interest, for example a speech therapist's use of tests of language (see Chapter 5). The more general tests fall into two groups.

Formal tests of development or intelligence

Usually given by a paediatrician or a psychologist, a developmental test is used with children up to the age of about two years. Children are presented with a series of graded tasks which might involve following a moving object visually, putting bricks in and out of boxes, naming pictures or scribbling and copying with a pencil. The result of this form of assessment is a score sometimes expressed as a 'mental age', i.e. the age at which one expects that set of tasks to be attained by an average child.

Intelligence tests are given by psychologists, generally to children of two years and over. They, too, consist of a variety of graded tasks, in which the children are expected to show some ability in ways that are thought relevant to academic achievement. So children are asked to demonstrate powers of verbal and non-verbal reasoning, memory, the ability to discriminate different shapes and so on. These tests give an Intelligence Quotient (IQ) with an average of 100 and with most children scoring between 85 and 115.

All formal tests have come under attack recently and some psychologists refuse to administer them because, they say, the results are of no value. In considering this, the following should be kept in mind:

(1) Tests of this kind are, essentially, comparisons: they look at the perform-ance of an individual child and compare this with the results obtained by a large number of children of the same age, living in similar circumstances. So if the individual child has been brought up in circumstances radically different from those on whom the test was originally based it will be of questionable value. For example, one would be wary of giving an Amer-ican test to a child who had been brought up in a Bombay shanty town.

(2) All tests are, to some extent, unreliable. That is, a test given on one day may give a different result from that obtained a month later. The child may be in a better, or worse, mood; the examiner's mood may be different; the child may have a cold one day and be healthy the next, and so on.

(3) Tests given to babies are not very good predictors of later IQ. One cannot guess a seventeen-year-old's IQ from a test given at seventeen months. But as children get older so the predictive power of tests improves; by six years of age it is quite good. It should also be noted that even baby test results are stable at the very low end of the scale: a severely mentally handicapped baby is highly likely to have a poor score on a developmental assessment and later tests are likely to give similar results.

(4) Tests of this kind can be helpful when a specific difficulty is suspected. If a child is not talking at four but can complete age appropriate non-verbal tests one has a valuable piece of information to help in future planning and to avoid the trap mentioned above of thinking that the child is slow all round.

(5) Tests of this kind, or of any kind, should never be used in isolation; they are a useful part of the assessment procedure but no more.

OBSERVATION RATHER THAN TESTING

Recently there has been a move towards the use of observation rather than testing, the aim being to make some assessment of the ways that children learn. Using this technique, observers hope to be able to pinpoint children's areas of strength and weakness, regarding each child as an individual, rather than comparing one child with a large group. Observation should not be seen as an alternative to formal testing; the two serve different purposes.

HELPING CHILDREN WITH LEARNING DIFFICULTIES

Fundamental principles

There is one point that should always be kept in mind when working with children, handicapped or not: they need to be helped to come to a realistic understanding of the extent to which they can gain control over themselves and their world.

This is something that most children learn anyway. They interact with their parents and learn that a smile or gurgle can elicit a smile back from an adult. At twelve months or so they stagger to their feet and learn that they can find out all manner of things by walking out of the house. They learn to open cupboards, to explore everywhere they can, with hands, eyes and feet. They learn later that they can be independent ('me do it') and they also learn, it is hoped, that they cannot be totally independent. A disability gets in the way of this process and, sadly, children often learn to be helpless, to have everything done for and to them. A basic principle of work with children whose learning patterns and capacity is different from most is to ensure that they come to develop a sense of being able, within their limits, to master their environment and to have a sense of control over it and over themselves.

Along with this is the need to maintain children's self-esteem. The crucial point here is that children should never feel that adults are fundamentally disappointed in them. This is not to say that adults should never show disapproval, far from it. But they should try as far as they can to avoid giving the children the message that they are basically worthless and unwanted. Related to this is the wisdom of not comparing one child with another in either child's hearing.

Adult expectations have to be geared to their children's abilities; easy to say but sometimes hard to achieve. In essence this means that we have to make allowances for a degree of slowness without treating the children as though they were babies. Adults might ask themselves these questions:

Do I answer for the child when he or she is asked a question?
Do I find myself helping more than I really need because it is so much quicker to get things done that way?
Am I really encouraging independence?

The final general principle is that all children can learn to some extent but some need far more help to do so than others.

In particular, slow learners need actions to be broken down into small steps. For example, children who are learning to feed themselves may do this simply by imitation. But for slow learners imitation is not likely to be enough, they will need directed help, first to hold the spoon, then to take it to their mouth, then to load it themselves, and so on. The secret of this is always to anticipate what the next learning step will be and to try to keep that in mind: the adult is likely to have to provide a bridge from one step to the next.

PARTICULAR WAYS OF HELPING

The more profoundly affected the child the more necessary will be help from a psychologist and/or a therapist. Whoever helps, though, is increasingly likely to involve the parents as partners in the child's teaching. One example of this partnership is the use of the Portage Project material which has become so widely used with children with a developmental delay.

There are three elements to the Portage programme. The first is the checklist, consisting of questions about children in six areas:

Categories	Examples of questions
(1) Infant stimulation	Does the child kick vigorously, or laugh?
(2) Socialisation	Is peek-a-boo imitated?
(3) Language	Can the child point to parts of the body?
(4) Self-help	Are zippers managed well?
(5) Cognitive	Can the child match objects that are similar?
(6) Motor	Has sitting alone been achieved?

Nearly 600 questions of this sort are in the checklist, although, of course, not all are asked of any one child since it has been designed to cover a wide range of ability. Each question is accompanied by a card which gives suggestions for what one can do to help children achieve that skill. These cards form the second element of the programme. The third is the people who implement it, usually parents assisted by someone who visits the home regularly to give help and encouragement.

The Portage approach is not, in itself, an answer to all problems; it can be misused if it is applied mechanically and it can lead to over-inflated expectations. It is not the only way to help parents help their children, but its popularity indicates what a large gap it has filled.

Project Headstart

Can some slow children be helped well before they go to school to make the most of their educational opportunities?

To answer this question we can look to Project Headstart. This work began in America in 1965 and has been the most expensive, largest and most heavily researched educational programme the world has ever known; around 450,000 children go through it each year.

The goals are to offer preschool programmes to deprived children in order to bring about improvements in their physical health, emotional and social development, their parents' attitudes to the children and to society and in the children's mental capacities.

Various findings have emerged from the evaluations of these programmes. It is important to note that the name Project Headstart can be misleading, suggesting that there is one approach; in fact there is a wide range of types of preschool provision offered within the general scheme.

One finding is that the more effective programmes are those that are home based or, at least, which involve one or both parents. This is not to say, of course, that if parents cannot be involved preschool help is of no value at all.

A second finding, causing great disappointment to early enthusiasts, is that while children's IQ goes up in the short term there is a washout effect once the extra help stops. When they join an ordinary mainstream school their IQ gain is generally lost.

However, it is often forgotten that the aims of the project encompassed far more than just gains in measured intelligence. There have been some recent studies which suggest that young adults who had been through a good programme had less need for special education, fewer brushes with the law, higher rates of employment and fewer early pregnancies than those who had not.

Commentators on these results have argued that what is crucial is a change in attitude of those who have enjoyed a good preschool experience. Perhaps they entered school feeling positively towards themselves and their teachers. This positive feeling communicated itself to the teachers and possibly to parents and so there began a spiral of success. One cannot look to preschool provision to solve all society's ills, nor to prevent all learning problems. But the Headstart experience should give heart to those who seek to offer similar assistance elsewhere, and an emphasis on the children's self-concept should help to sharpen much of what is done.

CONCLUSION

Return to Mary, mentioned at the beginning of this chapter. It is easy to understand why her mother was anxious. But, as has been discussed in the pages that followed this account, anxiety is the starting point for action: it is hoped that this chapter has given some indication of the lines along which Mary and her mother might proceed.

FURTHER READING

The Warnock Report was published in 1978 by Her Majesty's Stationery Office. It is entitled *Special Educational Needs Report of the Warnock Committee of Enquiry into the Education of Handicapped Children and Young People*.

Many practical books have been written to help people working with children with learning difficulties. A good place to start is the Human Horizon Series, published in London by Souvenir Press, distributed in Canada by HBJ Canada, 55 Barber Greene Road, Don Mills, Ontario, M3C 2AI.

Problems of Preschool Children
Edited by N. Richman and R. Lansdown
© 1988 John Wiley & Sons Ltd

CHAPTER 8

Child Abuse

NAOMI RICHMAN, MARIANNE TRANTER and ARNON BENTOVIM

Child abuse has always existed but only recently has the extent of the problem been recognized. A series of dramatic cases like those of Maria Colwell and Jasmine Beckford has focused public attention on the responsibilities of the community to protect children and to help their parents so that abuse does not happen again. The issues raised in dealing with abuse are complex and often involve challenging parents' rights to take sole responsibility for their children. Where there is a conflict between parents' and childrens' rights, the law now recognizes that children's needs for safety and adequate care must come first.

TYPES OF ABUSE

A wide range of conditions likely to affect either children's physical or emotional well-being or their normal development are included in the term child abuse.

PHYSICAL ABUSE

This term covers physical trauma, or 'non-accidental injury' inflicted on the child. Injuries which cause suspicion that child abuse has occurred include the following:

(1) Multiple injuries like fractures, cuts, or bruises in different parts of the body.
(2) Injuries of different ages.
(3) Bruising in unusual sites. The ordinary falls and bumps of childhood produce bruises in places like the shins, knees and forehead; in non-accidental injury bruising may occur on the neck, the inner side of the arm or the inner thighs.

(4) Evidence of burns, scalds, scratches, bites or finger marks.
(5) Brain haemorrhage — produced in young children by shaking, or in any age child by blows to the head. Fractures of the skull may also occur.

Physical abuse can occur over an extended period of time or be the result of one episode of violence.

FAILURE TO THRIVE (see Chapter 11)

This occurs when growth in weight and particularly in height is seriously below that expected. As described in Chapter 11 'non-organic' failure to thrive occurs when, through neglect or deliberate starvation, children are given inadequate food. Failure to thrive is often associated with understimulation and emotional deprivation.

NEGLECT OR LACK OF ADEQUATE CARE

Sometimes parents or other caretakers fail to protect children from everyday dangers. The child may suffer serious burns or falls, be found wandering in the streets, or left at home without adequate supervision. By law children should not be left alone in the house before the age of ten and children of less than fourteen should not be left in charge of younger children.

Another type of inadequate care occurs in some cases of chronic mental or physical handicap when necessary medical treatment for the child is refused.

FAILURE OF STIMULATION

This form of neglect occurs when children are deprived of adequate stimulation, often spending hours alone in their cots without toys or company. In its most extreme form this may result in an autistic picture (see Chapter 5) with social withdrawal and delayed development.

EMOTIONAL ABUSE

This is difficult to define precisely but it is said to occur when children are subject to markedly cruel or inappropriate care such as severe bullying or restriction of normal activities. For example, one father locked his four-year-old son in a cupboard for prolonged periods.

Signs that a child's social and emotional development are being seriously affected and that emotional abuse might be occurring include:

(1) Extreme wariness with adults, inability to play freely or explore the environment, sometimes called 'frozen watchfulness'.
(2) Children who shy away from their main caretaker and seem to have no

special attachment to them, for instance marked lack of concern about their absence. Such children may show over-friendliness to strangers.

These behaviours can also be seen in children who have been physically abused. Emotional and physical abuse frequently occur together.

ILLNESS-INDUCED SYNDROME

Only recently recognized, this term refers to a variety of situations in which parents fabricate evidence of illness in their child in order to gain medical attention. In some cases they may exaggerate or invent symptoms such as fits; in other cases they actually produce symptoms in the child by giving substances like medicines, salt or poisons.

SEXUAL ABUSE

Sexual abuse is discussed more fully later (see page 106). It can be defined as the sexual exploitation of children.

THE CAUSES OF CHILD ABUSE

Many different factors contribute to child abuse: the life experiences of the parents; their relationships with each other, their families and the wider social network; the current social situation. Child abuse occurs across the social spectrum but families in which abuse occurs are more likely to have a number of difficulties and stresses.

PARENTS' OWN EXPERIENCES AS CHILDREN

It is common for parents who have abused their children to have experienced similar abuse themselves. Disrupted homes, lack of love and care in childhood, or a harsh and violent upbringing lead the parents to feel rejected and unvalued. As adults they may have a backlog of anger and hostility because of these early injustices and a low opinion of themselves. There is a tendency to choose a partner with a similar background and such couples often become socially isolated and ill-prepared to cope with the demands of children.

It is important to note that most parents with adverse experiences in childhood do *not* abuse their children. As discussed in Chapter 2 later good experiences and rewarding relationships can compensate for early adversity.

PARENTS' CHARACTERISTICS

If their view of a young child's behaviour is unrealistic parents will not be able to respond appropriately to them. The child may be considered to have feelings and understanding far beyond their capacities, and the parent may want them to respond like an adult. For example, one mother of a nine-month-old boy wished he would make her a cup of tea, and complained that she was always having to prepare his food. These wishes for care from the infant usually occur in parents who felt unloved or neglected in their own childhood.

Other parents expect their children to be quiet and undemanding and to stop crying when they are told to. Understandably parents with these expectations become frustrated and angry when they are faced with the realities of child care. The infant may respond with irritability, unsettled behaviour, or feeding and sleeping problems, producing yet more tension in the parent.

MARITAL CONFLICT

Tensions between parents are commonly found in cases of child abuse. If the parents are unable to support each other emotionally and resolve their disagreements, the level of tension in one or both partners can lead to outbursts of violence directed towards the child. A parent may attack the child rather than the partner for fear of provoking even worse marital problems.

EMOTIONAL STRESS IN PARENTS

Lack of emotional support or of someone to confide in, plus domestic responsibilities make some parents very vulnerable. Any additional stress like illness in the mother or other family members, loss of a job or bereavement can overload their capacity to cope with a young child. Child neglect is particularly associated with environmental stress, but it must be stressed that it is not poverty alone which causes neglect, since most poor families do not neglect their children.

Low intelligence, illness, alcoholism or drug abuse in the parent also predispose to difficulties in parenting.

EVENTS AROUND THE BIRTH

The attachment between parent and child may fail to develop for a number of reasons (see Chapter 3). Children who are unwanted are particularly at risk of rejection. An extremely difficult birth, or a child who reminds the mother of the partner who treated her badly may evoke negative feelings in the mother. Early separation owing to prematurity or illness and a prolonged stay in a special care baby unit have also been suggested as risk factors for later abuse.

FACTORS IN THE CHILD

Children who are premature, physically ill, or retarded are at increased risk of abuse. Anxiety in the parents and unwillingness to commit themselves to a damaged child gets the relationship off to a difficult start from which it may not recover.

Other children show characteristics which make them unrewarding. Children who are irritable, cry a lot, are difficult to soothe and slow to build up a routine for sleeping and feeding can be extremely frustrating for parents.

Certain vulnerable children seem to become the target for all the family's negative feelings and are scapegoated whenever tension rises in the parents.

In summary the occurrence of child abuse is usually the result of many factors which interact together. Actual physical abuse may be precipitated by a particular event, but in most cases the family and child are already vulnerable and there is often a chronic lack of adequate care.

HOW COMMON IS ABUSE?

Current knowledge suggests that approximately ten children in 1000 will suffer some form of physical abuse during childhood, four out of these ten will suffer severe physical abuse or neglect, and of this severe group it is estimated that one out of ten will die (this makes four deaths per 10,000 children). These figures may well be underestimates and are only approximate because there is overlap between different forms of abuse.

The nature of abuse varies somewhat according to age. The majority of severe physical abuse occurs in children under the age of two years and some of the most worrying cases occur under the age of six months, reflecting the physical vulnerability of babies. Physical abuse seems to be equally common in boys and girls, and mothers are said to be more often responsible, although this is not found in all surveys.

RECOGNIZING ABUSE

Child abuse is disturbing and many people find it hard to believe that parents, often apparently concerned and well meaning, can mistreat their children, so that evidence suggestive of abuse is overlooked.

Parents themselves may want to stop their neglectful or punitive behaviour and often draw the attention of professionals to the worrying state of the child. Such indications are often indirect and professionals need to be sensitive to these 'cries for help'. Frequent complaints about minor ailments or difficult behaviour, worries about health, drawing attention to injury or growth problems, are all ways parents use to make others aware of the underlying problem of abuse.

At the same time because of fear of the consequences parents may well try to prevent recognition. They may always be in a hurry so there is never time to discuss the child fully or complain about other issues thus distracting attention from the child. Other danger signs include:

(1) The pattern of physical injury, as described previously (page 97).
(2) An inadequate explanation of how an injury occurred, or delay in seeking help.
(3) An unusual lack of concern about a child's growth, development or injury.
(4) Behaviour towards a child which is bullying, rejecting or unconcerned.

WAYS OF HELPING

The first task in helping parents and child is to make an accurate assessment of the abuse and of the factors leading to it. A detailed history and careful observation of the child and parents together are important.

Following the recognition of abuse, decisions must be made as to whether it is safe to leave the child at home for the time being, and about the possibility of working with the parents so that the child can remain with them or return home eventually. If severe abuse or failure of care has occurred it is usually necessary to protect the child through the appropriate child care procedures (see Chapter 15). This will initially involve a case conference of the appropriate community professionals who together will plan what is needed.

In most cases efforts are made to keep the child at home. Where there is longstanding or severe abuse and previous efforts to help have failed, it may be decided that a permanent alternative place is necessary. However, these decisions about a child's future rest with the Court.

Social workers are often expected to ensure that the child has legal protection and also to work therapeutically with the parents themselves.

WORKING WITH PARENTS

Given the nature of the problem and the adverse childhood experiences of many parents, it is not surprising that the process of helping is often lengthy and arduous. It may take a long time before parents can trust others and feel confident enough to explore how they might change.

It is essential to test out whether parents can work effectively and change. It is helpful to make an agreed contract with the parent of what needs to change and the therapeutic process involved. For example a child who has previously failed to thrive has to gain weight at a specified rate each week; if they fail to gain this weight the possibility of removal must be considered.

If the defined goals are not met within the specific time, then it may be in the best interests of a child who has been abused to leave the family and long-term placement may be necessary.

The use of a wide variety of different interventions is required. These might include:

(1) 'Parenting' the parents by providing support and care. This gives them a new experience of what parents can be like.
(2) The development of home-making skills.
(3) Helping the parents find new ways of dealing with distress, defiance, or behaviour difficulties, e.g. management of tempers.
(4) Helping the parents to learn how to stimulate the child.
(5) Finding enjoyable ways of parents being together and playing with their child.
(6) Marital work focusing on the parents working together and resolving their difficulties without drawing the child into their conflicts.

HELPING THE CHILDREN

Abused children show a variety of developmental delays and disturbed behaviours depending on the nature of the abuse and the family situation. They may be clinging and miserable, apathetic and unable to play; wary of adults or overfriendly towards them. Some are very disorganized and emotional and may respond with provocative behaviour as though seeking punishment even in new situations. There is a risk that these children will be reabused through their ability to evoke negative responses.

It needs a high level of skill and commitment to cope with such difficult children, and this is particularly hard for parents who themselves may lack the emotional resources to cope easily even with 'normal' children.

It is often essential to have a special setting — like a therapeutic day nursery in which to carry out treatment. The nursery provides care and warmth, stimulation and appropriate limits, helping to reverse the child's expectations of punishment and neglect.

If the child is in foster care, the nursery provides a safe place where parents can be with the child and learn new patterns of responding to them, so that their child can return home.

When the child is finally returned home the family can still come regularly to the day nursery to continue working on their problems. Usually the return home is done in stages and not completed unless there appears to be no risk of further abuse. It is of course not easy to decide whether it is safe for a child to return home. Sometimes the only way to assess whether parents can now manage, e.g. in cases of failure to thrive or emotional abuse, is to have a trial period at home under careful supervision.

When treatment is not successful or if it is not thought advisable to return the child home, an alternative placement must be sought. Although there must be concern about separation from natural parents, the choice must be made of the 'least detrimental' alternative for the child.

OUTCOME

It has already been indicated that in severe abuse there can be a death rate as high as one in ten and that young children are particularly at risk. Brain damage, or mental retardation can occur in as many as one in four cases of severe abuse, and social, educational and emotional disturbance and high rates of reinjury are characteristic of those cases which have had inadequate treatment.

Approximately one in three children who have experienced severe abuse and remain at home show normal patterns of behaviour given intensive treatment.

There is often a great improvement in language and other skills. Residual difficulties include withdrawn behaviour, poor self-esteem and learning difficulties.

The most powerful factors influencing outcome are not necessarily the severity of the abuse itself. The ability of the family to take responsibility for what happened to the child, their willingness to work on changing patterns of interactions within the family, the nature of the relationship between parents and child are all important. Where there is an unwillingness to own responsibility for the abuse, an absence of attachment between parents and child or very poor capacity for working towards change, it may be necessary to organize alternative placement.

The Browns are an example of a family in which physical abuse occurred and where treatment was carried out.

Sam, aged nine months, was admitted to a paediatric ward with a severe scald on his right upper arm and chest, which the parents said had been caused by his four-year-old sister Sara. Their description of how the burn had happened was very vague and they had delayed seeking help. The ward staff noticed some bruising on Sam's left leg and arm which looked like finger marks; the parents said they did not know how these had occurred. An interim care order was taken out by the hospital social worker who called a case conference. This was attended by the paediatrician and ward sister, plus the general practitioner, health visitor and community social worker.

It appeared that the family had recently been under considerable stress. The father had been made redundant and the mother had lost her own mother a few months previously, a great loss to her. The parents were unable to support each other when distressed. Sam was developing normally but was a quiet, serious child, tentative in play and wary with the parents. Sara was also a sombre girl, who had outbursts of provocative behaviour; there was no evidence of abuse in her case.

It was planned to place Sam on the 'At Risk' register, take out a Care Order by the local social services and place Sam in a foster family when he left the hospital. The parents denied causing the injuries and contested this plan but the magistrates' court upheld the decision. It was agreed by the court that the parents should be helped by a therapeutic nursery to deal with their difficulties with the aim that Sam might return home.

Initially Sam was brought to the therapeutic unit twice weekly by his foster mother, and met his parents and sister there. They spent the day together under supervision. Work involved weekly meetings with the parents in which they were encouraged:

(1) To accept responsibility for what had happened and the need to change if further abuse was to be prevented;
(2) To confide openly in each other and provide support at times of stress;
(3) Respond appropriately to both children.

Mrs Brown was helped to express her sadness over her mother's death and become aware of her need to find other people to confide in.

Eventually the parents were able to talk about their difficulties in coping and also tell Sara that she was not responsible for Sam's burn but that it had been their 'carelessness'.

They attended the unit for nearly a year, and during that time Sam was introduced back home for gradually longer periods. He remained on the at-risk register with support from a social worker for another two years.

PREVENTION OF ABUSE

Many factors which place a child at increased risk of being abused have already been mentioned. They include:

(1) The child being unwanted.
(2) Difficulties around the birth such as illness of mother or child.
(3) Lack of social support.
(4) Family and social stress.
(5) A parental history of a disrupted home or of ill-treatment.
(6) Mental illness or addiction in the parents.

Sensitive observation in the period around the time of birth may alert staff to the presence of increased risk. In practice, prediction of abuse is probably not very accurate, but there is some evidence that the provision of additional resources such as extra health visiting to infants thought to be at risk does act preventively.

General social factors like improved housing, preschool facilities and education, described more fully in Chapter 2, may well have an influence by reducing stress and providing support to families.

As mentioned earlier there are often warning signs that abuse has occurred or is about to occur, and prompt action may prevent further damage. The keeping of case registers of abuse and 'At Risk' registers within each area by social services is an important means of recording vital information about children and families and ensuring that the child's progress is monitored. Whilst their child's name is on the register the family has to be visited regularly by a social worker.

In established cases of abuse, prevention involves using appropriate legal measures plus work with the family. Decisions need to be made as quickly as possible so that a child is not left at risk or in uncertainty. They should be placed in a stable and caring home as soon as possible if they cannot remain with their parents.

There is some evidence that preventive measures have reduced the rates of physical abuse in recent years, although recently these have begun to rise again.

SEXUAL ABUSE

It is only in recent years that sexual abuse has been recognized as a form of child abuse, especially in young children. The recent increased number of referrals in the younger age groups probably reflects increased awareness rather than an increase in incidence.

Sexual abuse involves a spectrum of inappropriate sexual contacts between adult and child including exposure, molestation and intercourse. One could also include the use of children to make pornographic material.

There is a good deal of controversy about identifying sexual abuse in young children. Doubts are expressed about relying on their testimony and it is suggested that it is easy to make them say what the interviewer expects to hear, or that the children are merely expressing their fantasies. However, there is no doubt that sexual abuse occurs in younger children more commonly than was once thought, although there is no accurate information about how common it actually is. Most often the abuse is by someone in the child's family or a person well known to them, e.g. a babysitter or family friends.

CAUSES OF SEXUAL ABUSE WITHIN THE FAMILY

Sexual abuse occurs in families of all social classes. Many of the risk factors are similar to those associated with other types of abuse such as poverty, social disadvantage and social isolation.

Parents may be of low intelligence, have a history of mental illness, alcoholism or drug abuse or have been physically or sexually abused themselves as children. Male perpetrators may always have been sexually interested in children or may develop this interest in response to particular stresses. Where there is an unsatisfactory or absent sexual relationship in the marriage, the father or stepfather may turn towards his child(ren) for affection and gratification. In turn, young children who are neglected or unloved are at risk of sexual abuse because they seek affection from adults who then take advantage of them.

IDENTIFYING SEXUAL ABUSE

A number of signs are reported to be associated with sexual abuse, but it is important to remember that most of these signs are non-specific and can arise from a variety of causes. Although suspicions that sexual abuse has occurred may be high, without clear corroborative evidence from the child it may be impossible to establish that it has happened.

Physical signs

(1) Anal or vaginal inflammation, infection, tears or bleeding.
(2) Other signs of abuse such as bruising or evidence of neglect may be present.
(3) Persistent stomach aches and pains in the genital areas; however, most stomach pains are *not* a sign of abuse.
(4) Urinary tract infection, constipation, wetting or soiling may be a sign of sexual abuse, but in the majority of cases they are not.

Psychological symptoms

(1) Behavioural difficulties or emotional reactions such as withdrawal, misery, apathy, loss of appetite, poor sleep, and other general symptoms of a lack of well-being.
(2) Precocious sexual behaviour. One of the major effects of premature experience can be that ordinary sexual exploration or masturbation become exaggerated, and the child's behaviour becomes overtly sexualized. With adults there may be over-closeness and inappropriate touching, and this obviously puts the child at risk of further abuse, since predisposed adults might perceive the child as being seductive rather than requiring help.

Interviewing the child

If suspicions are raised that this type of abuse has occurred, it is important for the child to be seen by an experienced interviewer. It is not easy to obtain a clear account of their experiences from young children, especially if these are frightening or confusing, and there are a variety of ways of helping them to communicate, including the use of drawings, play and puppets. Dolls with explicit anatomical sexual features can be used to explore their understanding of sexual matters and to help them describe their experiences. One study found that young children who have been abused played differently with anatomical dolls and showed more sexual knowledge compared with controls.

Because of the distress for the children involved it is becoming common for videos of these interviews to be shown in court, rather than subjecting them to further interviews.

It is not uncommon for experts to disagree about the meaning or value of a young child's evidence, and further work is required to clarify the best way of obtaining evidence.

Medical examination

Medical examination and tests may provide confirmation of sexual abuse, but in the majority of cases it is not conclusive, especially as many forms of abuse do not leave any physical signs.

HELPING THE FAMILY

As with any form of abuse it is important to hold a case conference of involved professionals — social workers, paediatricians, psychiatrists, etc. and if necessary police, to decide whether there is adequate evidence that abuse has occurred and how to proceed in order to best help the child and family. The court is involved if criminal proceedings are taken against the perpetrators or if the case is contested by parents. The identification of the problem is a very painful affair which can lead to total disruption of the family and even imprisonment for the father. When deciding on a plan of help, an assessment of the possibility for change within the family is required similar to that described for physical abuse. Pointers to a good outcome include an acknowledgement of the problem and acceptance of responsibility by the parents, a willingness to make changes, and acceptance of the need to protect the child. Parent groups can help couples to face these painful issues and work on change. Unfortunately reports suggest that in only about a third of father–daughter incest cases who have received treatment does the family stay together as a functioning unit.

HELPING CHILDREN

Children are often confused and worried about events which follow their disclosure of abuse. They easily blame themselves for the fact that a parent has gone to prison or is living away from home. It is essential that they do not continue to feel responsible, and if possible and appropriate, i.e. with older children, the adult involved should explain to the child that they take full responsibility for what has happened and that the child was in no way to blame.

Young children can be helped to sort out the issues of guilt and responsibility in groups of the same developmental level. Groups avoid a close therapist–child relationship which can be frightening to these children and are useful for teaching assertiveness and self-protection skills. Issues dealt with in the groups include:

(1) The distinction between 'good' touching which is affectionate and enjoyable and 'bad' touching which is inappropriate and unpleasant.
(2) Having the right to say 'no' to unwanted touching.
(3) The difference between private and public parts of the body.
(4) Appropriate behaviour between adults and adults, and between adult and children.

Photographs, role play and videos are used for teaching about how to respond when approached by a stranger, or when approached inappropriately by familiar people, including even family members. The children practice how to say 'no' or 'go away' with confidence and force, and learn how to get help should they be faced with improper behaviour in the future. These methods have been used for the four to six-year-old age group.

OUTCOME FOR THE CHILD

There is little precise information about the long-term outcome of sexual abuse in young children although it is suggested they may suffer from a variety of emotional and behaviour difficulties and problems in forming close relations.

The outcome may be worse the closer the child is to the perpetrator and the more unpleasant, violent and frightening the experiences. The nature of the child's family will also affect outcome. A child who is blamed for the break-up of the family and lacks emotional support, is likely to feel extremely guilty, and find it hard to come to terms with their experiences.

PREVENTION

It is suggested that all children should have education in assertiveness and self-protection skills similar to the programmes described on this page but there is uncertainty about how this is best done, and at what age such programmes should begin. The issue is controversial because although parents are happy to warn children about strangers they feel very uncomfortable about focusing on improper behaviour from familiar people, especially close family; however since most sexual abuse occurs within the family a preventive programme has to deal with this issue.

FURTHER READING

A. Bentovim, A. Elton, J. Hildebrand, M. Tranter and E. Vizard (1988) *Child Sexual Abuse: Assessment & Treatment*. Bristol: John Wright.

R. Helfer and C.H. Kempe (1987) *Child Abuse*, 4th ed. Chicago: University of Chicago Press.

R. Porter (ed.) (1984) *Child Sexual Abuse Within The Family*. London: Tavistock Publications.

CHAPTER 9

Overview of Behaviour and Emotional Problems

NAOMI RICHMAN

This chapter discusses definitions of abnormal behaviour, current knowledge about why emotional and behaviour difficulties develop, how to assess these and the kinds of help we can offer to children and their families.

WHAT IS NORMAL BEHAVIOUR?

John, age three, is a nervous child, frightened of all sorts of things like the dark, clocks that tick loudly, dogs, going to the doctor.

Elizabeth is an extremely excitable and intense three-year-old who gets herself worked up into a state about occasions like going to a birthday party, and has frequent arguments with her mother.

Peter is four years old. He is always getting into fights at nursery, and other parents often complain about him to his mother.

How do we decide whether these behaviours are a sign that there is something to be concerned about, or just part of everyday development? We all have in our minds an idea of normal behaviour, although our ideas of normality probably vary. To some extent a child's age and sex affects our expectations, and so does the social climate. Different societies and different families vary in their expectations of how independent or how assertive children should be. For example some fathers want their sons to 'stand up' for themselves, even if this means being quite aggressive; some parents demand immediate compliance to requests, other parents are more easy going.

Most young children go through patches of difficult behaviour; only if a child's conduct or emotional reactions are handicapping, if they seriously interfere with getting on with other adults or children, affect learning or play, or interfere with ability to enjoy themselves, do we need to look further at the problem. Sometimes the cause of difficult behaviour seems obvious, a new brother or sister in the family, a stay in hospital, an unexpected separation from parents, sometimes difficult behaviour seems to come out of the blue. Whether there is an apparent cause for the behaviours or not, they are a sign that children are distressed or confused. We need to consider for each individual child whether *their* problems require further help.

John, the nervous three-year-old mentioned above, was also afraid of mixing with other children and of leaving his mother. He had nightmares and ate poorly. He was handicapped in several ways by his symptoms, and it seemed he might benefit from some help.

On the other hand, Elizabeth mixed well with other children, was independent, played imaginatively, and usually ate and slept well. Her outbursts seemed to be related to her extreme temperament and were not affecting her life generally.

Peter, by comparison, wanted friends but other children would not play with him because of his fighting. He had poor concentration, was disobedient and very difficult to manage both at home and at school where he was threatened with expulsion. In his case too, it seems worth considering if he can be helped.

DEVELOPMENTAL CHANGES

Isolated difficult behaviours are common as children develop and are usually not serious, although they can be very distressing to parents. For instance, about 20 per cent of one to two-year-olds wake regularly and although the majority eventually sleep well, when nights are disturbed parents can become quite desperate from lack of sleep.

There are changes in the sorts of behaviours that predominate at different ages. Wetting and soiling as well as night waking are more common in younger children. Difficulties in mixing, tempers and worries occur in older children.

There are developmental changes in the kinds of fears that children show presumably related to changes in understanding. A baby under six months is not afraid of masks, strangers, or loud noises, but towards the end of the first year these fears usually appear. The toddler is afraid of real objects like the hoover, or dogs, the older child of imaginary things like witches and monsters as well.

Table 9.1 shows rates of various behaviours in a representative sample of normal London children (not a clinical sample) seen at three and four years. Amongst the changes in the rates of different behaviours we can see that between three and four years there was a slight increase in the number of children described by their parents as faddy eaters, as worriers and as having

Table 9.1   Problem behaviours in a community sample of 98 London children

	Three-year-olds (%)	Four-year-olds (%)
Poor appetite	19	20
Faddy eater	15	24
Difficulty settling at night	16	15
Waking at night	14	12
Overactive, restless	17	13
Poor concentration	9	6
Difficult to control	11	10
Tempers	5	6
Unhappy mood	4	7
Worries	4	10
Fears	10	12
Poor relationship with sibling	10	15
Poor relationship with peers	4	6
Regular day wetting	26	8
Regular night wetting	33	19
Regular soiling	16	3

poor relations with their sibs. The most marked change is the reduction in the number of children who are wetting and soiling. In general as children get older, their concentration improves and overactivity is less of a problem.

Some behaviours worry parents a lot although they are common and not a sign of emotional disturbance. Habits like rocking, head-banging, and thumb-sucking occur as a normal phase of development, beginning in the second six months. Only if these habits persist, and occupy a child for long periods should they give rise to concern. The same applies to masturbation and nailbiting, which appear later. Similarly many children are fussy about their bedtime ritual, tidiness and cleanliness, their clothes and how their food is presented. This perfectionism becomes worrying only if it is carried to extremes, if play is very stereotyped, i.e. repetitive and unchanging, and the child becomes very upset by any change (see the section on autism, page 212).

Wetting is not a sign of emotional disturbance in young children, although from the age of two to three years soiling is likely to occur in association with other signs of disturbance.

Other more serious behaviours tend to be overlooked by adults because they cause no bother. The child who is unhappy, withdrawn, failing to communicate or not growing well should always give rise to concern but may not be noticed, especially in a large group (see Chapter 5).

As well as knowing about the kinds of problems that children show at different ages, it is important to keep in mind what children *can* achieve at each age, so that expectations do not fall too low. Those who work with difficult or developmentally delayed youngsters, begin to have lower expectations. They may forget what good concentration a three-year-old can have, how well they can express themselves, or how creative their play can be.

PERSISTENCE OF BEHAVIOURS

Individual problem behaviours tend to improve over time. The most persistent seem to be eating problems.

Although short-lived difficulties are common, we do not know which problems are going to disappear quickly. It is useful to think about the best way of managing a particular behaviour when it does occur, like biting, tempers or fearfulness, to lessen the chance that it will persist (see Chapter 10).

John's fear of dogs and going to the doctor (see page 111) began after an admission to hospital. If his parents gently encourage him to face up to his fears and cope with the things he finds difficult, he has more chance of getting over them; if he is not encouraged, perhaps the fears will increase, and his life will be even more restricted.

To summarize this section: it is important to keep in mind the range of behaviours shown by children of different ages so that abnormal or unusual behaviour is noted. Children with severe and persistent behaviour problems which are handicapping their social, emotional or learning capacities, need further assessment.

RATES OF BEHAVIOUR PROBLEMS

A survey carried out by the author and colleagues of three-year-olds living in outer London, estimate that 7 per cent of children had moderate to severe generalized problems, and 14 per cent had milder problems. If the three children described on page 111 had been in his survey, John would have been considered as having a mild problem and Peter a moderate problem because of the degree of impairment they showed in everyday functioning. Elizabeth would have been rated as showing no significant problems because her overall functioning was very good.

The survey children were seen again at four years and eight years and about two-thirds of those with generalized problems at three years, continued to have generalized difficulties at home at four and eight years. In school they also had more learning and behaviour difficulties at eight years compared with children described as having no problems at three years. Children with delayed language development at three years and had more behaviour difficulties at this age, and at eight years did less well at home or school than the others; they seem to be particularly at risk of having behaviour problems (see Chapter 5).

It seems that, unlike with single problem behaviours, generalized problem behaviour does not necessarily improve with time; severe toddler problems are not just a passing phase. Styles of interaction in the family and patterns of response in the child may well become entrenched.

Problems are more likely to persist in boys, in children with developmental delays, neurological problems, and if there is continuing family tension.

TYPES OF DISORDER IN EARLY CHILDHOOD

In young children it is not always easy to clearly define distinct types of disorder, many children show a variety of symptoms or difficult behaviours which do not fall into a particular pattern. However, some studies based on information from home and preschool settings are able to identify two main groups of difficult behaviours. The first group consists of conduct difficulties such as defiance, disobedience, aggression and destructiveness, restlessness and poor concentration. The second group consists of emotional difficulties like misery, apathy, fears and worries. There is disagreement as to whether there is a third small group of hyperactive children who are very active, restless and with poor concentration or whether these children should really be grouped with the conduct disorders.

Conduct difficulties and restless overactive behaviour tend to occur together or to have some characteristics in common. They are both more common in boys and are both likely to persist into school life, whereas emotional problems are more likely to clear up.

Aggressive children more often come from family backgrounds where there is discord and where there are family patterns of aggressive behaviour.

A classification of types of disorder is shown in Table 9.2. As well as the three groups already described, these are habit disorders, like soiling, sleeping problems and head-banging; failure to thrive; child abuse and neglect; and infantile autism. The last is perhaps the most clearly identifiable disorder in young children. It is characterized by delayed language development and deviant use of language, impaired understanding of social relations, lack of fantasy play, and interest in repetitive activities.

The lack of social learning by autistic children appears to derive from their difficulty in understanding and responding to social cues and in understanding the 'humanness' of other people. Thus it is extremely hard for them to sympathize with others' feelings or to understand their behaviour, or to develop the give and take necessary for normal social relations.

Autism is probably the end state of a number of different conditions and both genetic factors and brain disorder appear to be involved. Blind and deaf infants may show autistic features, especially children affected by rubella during early pregnancy.

Table 9.2   Classification of early childhood disorders

Conduct disorder
Emotional disorder
Hyperactivity
Habit disorders
Failure to thrive
Child abuse and neglect
Childhood autism

Although autism is rare, occurring in two to four children per 1000, it is important to identify autistic children early so that they can benefit from special educational help.

It should be noted that child abuse and neglect are not strictly disorders, since they are events which happen to a child rather than behaviours shown by the child. Children who have been abused may show a variety of difficult behaviours including both conduct and emotional difficulties.

CAUSES OF BEHAVIOUR DIFFICULTIES

It is very unlikely that we will find one 'cause' of a child's difficulties. In most cases they arise in response to a combination of factors lying to various degrees in the child, the family and the social circumstances (see Chapters 1 and 2). In some instances a child has an obvious disability like infantile autism, retardation or epilepsy with cerebral palsy, which makes a major contribution to the problem. Even with such vulnerable children family and social circumstances are important, and can tip the balance, enabling a child to cope well in spite of the handicap.

FACTORS IN THE CHILD

Temperamental differences

How is it some children seem to cope well with challenges and others not? Differences in temperament or *style* of behaviour seem to play a part. Children who are cheerful in mood, easy going, adaptable, easy to settle into a routine, cope better. Children who are reluctant to try new experiences, unadaptable, moody, very intense in their emotional reactions, are more likely to develop behaviour difficulties. An example of how temperament might affect behaviour was shown in a study of how children react to the birth of a sibling. Children who were extreme in their emotional responses and negative in mood, were more likely to respond negatively to the birth. Adults can obviously influence how well a child with a difficult temperament copes;

patience and sympathy, and introducing new situations gradually can help such children to adapt and reduce upset or confrontations. To some extent temperamental differences are probably inborn but starting from birth parents' responses will affect and modify the infants' innate predispositions.

Health and development

Children with physical illnesses like asthma or cystic fibrosis are more likely to have associated behaviour difficulties. They have to cope with going into hospital, reduced activity, anxieties about themselves and the future. In addition, parents' anxiety may affect how they deal with their child, and lead them to be over restrictive, lax or uncertain in their approach. Children with neurological and brain disorders have the highest risks of developing behaviour or emotional problems (see Chapter 4).

General developmental delay and language delay are also associated with behaviour difficulties. This may be related to immaturity, difficulties in communication, or an unstimulating background.

FACTORS IN THE FAMILY

Vulnerable children have a much better chance of managing if they are in an understanding and supportive family where the adults get on well. On the other hand, when faced with stresses like quarrelling parents, a depressed mother or a stressful separation, it may be very hard for them to cope (Chapter 1).

As was discussed in Chapter 1, marital difficulties are very often associated with behaviour problems in the children. When parents or other caretakers do not work together or consistently in guiding children, this confuses them. A common situation is for one parent to become more and more indulgent, as the other in desperation tries to be more and more strict; meanwhile the child is playing one off against the other. In other families, the parents are unable to deal with their own relationship and focus all their pent-up anger on to the child. Where there is overt discord between the parents this may be even more distressing.

Adult quarrelling is frightening and upsetting for young children who may become withdrawn and unhappy. On the other hand, they may themselves copy the aggressive argumentative behaviour they witness.

ADULTS AS MODELS

Adults are a powerful influence on how children deal with life (see Chapter 1). They provide models of how to communicate and get on with others, how to cope with frustration and difficulties, they can teach self-control and social rules. Parents who themselves easily become anxious or angry or who lack flexibility in responding to problems, will be less able to provide children with useful coping strategies. There is evidence that adults and children who cope best have a wider range of problem-solving skills which enables them to be more adaptable. If one solution is not successful they can try out others when they are faced with challenges. People who respond inflexibly, for instance losing their temper whenever they are frustrated or anxious, are more likely to exacerbate their difficulties.

Some forms of therapy, in particular that known as cognitive therapy, have a specific aim of helping people to understand the way they usually respond to difficult life situations and then to develop alternative, more appropriate strategies.

CHILDREN 'IN CARE'

Studies show that children who have been 'in care' (i.e. away from home either with foster parents or in a residential home), or who are currently in care are at increased risk of showing behavioural and emotional problems.

Those who go into care under the age of two years or who have several admissions into care are at the greatest risk. Probably a number of factors relate to this increased risk. Firstly the children may come from homes where there is a lot of discord or unhappiness or stress. Second, they may have many changes of caretaker and may move from home to home, so they do not have the opportunity to form any stable relationships with specific adults. One study showed that the outcome for children who have been in care varies according to what happens to them. Those who return home do worse in terms of both learning and behaviour, perhaps because they rarely settle back comfortably in the family of origin, especially if the mother has meanwhile formed a new family. Those who are adopted are the best adjusted although they remain with some problems in behaviour (see Chapter 13). The children who remain in institutions are intermediate in outcome.

COPING STRATEGIES

Young children are continually facing new challenges. They have to deal with developmental changes like toilet training, meeting other children and learning to share, starting playgroup or nursery. Besides these normal steps in growing up, most children have to deal with unpleasant or difficult situations like going to the doctor or dentist, or being in hospital. Even more seriously they may have to face illness, death, divorce, or separation from both parents. What affects how children manage these situations? It seems that a number of factors affect how they cope. These include:

(1) The nature of the situation.
(2) Previous experiences.
(3) Developmental status and age.
(4) Sex.
(5) Temperament of the child.

Adult reactions are also influential, for instance how they prepare and explain things to children, the models they offer for dealing with difficulties.

As an example of these various factors, let us take hospitalization. In very young children, say under six months, separation is not too upsetting as the baby does not fully discriminate between familiar caretakers and others, and can usually be comforted by strangers. From the second half of the first year there is a need for customary figures, as the infant can still not yet understand that people or objects can come and go. For them parents disappear or appear inexplicably. A characteristic series of responses has been described following hospitalization at this age. Initially there is protest, with crying and upset followed by 'depression', withdrawal, and apathy. Finally there is 'denial' when the child appears to be recovering but no longer responds differentially to the parents and will be friendly to anyone. The length of these three responses may vary in different children. It is to be hoped that the extremes of withdrawal or 'denial' are rarely seen nowadays on wards where there is open visiting, although there are unfortunately still hospitals which do not allow parents to stay overnight.

As children move into the third year they begin to appreciate that their parents will return and they can be comforted if there is a familiar person present when the parents are away.

Parent and staff reactions will strongly influence how a child copes. Parents who are extremely worried or upset can make it harder for their children, who often try to hide their feelings so as not to upset their parents more.

If children's natural anxieties are passed over unsympathetically this too is not helpful. The fears may increase and be much worse than the actual reality they have to face.

A previous experience of hospitalization which was unpleasant or frightening will increase fearfulness. On the other hand, previous separations which have been pleasant for the child and carefully planned will probably help them deal better with hospital.

OTHER FACTORS

It has already been mentioned that children with difficult temperaments are likely to have more adverse reactions in stressful situations. Boys are generally more affected than girls when faced with difficulties. They may be more vulnerable because of temperamental or developmental reasons; in addition expectations are different for boys and girls, and perhaps boys receive less support and sympathy when faced with a difficult situation (see Chapter 12).

Although a child appears not to be disturbed by an experience at the time, difficult behaviour may appear later. For example, on return home from hospital, many children become demanding and clinging, possibly with sleeping and eating disturbances.

Reactions to a disturbing experience, like hospitalization, can last up to a few months and it is difficult to predict which reactions are going to be prolonged. There is probably an interaction between the disturbing experience, the parents' responses and the child's personality. As an example of such an interaction we may take the case of Ben, who was involved in a car accident and admitted to hospital for a few nights. Although he was not seriously hurt and had not been concussed, he subsequently had nightmares and disturbed sleep, and was afraid of travelling in cars. He had always been a difficult boy to manage and this became worse. His parents were extremely shocked by the accident, both felt very insecure and anxious and were preoccupied with fears for the future and thoughts of death. As they began to feel better they were calmer and firmer with Ben and his behaviour improved. Here the nature of the event, the parents' responses and Ben's character probably all played a part in the development of a prolonged reaction.

ASSESSMENT OF BEHAVIOUR PROBLEMS

Discussing a child's behaviour in detail helps to sort out how serious it is and whether something further needs to be done.

(1) Sometimes it is helpful to complete a behaviour questionnaire about the child as this shows the extent of the problem and where further attention should be focused. There are such questionnaires available for use by parents (Behaviour Screening Questionnaire (BSQ*)), and by staff working in group settings (Preschool Behaviour Checklist (PBCL†)), but it must be remembered that questionnaires do have limitations and if there is concern this must be followed through by more detailed assessment.

(2) *Observations of behaviour*. It is surprising how much can be learnt just by watching a child. Peter, a boy who was always fighting, was observed in his nursery class by a nursery nurse for fifteen minutes. She wrote a running commentary of everything he did, looking particularly at whether he approached other children, whether other children approached him, how long he concentrated on a table activity, how often he attacked other children. She saw that he only concentrated on something when a member of staff was with him, that he tried to get attention by hitting other children

---

* Available from Dr Naomi Richman, Department of Psychological Medicine, The Hospital for Sick Children, Great Ormond Street, London, WC1.
† Available from NFER Publications, Windsor.

and did not talk to them or play in a friendly way; and that no child responded to him or approached him. She concluded that he needed help in learning how to relate to other children and in concentrating.

Observing Stephen, another boy in the same class who also fought a lot, she saw that his fighting tended to be in a boisterous group of other boys, but that he also made many positive approaches to others who responded positively to him, and that he was able to concentrate on building activities for long periods. She concluded that Stephen did not need special help but that classroom management of boisterous behaviour could be tightened up. Observations were made in a similar way of a mother and her daughter Susie in a day-care setting. Susie had many tempers at home and in the day nursery, and was aggressive to her baby sister who also attended. It was seen that Susie often made comments or requests to her mother but these were usually ignored as the mother was preoccupied with the baby's needs. After repeated attempts to get her mother's attention, Susie finally succeeded in this by doing something naughty, she then had a temper tantrum when her mother told her off. The conclusion was that her mother needed help to notice Susie more, especially when she was being quiet and good.

Observations of sequences of behaviour like these can be very useful for parents and staff who are often unaware of what leads up to naughty behaviour.

(3) *Observations of development.* Observation of play activities are often more useful than formal testing in showing how a child actually functions (Chapter 14). The observer looks at features like concentration, use of language and of imaginative and symbolic play, complexity of play, and play and communication with other children. If necessary these observations can be supplemented with formal developmental and language assessments (see Chapters 5 and 7). Suspicion of impaired hearing should always be high, especially when language is delayed or articulation is poor (Chapter 5).

(4) *Growth and failure to thrive.* Growth is an important indicator of well-being in young children. From birth, height and weight should be plotted regularly on standardized growth charts to ensure that growth is proceeding normally (Chapter 11).

(5) *Understanding the child.* We can learn a lot by watching children even before they are talking much, although we must be careful not to jump to conclusions about their thoughts. Sometimes parents or nursery staff infer planned or malicious intent from children's behaviour when detailed observation shows that the child is merely confused or responding to the behaviour of others.

Play materials help a child to feel at home and provide the opportunity to observe various activities. Here are descriptions of two children who were seen for assessment.

John has come to the clinic because he does not talk at nursery school; he is four years old, serious and quiet. He stays close by his mother, approaches toys tentatively and in a rather clumsy way, but enjoys puzzles and lego once he gets going and seems happy. His conversation to his mother is limited in quantity and quality and he does not talk to the interviewer or approach her.

Peter, also age four, is a management problem. He rushes into the room in an excited way, touches everything, often roughly, but concentrates very little. He talks a lot and loudly with good articulation, interrupting others. There is frequent whining and shouting as he demands things from his parents. He is disinhibited in the way he comes up to a strange interviewer to talk and ask for things.

We can see there are marked differences in these boys in:

mood and intensity of expressing feelings,
activity level and restlessness,
concentration,
confidence,
use of play material,
level of play,
quality and use of language,
ways of relating to parents and to strangers.

Further exploration is needed to see whether these behaviours occur in all settings and what factors seem to be contributing to them. These could include:

(1) Temperamental differences in both boys, perhaps John is temperament-ally timid whereas Peter is outgoing, restless and active.
(2) Developmental delay in John.
(3) Parental behaviour to the child in both cases; possibly John's parents have sheltered him from new situations or are themselves anxious; on the other hand, Peter's parents may enjoy his boisterous behaviour and encourage it.

As they get older, some children can talk to us directly about their feelings. They can tell us about their fears and anxieties, their wishes, whether they would like help, for instance not to be naughty or to make friends. An atmosphere of trust and understanding must be built up before children can express their feelings in this way and often they do not or cannot talk easily. Play is frequently a more comfortable way for children to express themselves. The content of play may reflect an overall mood of sombreness or anxiety, there may be an inhibition of thought and creativity or activities may be repetitive. In some disturbed children play is extremely restless and dis-organized with no continuity or structure.

During assessment, fantasy play can be used to express anxieties or a child may choose an object like a puppet or a telephone to talk through. This is discussed at more length in Chapter 14.

Although training and supervision are required when using play for assessment and treatment, the provision of time and space for children to express themselves in the presence of a supportive adult (an experience that many children lack) should be encouraged at home and in preschool settings.

The way parents and children interact often helps us to plan ways of helping with difficult behaviour (see Chapter 11).

Observations of children's responses to their parents are particularly important in assessing cases of non-accidental injury and in determining whether children should live with their parents.

Signs which suggest an impaired relationship are:

(1) A lack of warmth or interest between parent and child.
(2) Minimal contact or conversation between them during the assessment.
(3) Wariness of the parent by the child.
(4) A marked deterioration of the child's behaviour in the presence of the parents. He may become very inhibited and withdrawn or show signs of great tension by head-banging or other habits.

HELPING PARENTS AND CHILDREN

SOCIAL MEASURES

The importance of general social measures and adequate day care facilities for families with young children have been discussed in Chapter 3.

THE PRIMARY HEALTH CARE SETTING

The majority of help offered to young children and their families is given in the primary health care setting, i.e. family doctor's surgeries and child health clinics, by general practitioners, health visitors and community paediatricians or clinical medical officers. Day nurseries too are an important resource for parents and children (see Chapter 13). There are now some special under fives advisory clinics run by health visitors or community psychologists to which problems of behaviour (like eating or sleep difficulties), or problems of development, can be referred.

Physiotherapists, speech therapists and educational home visitors may also become involved in providing special help for young children at home or in preschool.

Various kinds of help are available at the primary health care level; the choice depending partly on the type of problem and also on the particular skills and interest of those offering help. Management advice based on behaviour principles is used for dealing with specific problems like sleep difficulties, tempers, or some fears (see Chapter 11). Counselling focuses on parents' needs, for instance difficulties in the parents' own relationship, anxieties over a sick child.

An increasing source of help lies in the many support groups now in existence. These are run by parents themselves or by primary care workers. The groups may form themselves or be formed by primary care workers. The groups may form to deal with specific issues — a stillbirth, particular handicaps in children — or a specific time in life — pregnancy or postnatal groups.

REFERRING ONWARDS

Situations in which more specialized help should be considered are listed below.

(1) A child has severe and persistent problems which have not improved after parental counselling and supportive measures, and are seriously affecting social or family relations.
(2) Parents are very distressed or anxious about their child.
(3) Family discord or child rearing appear to be seriously affecting a child's emotional or general development.
(4) There is evidence of a slowing down in weight gain or growth.
(5) The child has a physical illness which parents find difficult to manage and which is causing a great deal of distress.
(6) The child appears to be delayed in general development or in language.

Problems (1) and (3) could be referred to a child and family psychiatric clinic, although social services might have to be involved immediately if there is a risk of child abuse. Children with slow growth will probably be seen first by a paediatrician; ideally growth and physical problems would be seen jointly by a paediatrician and a member of a child psychiatric team. A child with delayed development needs to be assessed by a psychologist. Most children with delayed speech are seen first by speech therapists.

CHILD AND FAMILY PSYCHIATRIC CLINICS

Staff working in these clinics include social workers, psychologists, pyschiatrists and possibly a psychotherapist. All these are involved in assessments and treatment of children and families and there is overlap in the work they do, but they also have specific roles.

Social workers

Most social workers are employed by local authorities. They have responsibilities for a wide range of services such as counselling and organizing practical help for those with special needs like the handicapped.

They have a special responsibility in law whenever there is any question of a child being received into care, or of child abuse, and in adoption and fostering procedures.

When working with families with young children they can give advice about resources and provide support for families in difficulties.

Depending on the setting they may be involved in residential or day care work with children, in individual counselling and in family and marital therapy.

Psychologists

Psychologists working with children generally do so within the framework of education or the health service, although some are employed by social services departments.

Educational psychologists train as teachers and have had at least two years' teaching experience before going on to further training in educational psychology. They work mainly as advisers to teachers and others concerned with schools but recently there has been an increased interest in work with preschool children and their parents.

Clinical psychologists train and work within health services, usually, but not always, being based in hospitals.

The role of the psychologist varies according to the setting in which the work is done. Those coming into contact with preschool children can usually make an accurate assessment of the child's developmental level, advise on management either of individual children or groups and sometimes offer therapy for children and their families.

Psychiatrists

Psychiatrists are doctors with a training in assessment and treatment of adults and children. They have a special role in the assessment of children with failure to thrive, physical illness, severe developmental disorders like autism, and where drug therapy may be necessary.

Child psychotherapists

Psychotherapists may also be psychologists, psychiatrists or social workers. Their training focuses on understanding child development and in how to communicate with children in order to help them. There are many types of child psychotherapy. In psychoanalytic therapy the child's play is used along with what they say and other aspects of behaviour as a source of information about inner concerns and ways of coping. Bringing to the surface and the gradual sharing and elaboration in language of the concerns is the primary means of intervention.

Other professionals may also form part of a treatment team especially in therapeutic day centres or hospitals. These include speech therapists, physiotherapists, occupational therapists, nursery nurses, nursery teachers and play leaders.

TYPES OF TREATMENT

In many cases a review of the child's problems with parents, and a discussion of their significance is all that is needed. In more complex cases a variety of treatments are available, and are often used together.

FAMILY WORK

This involves seeing as many as possible of the family together at least initially, to assess how they interact with each other. It is possible to see how each parent plays with the children and controls them, expressions of affection within the family, how brothers and sisters get on together, what precipitates difficult behaviour, how parents deal with this, whether one child is favoured, and so on.

> Jamie, aged four and Teresa aged two-and-a-half, came with their parents to the clinic because Jamie was considered to be so overactive and out of control. During the interview it was observed that Teresa was actually more restless and disobedient than her brother and that she provoked him, but her parents laughed at her behaviour whereas they seemed to expect Jamie to sit quietly without fidgeting. The parents said they felt too tired to talk over problems together at home.

Differences in approach to the two children could be because Teresa is younger or because she is a girl. Possibly Jamie is more difficult at home or had been very difficult in the past and his parents no longer noticed his good aspects. These different ideas can be explored with the parents, looking at their expectations and attitudes towards the children.

Management advice can be combined with attempts to help the family change the way they interact together, e.g. by focusing attention on Jamie's good points, by encouraging parents to have time for themselves and to consider their own needs and their own relationship. This multifocal approach is typical of the manner in which family problems are often tackled.

There are many kinds of family therapy and different therapists use different models in their work. For example, some therapists base their work on the aspects of family functioning described in Chapter 1. Their work with families might deal with any of the following issues:

(1) *Developmental stage of family*, e.g. discussing appropriate dependency and independency for children, or the effect on parents of grandparents' lack of interest.

(2) *Facilitating the expression of positive feelings.*

(3) *Issues of control* or setting limits (see Chapter 11).

(4) *Decision making* and daily organization.

(5) *Communication* in a more open and clearer manner.

(6) *Appropriate role taking*, e.g. parents deciding on issues together; an older sister not acting like a parent.

(7) *Involvement.* Helping parents to be equally involved with *all* the children; encouraging a child to be appropriately independent.

(8) *Relations with the outside world.* Encouraging parents to accept support from others.

These aspects of functioning are interrelated. For instance, lack of control is often associated with unwillingness by the adults to take a parenting role or be the one in charge.

The Lesley family illustrates a number of aspects of family functioning. There were three children in the family: a girl aged nearly six, Lara; a girl of four who had severe epilepsy; and another girl of two years. The children screamed and squabbled continuously and the mother screamed back at them, often feeling hopeless and depressed and never getting her work done. She complained to the father about the children as soon as he came back from work, consequently he felt annoyed with her and the children and the two of them were irritable with each other because life was so tense. They had lost contact with friends and rarely went out, and had little support or sympathy from the grandparents. Lara bore the brunt of her parents' complaints and seemed miserable and lonely.

These problems were tackled in various ways.

(1) *Expression of positive feelings.* Lara and her parents filled in a daily chart about all the *good* things Lara had done that day.

(2) *Issues of control* were discussed, e.g. the importance of consistency (see Chapter 11).

(3) *Decision making*, e.g. organizing more routine and planning evenings and weekends.

(4) *Communication* (a) Explanations to Lara about her sister's epilepsy, (b) parents discussing together their feelings about having a handicapped child.

(5) *Role taking.* Lara not to be held responsible for the problem or expected to give in all the time to the other two.

(6) *Involvement.* Parents to consider being more involved with each other and making time to be together and talk.

(7) *Relations with outside world.* Parents to consider organizing a baby-sitter and contacting old friends.

Depending on the situation it might be advisable to look more deeply into the parents' own backgrounds. Perhaps one of them had a handicapped brother or sister and this makes it more difficult for them to cope with their own handicapped child. Or it could be that their own relationship is very tense and their irritation is inappropriately spilling over on to Lara so that the focus of work needs to be their relationship.

In some cases work will focus almost entirely on the marital relationship because it is agreed that this is the prime difficulty, in other cases the work will be primarily behavioural management, with the parents acting as 'therapists' themselves and carrying out the treatment programme at home (see Chapter 11).

PRESCHOOL ATTENDANCE

Attendance at a preschool centre can be of benefit even if home circumstances remain stressed.

In the preschool setting children can be helped to concentrate better, learn how to play and mix with other children, develop language and other skills. The relationship developed with a teacher, nursery nurse, speech therapist or physiotherapist is often extremely important to the child. If such a relationship is warm and accepting, it helps a child to feel confident and worthy.

Parents attending the preschool may observe how staff and their child play, and begin to change their own behaviour, perhaps finding things to enjoy with their child and responding more positively to them.

WORKING WITH CHILDREN INDIVIDUALLY

Individual help is useful for dealing with particular situations, like going to hospital. If a child has a marked fear, say of dogs, dentists, or injections, techniques based on relaxation can be helpful (see Chapter 11).

It is worth emphasizing that as with adults, most children are not helped by dismissing their fears and worries. It is much better to acknowledge these and then work out ways of coping with them.

Children in care or being prepared for adoption or fostering are particularly in need of help in trying to understand their situation and come to terms with it. Depending on their age, different techniques can be used. A life story book has photos, writing, drawings (perhaps by the child) and can show the family tree, who the child has lived with and where, the significant people in the child's life and where they are now.

Calendars and charts are used as concrete indicators of how long the wait will be before seeing someone again, going home or being adopted. Puppets, dolls or animals will be used by some children to express worries or feelings that are difficult to talk about. One character may be selected to represent themselves and other figures will represent their families, social workers, foster parents, etc.

For many deprived children, a long-term relationship with one person who can accept their tumultuous feelings can be very helpful. For a few other children with severely impaired relationships individual psychotherapy may be indicated. With most young children family and management work is probably the best means of help; there is no evidence for the majority that long-term psychotherapy is beneficial.

SPECIALIZED DAY CENTRES

There are a variety of family day-care centres. In some of these, parent involvement is slight, with perhaps a separate parents' room and encouragement of parents to spend time in the centre. In other day centres there is an active policy of providing support for parents, with home visiting, parents' groups, etc. Special therapeutic day centres are usually attached to a child and family psychiatric clinic. Some cater mainly for the children through play and educational sessions, others have a treatment programme involving parents. This is particularly useful when dealing with complex and difficult cases.

CONCLUSION

It is often said that young children with behaviour difficulties grow out of them. We have seen that this is not always so and that many children and parents might benefit from short-term counselling on management. Certain problems need further assessment as soon as they are identified, these are:

Language or developmental delay.
Failure to grow or put on weight.
Situations where parental care is leading to avoidable impairment of physical or emotional development.
Severe management problems.

Children who are in care or who have been in care are particularly at risk, and consideration should always be given to providing extra help for them.

In most cases a problem of behaviour arises through an interplay between family circumstances and the child's characteristics. It follows that when assessing a situation and in planning a treatment programme, it is important to consider all aspects of child and family function. It also follows that there are usually several ways in which help can be given, and a flexible, multidimensional approach is more likely to be successful than a rigid one which offers the same type of help to every child and family whatever the situation.

Finally, careful observations are always useful in further understanding and planning ways of helping.

FURTHER READING

N. Richman, J. Stevenson and P. Graham (1982) *Preschool to School: a Behavioural Study*. London: Academic Press.

M. Rutter (1977) *Helping Troubled Children*. Harmondsworth: Penguin.

E. Taylor (1985) *Hyperactivity: a Parents' Guide*. London: Martin Duwitz.

L. Wing (1980) *Autistic Children: a Guide for Parents*. London: Constable.

Problems of Preschool Children
Edited by N. Richman and R. Lansdown
© 1988 John Wiley & Sons Ltd

CHAPTER 10

Behaviour Disorders: Principles of Management

Jo Douglas

Many of the behaviour problems shown by young children are an extreme form of everyday behaviour which occurs in most children sometime or another. As described in Chapter 9 behaviours such as temper tantrums, defiance, sleeping and eating difficulties are common. Often, adults develop their own methods for dealing with these behaviours using techniques like distracting or ignoring a child who is whining or on the verge of having a temper. Behavioural management uses these familiar techniques but in a more systematic and precise manner.

One of the key principles of behavioural management work is that the *results* of a particular behaviour affect the likelihood of that behaviour occurring again. As an example: if a child is given sweets to stop temper tantrums, then this will increase the likelihood that tempers recur. Or if the consequences of refusing to eat is a great deal of parental attention then the problem is likely to increase. Consequences that increase the likelihood of preceding behaviour being repeated are called 'reinforcers'.

ASSESSMENT OF THE PROBLEM

A clear assessment of the presenting problem is vital in planning management. Although behavioural techniques are easy to understand they can be used inappropriately unless the context of the child's difficulty is clearly understood. Suddenly launching in with management ideas may fail or make the difficulties worse. The following areas of questioning are crucial in identifying the problem and the ways in which treatment should be planned:

(1) Description of the problem behaviour
(2) The context of the problem behaviour
(3) General information about the child
(4) General information about the family
(5) Observations and recordings of behaviour

DESCRIPTION OF THE PROBLEM BEHAVIOUR

It is common for adults to talk in generalizations when describing a child. A description like 'he's very naughty and irritating' is imprecise and gives no indication of how bad the behaviour is or how often it occurs. The first stage in assessment is to obtain a clear description of the problem as an adult sees it. A detailed account of a recent event is most helpful in throwing a light on what causes concern.

Useful questions to ask might be: What do they do that is irritating? Can you describe the last time they were very naughty? What seemed to set it off? What did they do exactly? What did you do? How long did it last? How often does it happen? How long does it usually go on for? Does this happen only with you or with other people as well?

The application of these ideas requires a sympathetic understanding of the feelings of those adults who are working with the child. The history of the problem and the context in which it occurs means that intervention using behavioural principles is not necessarily straightforward.

It is rarely possible for parents or other adults just to accept and carry out a programme which is given to them on a plate. It is much better for the adults concerned to work out for themselves why the child is continuing to misbehave and then to come to their own conclusions about changes in management. They may need some guidance in this and if so the guidance will have to be offered sensitively.

Adults' main concern at the beginning of a change in management plan is 'what caused the problem?' But often it is not possible to identify this as the problem may have been very longstanding or may have gradually evolved without anyone realizing that it was building up. The combination of temperamental factors, emotional atmosphere at home, past learning history and current conditions all contribute to the present situation. The search for the 'cause' can be a fruitless and pointless one, and often it is better to focus on the 'here and now', trying to alter whatever it is that is maintaining the problem.

A wide variety of behaviours can be tackled using management techniques. These include isolated difficulties like sleeping problems or toilet training, and generalized difficulties as in defiant or withdrawn and fearful children.

THE CONTEXT OF THE PROBLEM BEHAVIOUR

Behaviour problems are shown at different times and places and with different people, so it is important to identify what is influencing the child.

(1) *What triggers the problem?* The behaviour may be more common in public or at home with the mother alone, when a sister comes from school, or at the meal table. This is all vital information as it identifies the situations in which change is required. The trigger for bad behaviour may be the presence of a sibling who evokes feelings of jealousy. In such a case some additional work will be required to help the parents and children face up to these feelings and cope with them rather than just rely on management work. In other instances the difficult behaviour may be related to parental arguments or mood changes and work may need to be focused on these aspects of family functioning.

(2) *What is maintaining the problem?* For example, reactions to the child's behaviour from parents, brothers and sisters, nursery staff and others. It is vital to identify the consequences of the behaviour as they are the major focus in any plan of change. Consequences can either increase or decrease the occurrence of the behaviour. It will often be necessary to think through the chain of events linked to particular behaviour.

Luke, a two-year-old, throws his toys at the door every time he is playing in the kitchen. His mother may tell him three or four times not to do it, she then shouts at him to stop a couple times, smacks him and then picks him up to stop him from continuing.

This example demonstrates how the mother has finally reinforced the child's throwing by eventually picking him up. Her view was that he never does what he is told but in fact he has learned that he gets a cuddle if he throws his toys.

GENERAL INFORMATION ABOUT THE CHILD

Specific questioning is also required about the children and their background before an intervention is carried out. This should include:

(1) *Other problems.* Children often show a wide range of problems. A child who has problems with toileting may also be a faddy eater and uncooperative. Tantrums may be associated with aggressive actions towards friends or siblings. The sleep disturbed child may also have behaviour problems during the day and a wide and more comprehensive management approach will need to be considered.

(2) *Past history.* There may be events in the past history of the child that have great emotional significance. These could be deaths, losses, parental disharmony, break up of the home, adoption or fostering, or birth of a sibling. Each of these events can affect a child's emotional state. If daily functioning is significantly disrupted the child might benefit more from a therapeutic approach that faced these issues rather than from behaviour

management, or a combined approach of behavioural management and other therapy might be needed.

(3) *Developmental level.* Parents' expectations of a child's behaviour some-times outstrip the developmental level of the child, conversely some parents have difficulty accepting that their 'baby' is growing up and needs to develop more social skills and self-control. Behaviour that is age appropriate at two years may not be so at four years of age. For example, both wetting and soiling in a two-year-old is not considered unusual but in a five-year-old would be cause for concern. Management work can be very effective in training new behaviour in children but the behavioural expecta-tions should match the child's developmental level.

(4) *Medical history.* Significant illnesses, accidents or other events may be linked to the behavioural problem. Particular attention should be paid to hearing, eyesight and language delay as these can be overshadowed by the behavioural problem. Neurological difficulties are associated with be-havioural problems and it is important that any necessary investigations and treatment should occur alongside the behavioural management work.

GENERAL INFORMATION ABOUT THE FAMILY

Family members and relationships

Marital disharmony is often an underlying feature leading to parental disagree-ment about managing the child or inconsistent and erratic discipline and control. Inappropriate anger and irritation towards the child, inconsistent demands, conflicting messages, lack of clear limits or rules all disrupt the child's ability to learn appropriate behaviour. Management work can be very effective in these circumstances.

Sometimes the marital relationship is so bad that it is not possible for the parents to work together in changing management methods. Work then needs to be aimed at the parents' problems before the child's problems can be approached.

General stress level

Financial, employment and housing stresses can all add up to a great burden on parents. They will have little patience or tolerance to deal with a couple of lively preschoolers when they are worrying about making ends meet. Aware-ness of these factors might limit the range of change that anyone could ask. The emotional stability of the parents is also important. Illness, depression, ten-sion, anxiety, alcoholism or drug abuse affect relationships with children and may require help in their own right. About a third of women with preschool children suffer depressive symptoms which interfered with their ability to respond to their child's needs. Emotional support and relief from child care may be more helpful in these cases than expecting the mother to change her reactions towards her child.

Parents' attitudes to their child

Sometimes parents' expectations about their child are unrealistic and they need help in understanding what behaviour is age appropriate. The child may be seen as vulnerable or special because of illness or other reasons, or as a 'bad lot' that nothing can change. It is crucial to assess parental feelings about their child's character. Behaviour management can be carried out with such parents but they also require help in rethinking their views about the child.

OBSERVATIONS AND RECORDINGS OF BEHAVIOUR

Once the initial assessment has been completed it is helpful to observe the child in the home or nursery setting. These observations provide fuller detail of the events surrounding particular behaviour and can be recorded so as to monitor change.

A simple chart, as in the example below, can be given to parents to help them think about the factors that trigger the problem as well as the consequences of the behaviour.

Setting conditions	Behaviour	Consequences
Checkout of supermarket	Screaming and struggling for sweets	Give him sweets to keep him quiet

Parents can choose certain difficult behaviour to record and discuss over two weeks or they can try to record every instance on a particular day of 'not doing what I ask' or 'having a tantrum' and check how they are responding to the behaviour.

Other types of charts can record the incidence of the problem to see how often it occurs or whether there is any pattern in the day.

Behaviour	7.00 am	8.00 am	9.00 am	10.00 am	11.00 am	12.00 am
Tantrums	+ +				+ +	+ +
Hitting	+	+	+		+ +	

It is possible to combine the frequency chart above with one measuring how bad the problem is, so instead of a tick for each time it happens '1' could mean slight, '2' could mean medium and '3' could mean severe. Charting of this sort can be done with the co-operation and full knowledge of the child; sometimes they will fill in the chart themselves under guidance from the parents. Colouring in a square to indicate whether the temper was black (bad), red (medium), or pink (slight), can help the child become aware of their behaviour and try to control the outbursts.

A diary can be used to record a range of daily behaviour and show the problem in the context of the daily routine. With sleep disturbance it is important to assess the amount of sleep the child is getting as well as the number and duration of wakings. The timing of daytime naps can be quite crucial when planning earlier bedtimes.

	Monday	Tuesday	Wednesday
Time woke in morning			
Time and lengths of day naps			
Time went to bed in the evening			
Time settled in bed in the evening			
Times and lengths of waking in evening and what you did			
Times and lengths of waking in the night and what you did			

PLANNING TREATMENT

Once sufficient information has been gathered it becomes possible to plan a treatment programme if this seems appropriate. The programme will depend on the age of the child, the nature of the problem, and the family context.

It is necessary to be creative when suggesting strategies for change as these will work best if tailored to fit the particular child and family. It is also vital to be sensitive to the parents' wishes and ensure that they agree with the programme and feel themselves to be partners in the treatment project, even if it is taking place in a nursery.

Basic management strategies include:

(1) *Cueing or setting the scene*, for example, ensuring regular mealtimes or bedtimes with well established routines.
(2) *Extinction*, for example, ignoring tempers, silly or rude behaviour, preventing destructive or aggressive behaviour.
(3) *Shaping or step-by-step change*, for example, helping a child to sit for increasingly longer periods at mealtimes or go to bed at gradually earlier times.
(4) *Reinforcement* for desired behaviour. This can take the form of praise and encouragement. Star charts and stickers, or special treats, are helpful for older children and must be chosen carefully to suit a particular child's age and interests. Children with a verbal age of around three years can understand the use of this type of reinforcement.

Charts recording behaviour can be used as the basis for a reward or incentive. The child earns a sticker or colours in a square for having carried out a request or behaved well for a period in the day. Once a reward has been earned it must never be taken away. Rewards will only have an effect if the adults back them up with praise and positive comments about the child's achievements. Eventually praise will be more important and the child will no longer require concrete rewards. If progress is slowing down the requirements for earning a reward can be increased. For example, instead of earning a reward every time a child sleeps through the night in their own bed, the requirements could be increased to every two nights.

The rest of this chapter discusses strategies for dealing with specific problems.

MANAGEMENT OF SPECIFIC PROBLEMS

NON-COMPLIANCE

Many problems have their root in non-compliance manifested by such behaviours as refusing to do what is asked, persisting in naughty or dangerous acts, aggressive outbursts, destructiveness and tempers. When dealing with such a child adults often find themselves in an escalating cycle of continual nagging, threats and smacking; nevertheless the child is usually more tenacious than the adult who ends up giving in to the child's demands or letting them get away with things. Management work focuses on setting limits for the child with clear rules about what is allowed. The child's understanding that if they fight long enough against their parents' weak and inconsistent controls they will get their own way needs to be challenged.

Mr and Mrs Foster could not understand why seven-year-old Tommy was so difficult at home. They gave him everything he wanted and his mother had given up work so as to provide him with security. Nevertheless he never seemed to be happy or satisfied, the more he was given the more he demanded. This occurred in relation to sweets, toys and their attention. They frequently tried to limit what he had but nearly always gave in because he responded with prolonged screaming.

The first stage of establishing boundaries for a child is to ensure that any requests, demands or threats are carried through. The child has learnt that 'no' means 'possibly, try again' and the adults have to teach the child that they mean what they say. They need to reduce the number of demands and instructions and not to comment on every wrongdoing so that it is more likely that each request can be carried through. Particular behaviours are selected for encouragement such as eating a plate of food for dinner, not climbing on the table or putting on a coat before going out.

To help the child learn the new responses incentives can be offered for complying. Star charts or small surprises provide concrete evidence to the child that good behaviour has been noted and meets with approval. These incentives can initially be provided for every instance of good behaviour, but once the child has learned what is expected and that the adults mean what they say the reward can be given for longer periods that have passed without upset. Regular comments and attention when the child is being good help to consolidate the learning and maintain it after incentives have been dropped.

Wayne (aged four years) was a tough boy who was large for his age. He lived with his mother who had great difficulty in managing him. He was disobedient, would run off when out with her, could be insolent and verbally abusive. His language development was slow. Mother found him an unrewarding child to have around and their interaction was usually very negative. She never played with him or read stories to him but expected him to play on his own in the flat or watch TV. She often criticized him, shouted at him continually and found great difficulty in praising him for any good behaviours.

Refusal to comply should be met with indifference. Withdrawal of attention and cool disapproval is much more concerning to the child than shouting and anger, which by now are probably met with bravado. The emotional responses from adults that some children receive when they refuse to comply maintain non-compliance if this is the major form of attention that the child gets. It is essential that the adults make time for playing and talking to their child and attend to them when they are 'good'.

BITING, HITTING AND ATTACKING

Hitting and biting games often start in babyhood when adults think they are funny, but if they persist in the older child this causes a lot of concern in nurseries as well as to parents. Attempts may have been made to control the attacks through humour but when the child does not stop parents often also resort to aggression, shouting, smacking and threatening the child. Attempts to bite the child back are common but do not provide a good model of adult behaviour.

Sometimes these behaviours start after a period of emotional disturbance, frustration or distress. It is difficult to ignore such anti-social behaviour, as other children and people can get hurt. The problem may be situation or person specific, or it can be wide reaching and affect every interaction the child has with adults and children.

> Mary aged two-and-a-half years had a one-year history of scratching and biting her parents and other children. She was due to start nursery and her mother was very anxious about whether to tell the staff or even let her go there. She was an ex-teacher herself so was keen for her child to appear very well behaved and communicated her anxiety and tension to Mary. At home mother would hover around Mary if a friend had been invited in, to forestall any attacks. Mary had severely clawed the face of a cousin previously and had a tendency to scratch her baby sister if left unattended. She would often turn on her parents in a game and bite them on the shoulder or arm. She was a bright little girl who had difficulty sharing her toys and mixing with other children and had lived a socially isolated existence as her mother was frightened to let her go to parties or other friends' houses.

Whenever children start to hit or bite, adults need to indicate complete disapproval and immediately stop the sequence that will rapidly escalate if they respond aggressively. The adult needs to maintain calm and firm control and remove the child from the situation temporarily. This can entail taking the child out of the room or making them stop the activity and sit on a chair or the floor. Sometimes the child will need to be forcibly picked up to make them do what is required. This method was successful in helping Mary cope in the nursery.

After a short cooling down period of a few minutes the child can be reintroduced to the situation and shown how to cope more appropriately, for example learning how to share toys in a nursery, where grabbing, pushing and shoving can easily escalate into fights. Learning to ask, offering another toy in exchange or just joining in play with the older child are all more appropriate methods of coping.

Aggressive behaviours often occur when children are deficient in other social behaviour, their language may be poor and they have not learned to wait or develop elementary self-control. Frustration and anger easily build up and the child does not know what to do with their feelings. Learning to go to their mother or the nursery staff when upset and taking up another activity can reduce this build up.

TEMPERS AND TANTRUMS

Tantrums can occur in isolation from other behaviour problems or as part of generalized non-compliance. It is high intensity behaviour that evokes great embarrassment in public and that parents will try to avoid by giving in. Attempts to ignore the tantrums may well have been futile if parents capitulate before the child has stopped crying.

Tantrums occur when a child is thwarted, frustrated or not given their own way. They can involve screaming, crying, and shouting combined with collapsing on the floor and banging head or feet. Sometimes aggression is directed towards people with kicking and punching and at other times towards the room and furniture. In general, the children do not hurt themselves and the tantrum should be allowed to run its course without any interference from adults. Physical restraint may be necessary in some cases to stop the child hurting someone else or destroying the room. This can be achieved by standing behind the child and holding their arms across their body until they calm down. Once calm, life should carry on as if nothing had happened. The child should not produce any result by the behaviour or achieve what they want. Attention, cuddles and positive comments should be delayed until the child next shows cooperative and sociable behaviour.

TOILETING PROBLEMS

Daytime wetting (enuresis)

At two years of age most parents have started to toilet train their children and nearly 90 per cent of children are dry and clean by the age of three years.

For a child to be continent they need to learn how to use the potty or toilet and also recognize the sensations associated with needing to go. Complete bladder and bowel control is achieved when children realize their need and indicate this to the parent or goes by themselves. A consistent period of training is necessary to gain control so that the child has repeated experiences of when and where to go. Parents need to treat this like any other learned skill and not show anxiety, anger or aversion during the training period, but pleasure if the child performs appropriately. Some parents find the routine, and the reminding a difficult task particularly when they are in overstressed circumstances. Poor housing and sanitation provision can delay training.

Lapses in continence can arise from a variety of sources, stress and anxiety, excitement and anticipation, illness and fear. In some instances it is part of a wider behavioural problem. When parents cannot manage the child it becomes a focus of conflict between the parent and child. Management advice will aim at establishing a routine of going to the toilet, first with parental reminders and later without reminding. Accidents should be ignored and the child told calmly where they should have performed instead.

A star chart or small rewards can be used to help the child comply with parental reminders and to go to the toilet without arguing. Since it is common for young children especially boys to wet at night, medical examination of children with nocturnal enuresis is not usually warranted. If daytime wetting persists after three years the possibility of an abnormality of the urinary tract or a urinary infection needs to be considered. Urinary infections are particularly common in girls. Very frequent wetting in the day, pain or burning on passing water are suggestive of an infection and should always be investigated. Sometimes daytime wetting is related to a poor bladder capacity, where the child has the urge to pass water when only a small quantity of urine is present in the bladder. Training the child to hold on as long as possible after drinking fluids can gradually increase bladder capacity. This technique may also help night-time wetting.

Night-time wetting

There are wide variations in the ages in which children become dry at night. Forty-five per cent of boys and 31 per cent of girls wet regularly at three years and by four years these figures are down to 20 per cent. Bedwetting tends to run in families and is also more common in children with developmental delay.

Many doctors feel that night-time wetting should not be treated at all until a child is well over five years since usually normal developmental changes will lead to its disappearance. However, some parents do become distressed by continued wetting in the older child and a number of management approaches can be used.

The first point to be made is that it is important for parents not to show anger and upset at wet beds as this could exacerbate the problem. When children are anxious or upset they are more likely to wet.

Apart from ensuring that mattresses are protected by waterproof sheets the management methods used are:

(1) Waking the child during the night and making them go to the toilet or sit on the potty. The child needs to be fully awake and aware of what they are doing otherwise they are learning to empty the bladder in a drowsy state which is the complete antithesis of what is usually required. Many parents lift their children at night but usually do not wake them fully.

(2) Restricting fluids at bedtime is often tried by parents but this method does not teach the child bladder control. A deliberate teaching method would involve giving the child a lot to drink at bedtime but then to wake them several times during the night to use the potty. This provides the child with repeated opportunities to learn about full bladder signals and emptying the bladder in the correct place. The practice is used intensively for a few nights and paired with rewards for dry beds.

(3) Star charts can be used to encourage dry beds. The child earns a star in the morning or some other small reward to encourage attempts to stay dry. Lack of success should be treated casually and a comment about trying

again is all that is said. Parents should indicate great pleasure if the bed is dry rather than expecting it as a norm of behaviour for the child's age during this teaching phase. This method could be used for children from about five years upwards.

(4) The bell and pads, an alarm system which rings when the child begins to wet is widely used with older children but is not suitable for those under seven years of age.

Soiling (encopresis)

Most children have bowel control by the age of three years but if this has not occurred both physical and psychological aspects need exploring.

Children who pass motions normally but not in the toilet may never have learned correct toileting habits. Some are fearful of the toilet because of a previous bad experience of being locked in, or falling backwards, or because they worry about the toilet flushing. Regular training needs to be established if the history of the problem indicates erratic opportunities to learn. If the child shows anxiety and fear about sitting on the toilet they can be gradually encouraged to spend longer time sitting on it with the parent for company and toys and books for distraction. Rewards can help motivation. Once the child can sit for up to five minutes without distress then rewards and praise can be linked to passing a motion in the toilet. The child may need a demonstration by the parent to show how to push and expel bowel movements.

Constipation is often a major element in soiling. It frequently presents as loose stools or a watery discharge with stained pants because the bowel has become packed with hard faeces and only a small amount of liquid faeces can escape around this (known as constipation with overflow).

Children with constipation may have had an anal fissure as a baby which caused pain on defecting and then a tendency to hold back faeces to avoid the pain. This behaviour can continue long after the healing of the fissure but the faeces will be hard and painful to pass because of its size. Others may have had sluggish bowel contractions which will have caused a backlog of faeces which has become hard and impacted.

Management of such children requires a combination of a bulking agent to soften the faeces and a training programme. An enema to clear the rectum and start the child afresh will speed up the process although some doctors think that enemas are unnecessary. Rewards can be given for successful defecation in the toilet paired with a regular time for sitting on the toilet. Rewards should never be given for clean pants as this can encourage the child to hold back faeces and start the constipation cycle again. Young children need encouragement and support to try and pass a motion normally as they may have become very frightened and worried about bowel movements.

In some children constipation is caused by punitive toilet training with excessive punishment for accidental soiling or forced and prolonged sitting on the toilet. The anxiety this generated resulted in constipation. It is important not to punish children when they soil but help them learn what to do. If toileting becomes emotionally fraught and the major focus of interaction between parent and child it is unlikely to be controlled. As with other behaviour difficulties it is essential for the parents to have a calm and neutral approach.

HABITS

Nearly all children show some habits during their development. The most common are thumbsucking and nailbiting, but hair pulling, headbanging, masturbation and rocking are also frequent. Most habits diminish with age but if a child is unhappy, anxious or understimulated, or the habit receives a lot of attention, it may persist and increase in intensity. It is important to combine any behavioural intervention for a habit with adequate attention to the child's emotional needs.

Thumbsucking and nailbiting

About a third of children manifest these in the preschool years. Usually there is no need to interfere unless they become excessive. In instances where parents want to stop the behaviour the child can be rewarded for increasingly longer periods of not thumbsucking or nailbiting. Stories can be read and television allowed only when the hands are out of the child's mouth. Being angry and upset with the child does not help and usually nor does paying a lot of attention to the behaviour and reminding the child not to do it. Sometimes an alternative behaviour like clenching fists can be suggested whenever the child puts his hands in his mouth.

Head-banging, hair pulling, rocking and masturbation

These behaviours all start as comfort habits but under stress or with inappropriate management they can become marked problems. The child who gains parental attention only by head-banging is likely to escalate this response to the point of self damage. Similarly, the child who twirls hair can start to pull out handfuls in temper or frustration if they learn that this brings attention or their own way.

> Fourteen-month-old Clive started banging his head when he had earache and as soon as he started doing this his mother picked him up. He continued to demand this even after the earache had gone. The behaviour gradually escalated and his parents became more and more frantic until they were carrying him about all day long.

These habits are best managed by being totally ignored, but it may be necessary to use a helmet if the headbanging is very severe. At the same time it is essential to ensure that the child is not neglected or bored and receives attention when they are not exhibiting the habit.

Giving up the comforter

Blankets and large toys become difficult to transport once the child is more mobile and after a prolonged period of use tend to become dirty and rather bedraggled. Parents often want help in stopping their child taking the comforter with them everywhere but are concerned that if it is taken away to wash or is lost they could not cope with the child's distress.

Some families can confine the comforter to the bedroom only, but others find that the only way to reduce the child's dependence on the object is to gradually reduce its size over a few weeks until the child is left holding a few strands of blanket or a bit of fur. This is eventually lost and the child no longer demands the comforter.

> Judy was the eldest of three children. As a baby she had slept on a lambskin and had become very attached to it. At four years she still had four small pieces of it left that were scattered around the house and called 'nong-nongs'. Whenever tired, distressed or hungry she would find the fluff and stroke it along her cheek. Interestingly both of her younger brothers copied this attachment as each in turn had a lambskin to lie on as a baby.

SLEEP DISTURBANCE

Disturbed nights are one of the most exhausting aspects of rearing young children and many parents desperately try a variety of approaches to the problem. Medication is frequently prescribed but this is usually not very effective and there is concern about giving children drugs over long periods.

Disturbed nights may have continued from the early months of life when the child woke for night feeds, or there may have been a period of uninterrupted nights which were disrupted after a period of illness, separation or stress. Some parents feel very unsure about what demands to make about sleep patterns. They may want their child to sleep in their own bedroom but feel guilty about this, and have fears that the child will feel rejected and isolated. It is important to point out that the quality of interaction with the child during the day is far more important than 24-hour contact, and that a child can feel perfectly secure and loved even though limits for behaviour are imposed. Management methods try to identify any possible factors that are maintaining the child's wakefulness. Often this is related to parental attention during the night; frequently children have never learned to fall asleep on their own and so when they wake in the night they cry for company to help them fall asleep again. It should be the parents' decision how to manage the problem. If taking the child into their bed solves the problem and they are happy with this there is no further advice to offer. Help should be offered when the existing circumstances are difficult and uncomfortable for the parents.

The management methods should be discussed with the parents so they select a method that they feel they can carry out reliably. Expecting too much is a professional pitfall particularly with anxious and over-stressed parents. Sleep diaries are an essential part of gaining accurate information about the problem and also for monitoring the progress in treatment. They provide clear definitions of the difficulty and what the parents are doing.

The child who cannot fall asleep alone

These children may fall asleep on the parents' lap or the parent may get into bed and cuddle them to sleep. Because forcing the child suddenly to cope with falling asleep alone is often too distressing for them and their parents, 'leaving them to cry' often does not work. A gentler and more graded approach can be very helpful when the parent works through a series of steps that lead to separation. These can be very small changes that take several weeks to work through.

A possible sequence would be:

(1) Lying *on* the bed cuddling the child, rather than in the bed.
(2) Reducing the amount of contact but lying beside the child.
(3) Sitting up on the bed beside the child with a hand on them.
(4) Sitting beside the bed on a chair.
(5) Sitting on a chair halfway across the room.
(6) Sitting on a chair in the doorway.
(7) Sitting outside the door.

Some creativity is required to devise the sequence of steps appropriate to the problem and the parent and child. But once each stage is worked through and the child accepts it with no fuss the parents should not reverse their behaviour if the child suddenly starts to complain again. They should feel confident that their presence in the child's room is reassuring and that they will undo the limit setting that they have already achieved.

The child who cries at night

Bedtime problems frequently occur with night-time waking, but some children cry at night despite being able to fall asleep alone. Often parents try all sorts of activities to get the child to sleep again although these activities probably have little effect in reducing the problem and may actually be making it worse. Car rides at night, playing, drinks and food, watching the video, can all make waking at night rather fun. The parent needs to settle to one response and teach the child that nothing else will happen. Parents need to react like a 'block of wood' if possible and not respond to faces and noises the child may make or get involved in conversation. A graded sequence with a gradual reduction of social and physical contact as previously mentioned can be utilized to help children settle themselves back to sleep.

Some parents feel that being in the room will only agitate the child more and they opt to let the child cry it out. This procedure is more stressful and difficult. The parents should not comfort the child midway through the crying bout as this will teach the child that if they cry for a certain length of time the parent will eventually come in. A brief look in the bedroom and a firm voice saying 'go to sleep' can reassure the parent that the child is safe. The crying may last for a long time the first three or four nights but generally quickly reduces as the child learns there is no point to it.

The child who falls asleep on the breast or bottle

Many babies do this in the first few months of life, but in the second half of the first year mothers should start concentrating on helping their child fall asleep without being dependent on feeding. It does not mean that the child has to be weaned, but that feeding and falling asleep should occur as separate behaviours and not be linked.

The breast-fed baby can continue to breast feed during the day but after the first year does not require feeds in the night. The bottle-fed baby has the option of trying water at night if the parent is concerned about thirst, but generally this is rejected by the child who then learns to fall asleep without the bottle. Cuddles and comfort during the night waking can gradually be reduced so that the child does not become dependent on physical contact instead of feeding. In the three- or four-year-old a reward a sticker can be an extra incentive to help the child go through the night without a drink or parental attention.

The child who sleeps in the parents' bed

Sharing a bed with a small child can be enjoyable, but for many parents it is very disruptive to their sleep as most young children are restless sleepers. One technique of treatment is to take the child back to their own bed every time they come into the parents' room. This can be an exhausting process and the parents need to be extremely determined; if they allow the child to stay after several tries this teaches them to persevere all the more. The child should be allowed to stay after the first attempt or not at all. Some children creep in quietly and get into the parental bed without waking them initially. This can be countered by attaching bells to the door handle, moving the bed against the wall so the child has to climb over the lightest sleeper, or by putting obstacles around the bed.

Rewards and charts can encourage the child to try to stay in their own bed all night.

An alternative strategy is for one parent to sleep in the child's room for a short period until the child is settled there and then use a gradual separation to enable settling without parental presence.

The child who wakes early

Children cannot be taught to go back to sleep again once they wake although occasionally an early morning drink may give another hour's peace. Generally the management process aims at teaching the children not to disturb their parents. This can be achieved by encouraging them to go into their parents' room only when the child's bedroom light is on. A time-switch on a side light can be set for this. If the child wakes very early then the time-switch can be set to the time of normal waking so that there is no wait initially. Once this response is established the timing can be gradually altered so that the waiting time is increased from five minutes up to perhaps an hour. A reward can be linked to waiting for the light to come on.

SEPARATION DIFFICULTIES

Some children are very clinging and will not attend playgroup or nursery without their mothers staying as well. Tantrums and crying disrupt any activities in the nursery and the child may be uncooperative and distressed until the mother returns. Other children will show great upset on separation but settle down after about 5 minutes once the mother has gone. Often the separation problem is the mother's in such cases.

Brief separation periods should be encouraged during the second year of life to enable children to be accustomed to the longer separations expected later on. Mothers may need help to leave the child with a relative or friend for a few minutes. Repeated experiences of brief and safe separations are the best learning experience for children and allow them to realize that nothing dreadful will happen without their mother or father around.

If the child is upset then it would be best to wait until the child calms down slightly before the mother returns so the child does not mistakenly learn that crying makes them come back. Sometimes parents need help in how to say goodbye, excessive hugs and kisses are likely to evoke an emotional response in a preschool child, but leaving without any indication also makes the child feel mistrustful and more clinging. A quick and confident goodbye with reassurance that the mother will return to collect the child can need some practice. Children very easily pick up any ambivalence in a parent on parting and this can make them feel unsettled and unsure.

Laura had tried three different playgroups before she eventually settled into a nursery class at the age of four years. Her mother had started her at the first playgroup just after the birth of the second baby and Laura would not let her mother leave, crying and clinging on to her. After four weeks of being unable to separate Mrs S decided to stop the attendance at the playgroup. The same happened at two successive playgroups. Success was finally achieved in the nursery school as mother felt that this environment was more stimulating for Laura, and despite initial protests from Laura she was finally able to leave her there. Laura took several weeks to start to participate and play in the nursery despite the fact that she was a lively, bright and verbal child at home.

WITHDRAWN AND ISOLATED CHILDREN

Timid and withdrawn behaviour may reflect the parental style of communication or be demonstrating some emotional difficulty. If children are generally quiet, have always been so and show 'shy' behaviour with adults and other children they may need help in learning to relate and mix more appropriately for their age. A playgroup or nursery can often be the first place that the withdrawn behaviour is noted. Timid children will require support from the nursery worker or teacher to integrate into the class. They can be encouraged to join in games with others, and sit next to a sociable child who will make an effort to bring them out. Gentle encouragement to talk and join in activities rather than directly confronting the child to say something in front of the whole group yields better results. Once the child makes a particular friend and relates well to the teacher the problem begins to resolve.

The child who rarely talks should also be investigated for hearing and language development, as these problems can often go undetected in the quiet child.

CONCLUSION

Some children are much more difficult to rear than others due to temperamental differences and varying activity levels. Parents who have managed other children in the family very adequately may suddenly find that their normal style of control and interaction is not working and want help in management.

Other parents ask for advice on how best to cope with a wide range of behavioural difficulties. In addition a proportion of children suffer more severe disturbance. The child's behaviour may be a very effective barometer of the emotional stability and atmosphere at home and so all behaviour problems should be seen in the child's family context. Isolated and uninformed attempts at behaviour change using management methods can be doomed to failure from the start if an adequate assessment is not made of the factors triggering and maintaining the behaviour. Intervention may be required at more than one level in the family for enduring change to take place.

FURTHER READING

M. Chazan, A.F. Laing, J. Jones, G.C. Harper and J. Bolton (1983). *Helping young children with behaviour difficulties*. Beckenham: Croom Helm.

J. Douglas (ed) (1988). *Emotional and behavioural problems in young children. A multi-disciplinary learning pack*. Windsor: NFER/Nelson.

J. Douglas and N. Richman (1984). *Coping with young children*. Harmondsworth: Penguin.

J. Douglas and N. Richman (1984). *My child won't sleep*. Harmondsworth: Penguin.

J. Douglas and N. Richman (1985). *Sleep management manual*. Department of Psychological Medicine, Hospital for Sick Children, Great Ormond Street, London, WC1N 3JH.

R.L. Forehand and R.J. McMahon (1981). *Helping the non-compliant child. A clinician's guide to parent training*. New York: Guilford Press.

M. Herbert (1974). *Emotional problems of development in children*. London: Academic Press.

M. Herbert (1981). *Behavioural treatment of problem children*. London: Academic Press.

R. McAuley and P. McAuley (1977). *Child behaviour problems: An empirical approach to management*. London: Macmillan.

M. Rutter (1975) *Helping troubled children*. Harmondsworth: Penguin.

Problems of Preschool Children
Edited by N. Richman and R. Lansdown
© 1988 John Wiley & Sons Ltd

CHAPTER 11

Feeding Problems and Failure to Thrive

JENNIFER JENKINS AND PETER MILLA

INTRODUCTION

Most preschool children will, at some time or another, be a problem for their parents to feed. Some may not feel hungry. Others will be very finicky or fussy and parents will worry that they are not receiving a nutritionally adequate diet. At different ages they will want more food and their taste in food will change. For most children difficulties in eating are short-lived and they soon return to a more normal amount and variety of food.

However, some children are persistently difficult over their food and their eating patterns start to cause problems. For example, some children find it difficult to move from sloppy foods on to solids and can remain on liquid or puréed foods until they are three or four years old. Some children have tantrums at mealtimes and constantly throw food on the floor or refuse to eat. Some are slow to eat and meals can become prolonged to several hours. These kinds of behaviours can cause parents worry and tension and they often need help to stop the battle which has developed between themselves and their child.

A small number of children develop a much more serious feeding problem. These are children who for a number of different reasons do not eat enough to grow. Their rate of growth both of weight and height is well below what it should be because of their poor calorie intake. In this chapter we will consider first the normal patterns that children show in feeding. Then we will examine the range of problems that develop and their treatment.

NORMAL DEVELOPMENT OF PATTERNS OF FOOD IN-TAKE

The developmental patterns of chewing and feeding follow a sequential

151

pattern. The newborn baby takes an entirely liquid diet and initially may demand up to twelve feeds in 24 hours, including two at night. However, by one month of age over 60 per cent of babies prefer a three-hourly feed and by six months of age this has progressed to four-hourly feeds.

ROOTING REFLEX

Initially the baby exhibits a rooting reflex which assists in locating the source of nourishment. For the first few weeks of life this is a side-to-side head-turning response towards and away from something which rubs against the cheek. From three weeks old it becomes more direct: the head turns straight to the breast or bottle, the mouth grasps the nipple or teat and the baby sucks.

SUCKING AND SWALLOWING

Just like rooting there are two stages of development of sucking. The first is called suckling. At this stage the baby's lips only loosely grasp the nipple and the tongue moves in and out in a licking action. As the nipple is not firmly grasped some milk leaks out as the baby sucks and some air is swallowed. As the baby grows older mature sucking replaces suckling, with the lips holding the nipple much more tightly, the tongue moving rhythmically up and down, creating a vacuum in the mouth. There is practically no leakage of milk and no air swallowing. Thus the older baby is much less troubled by wind than the newborn infant.

Changes in the pattern of tongue movement are also seen during swallowing. The newborn baby's mouth opens prior to a swallow. The tongue protrudes, and retracts only as the mouth closes. By six to twelve weeks such tongue protrusion diminishes. By the end of the third month the baby is able to move food to the back of the tongue and only then is ready for the introduction of solids.

CHEWING

At about four months the baby starts to be able to chew and can begin to take solids. Initially munching occurs in which the jaw moves up and down but without the tongue moving sideways. By six months isolated movement of tongue, lips and jaw start to become integrated and the tongue carries food from side to side. Smoothly co-ordinated functioning of tongue, lips, jaw and cheeks occur. By 24 months jaw movements have progressed from up and down to round and round and the development of lip closure and cheek action helps keep food over the back teeth during grinding.

CUP AND SPOON FEEDING

From the age of five months the babies' hands constantly go to their mouths as does everything they pick up. This persists until they are really adept with their hands at which time such mouthing behaviour ceases. At the beginning of mouthing, babies' hands and eyes are co-ordinated well enough for them to feed themselves with a rusk or to put their lips to the rim of a cup. Progress in drinking from a cup requires the development of:

(1) Raising the tip of the tongue during swallowing.
(2) Controlling the lips.
(3) Stabilizing the jaw.

This sequence of events is completed by about two years of age. The development of lip control includes being able to close the side of the lips, clearing food from a spoon with the upper lip and then removing food from the lips with a wiping movement. These movements are essential for self-feeding.

SELF-FEEDING

Most six-month-old babies make some attempt to help feed themselves by holding the bottle, cup or spoon and can usually manage a biscuit or rusk. By nine to twelve months they like to help in their own feeding by holding a spoon, putting fingers in food, etc. They should be encouraged in this sort of play as it helps them to develop skills towards feeding themselves. At this stage infants play with food with their hands and will deliberately drop food on to the floor, smear it over their faces and even invert a dish of food over their head. These activities are not due to lack of skill but are deliberate, motivated by the pleasure of exploring the qualities of foods.

The ages at which infants manage a cup without spilling the contents and start to hold a fork and spoon are variable (see Chapter 7). Most children acquire these skills by the age of fifteen to eighteen months. By the age of two-and-a-half to three years most children can manage a knife and fork and can use an ordinary plate. The speed at which children develop good eating habits not only depends on their developmental level but also on the behaviour of other family members at mealtimes. Children learn behaviour by copying people around them. If eating a good sized meal and sitting at the table to eat it are not important for other members of the family, a three-year-old is unlikely to progress in this direction.

EMOTIONAL AND BEHAVIOURAL FACTORS AFFECTING FOOD IN-TAKE

Some children need to eat much more than others to achieve normal weight gain even when completely fit and healthy. In part this is related to personality and activity levels: more active children tend to eat more than passive children. It is also related to the child's build with larger, heavier children tending to have larger appetites than small, slight children.

Children's appetites tend to vary like those of adults: some children are hungry first thing in the morning, others do not feel hungry until later in the day. Failure to recognize and adapt to such variations may cause considerable worry. If a parent gets too anxious, food forcing techniques are used and these are almost always counter-productive.

Appetite may be diminished by a number of normal physical factors such as hot weather or infections. Appetite is also influenced by how a child is feeling: some children lose interest in food if they are feeling very unhappy. Reasons for this will be discussed later in the chapter.

Despite these variations of appetite and food intake, healthy children grow at a steady rate and provided such growth conforms to the standards outlined below there is no need for worry.

COMMON DIFFICULTIES IN BREAST FEEDING

Breast feeding can be a problem for some mothers and babies. Some babies may have a weak suck. This can occur for a number of different reasons including tiredness, the baby not being able to co-ordinate sucking and breathing because the nose is blocked, the short-term effect of drugs which the mother was given during the child's birth, etc. With most children the strength of the suck improves after a short time. Some babies find it difficult to feed in certain positions and mothers need to experiment with different ways of holding the baby until they can find a position which is comfortable for themselves and the baby. Some babies fall off to sleep shortly after beginning to feed and may need shorter but more frequent feeds. Changing their position to restimulate feeding can be helpful. Mothers may have difficulties with sore and cracked nipples or with the regulation of their milk. For mothers producing too little milk, more frequent feeds will stimulate milk production. Most of these difficulties are overcome after a short while.

PATTERNS OF NORMAL GROWTH

There is an intimate relationship between children's general health, their nutritional state and their growth. Examining a child's growth pattern gives a good indication of how adequate their diet is and a good indication of their general health. Normal growth is associated with a steady increase in body mass and height and an orderly pattern of developing biological functions. Although rates of growth may vary between individuals, measurements of large numbers of children at different ages and at different times in the life of each one have established normal population standards of growth, to which individuals from a similar population are expected to conform.

These standards are displayed on growth charts for weight, height and head

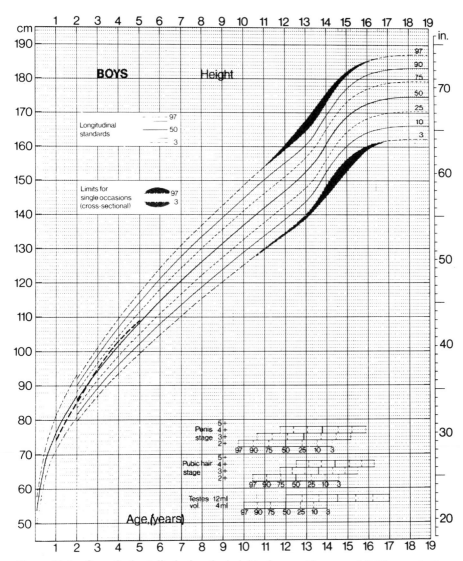

Figure 11.1   Growth chart displaying the height of normal boys aged 0–19 years in the United Kingdom. Superimposed is the growth pattern (in terms of height) of a normally growing boy, now five years old. (Growth and Development Chart, Ref 11A, prepared by J.M. Tanner and R.H. Whitehouse. Reproduced by permission of Castlemead Publications.)

circumference. Examples of growth charts, are shown in Figures 11.1 and 11.2, respectively for height and weight. As girls and boys grow at different rates there are separate growth charts for each. Figures 11.1 and 11.2 are for boys.

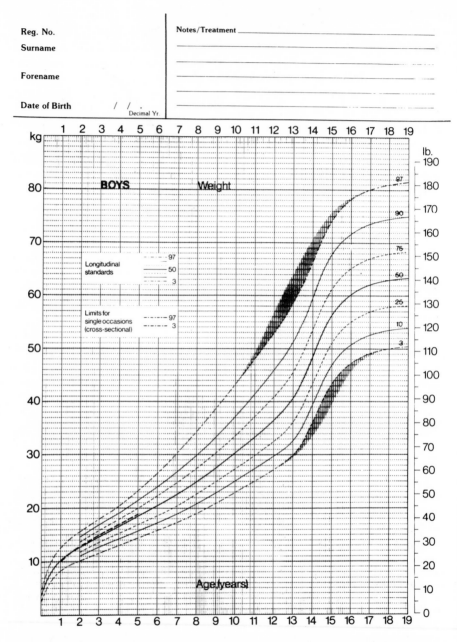

Figure 11.2   Growth chart displaying the weight of normal boys aged 0–19 years in the United Kingdom. Superimposed is the pattern of weight gain of a normally growing boy, now five years old. (Growth and Development Chart, Ref 11A, prepared by J.M. Tanner and R.H. Whitehouse. Reproduced by permission of Castlemead Publications.)

The lines sloping upwards and to the right on the growth chart are centile lines. A centile refers to a percentage of children in the population who are a particular weight or height at a particular age. The thickened dark line in the middle of the chart is the 50th centile line which shows the average weight for children at different ages. The bottom line on the chart is the third centile line, i.e. only 3 per cent of children have weights below this line. The top line is the 97th centile line: only 3 per cent of children will have weights above this. Knowing the average weights and the range of weight for different age children allows us to judge whether a child's growth is within the normal range for age or whether an abnormal pattern is present. Simple, regular monitoring of weight and height plotted over time on a growth chart provides an excellent means of confirming an infant's health and the adequacy of food intake. In general, infants will remain on, or close to, the centile line on which they were born. If their weight or height starts to deviate markedly from this line this indicates a serious problem and always requires medical investigation.

The growth pattern of James, aged five, is superimposed on Figures 11.1 and 11.2. He has grown normally. His height and weight are plotted as _ _ _ _ on the growth charts in Figures 11.1 and 11.2. He was born just below the 50th centile for height and for weight and he has remained very close to these lines as he has got older.

This chart also allows us to see how quickly normal children grow in weight and in height and when they grow fastest. It is clear from Figures 11.1 and 11.2 that children grow at their fastest rate during the first year of life as here the centile lines on the chart between birth and one year rise most steeply. Growth slows over the next year and thereafter continues at a steady rate until the pubertal growth spurt at about thirteen years for boys and eleven years for girls. Children under the age of one year are at particular risk for the development of nutritional deficiencies and growth failure, because this is the time of their fastest growth.

The rapid growth of the earliest period requires optimal nutritional intake. Energy intake must be sufficient for growth, maintenance and activity. During the first four months of life one-third of all calories an infant consumes are used for growth. By the age of one year this has decreased to one-tenth of the total energy consumed. Recommended amounts of food intake are based on the child's age and weight. As well as affecting height and weight gain prolonged malnutrition at this stage may be associated with brain damage, since the infant's brain is at a critical stage of development (see Chapter 4).

In children with feeding problems measurements of height and weight plotted on growth charts such as those shown in Figures 11.1 and 11.2 provide a simple way of demonstrating the seriousness of the feeding problem. If children's food intake is severely limited over a period of time their weight will fall well below the centile line on which they were born. If the child's calorie intake continues to be inadequate over a long period of time the rate of growth in height will also be affected and height will fall below the birth centile line. Growth patterns of this sort are serious and need immediate investigation.

FAILURE TO THRIVE

Failure to thrive is a term used to describe a serious failure in growth; it is caused by a variety of physical and/or emotional problems.

ORGANIC REASONS FOR FAILURE TO THRIVE

Approximately 20 per cent of the children presenting to hospitals with failure to thrive are found to have an organic (i.e. physical) cause. Table 11.1 lists some of the physical factors which influence food intake and utilization.

The growth failure may be due to an illness which limits the child's calorie intake as in some neurological disorders, chronic renal disease, or illnesses associated with excessive vomiting. Food may not be digested and absorbed, as in many disorders of the small intestine such as cystic fibrosis or coeliac disease. Some children are able to absorb but not utilize nutrients as in metabolic disorders such as diabetes mellitus. There may be increased energy requirements as in chronic inflammatory disorders, chronic lung disease and heart disease. An endocrine disturbance may result in a hormonal and biochemical environment which is unfavourable for normal growth to occur. Disease of any system of the body may result in failure to thrive and thus careful investigation is necessary before a diagnosis of non-organic or organic failure to thrive is made.

Table 11.1   Some of the physical factors which influence food intake and utilization

---

Illnesses which limit calorie intake
  Neurological disorders
  Chronic renal disease
  Excessive vomiting
Illnesses which impair digestion and absorption of food
  Cystic fibrosis
  Coeliac disease
Illnesses which impair utilization of nutrients
  Metabolic disorders such as diabetes mellitus
Illnesses which increase energy requirements
  Chronic inflammatory disorders
  Chronic lung disease
  Heart disease

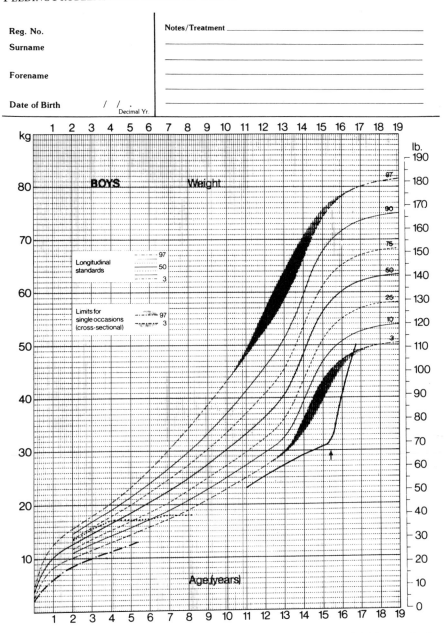

Figure 11.3   Growth chart displaying the weight of normal boys aged 0–19 years in the United Kingdom. See Figure 11.4 for key. (Growth and Development Chart, Ref 11A, prepared by J.M. Tanner and R.H. Whitehouse. Reproduced by permission of Castle-mead Publications.)

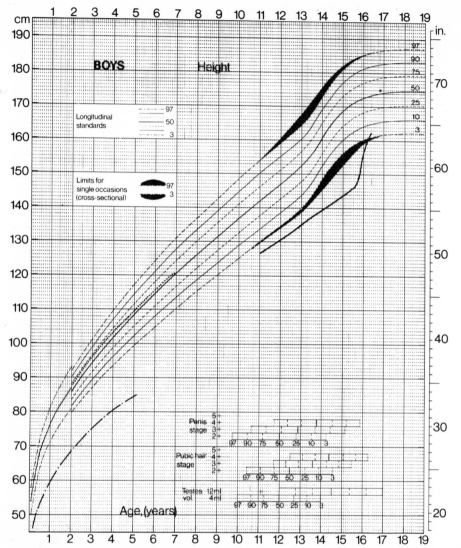

Figure 11.4   Growth chart displaying the height of normal boys aged 0–19 years in the United Kingdom. (Growth and Development Chart, Ref 11A, prepared by J.M. Tanner and R.H. Whitehouse. Reproduced by permission of Castlemead Publications.)
   Superimposed are three deviant patterns of growth:

(1) Decrease in weight alone ⋯⋯⋯
(2) Height and weight equally depressed .—.—.—.
(3) Catch-up growth following an intervention ———

   Referring to the next set of growth charts (Figures 11.3 and 11.4), certain deviant patterns of growth have now been plotted on the charts. These deviant patterns of growth are suggestive of certain kinds of disease processes:

(1) Marked decrease in weight centile alone, without an equivalent decrease in height centile, indicates a significant reduction in assimilation of nutrients either due to malabsorption or an inadequate food intake such as in a severe feeding problem.
(2) Height and weight equally depressed is more suggestive of endocrine, skeletal or genetic defects rather than a gastro-intestinal problem. However a gastro-intestinal disorder may be present if weight gain has been affected before height.

There is a further pattern of deviant growth which has not been shown in Figure 11.3 and 11.4. This is when there is a reduction in height, weight and head circumference and occurs in severe protein calorie malnutrition and in neurological disorders.

Also on Figure 11.3 and 11.4 we have shown what happens to a child's · growth following an intervention which improves their ability to take or utilize food. The solid line shows a period of poor growth until approximately fifteen years. Following an intervention this child begins to show catch-up growth in his height and weight.

NON-ORGANIC FAILURE TO THRIVE

This term is used to refer to children in whom no physical cause can be found to explain their poor growth in weight and sometimes also in height. Although there is some controversy amongst researchers in this field about what causes non-organic failure to thrive most agree that the primary reason for poor growth is a low calorie intake.

Non-organic failure to thrive is not a common problem. Approximately 2 per cent of children under three in an urban population fail to thrive for non-organic reasons. Many children who are failing to thrive for non-organic reasons also show delay in their other milestones and have behavioural difficulties. This is the most serious kind of feeding problem because it has long-term consequences for the child's growth, emotional and social development.

What then are the causes for a child having a low calorie intake? Most of the explanations have been in terms of parental factors which stop a child from getting enough food. But more recently clinicians have stressed factors within the child which contribute to the problem.

PARENTAL FACTORS — EMOTIONAL AND SOCIAL DEPRIVATION

The main explanation for non-organic failure to thrive has been in terms of the parents' inability to care adequately for the child. The parent is not able to provide the child with a physically or emotionally nurturing environment.

Children who fail to thrive because of poor or neglectful parenting start to thrive when they are in an environment away from their parents and they eventually show improvement in developmental functioning as well.

The primary problem is probably a difficulty in the mother–child (or primary caregiver) relationship; the mothers often being unresponsive and insensitive to their infants' needs (see Chapter 3). Social deprivation has also been associated with failure to thrive, with more children coming from homes with large families and overcrowded conditions. The mothers are sometimes suffering from depression or other psychiatric disorders and having difficulties in their marriage. However, it is probably not the deprivation as such which causes the child to fail to thrive, but the parents' inability to care adequately for the child when they live in adverse and stressful circumstances.

> Jane is a two-year-old girl. For eighteen months her weight gain has been very poor. She is much thinner than she should be and she is also not growing well in height. There are four other children in her family and the parents find it difficult to look after them all. Jane is the youngest child. Both of the parents find her irritating as she often cries and on the whole they tend to ignore her. At mealtimes one of the parents tries to feed her for a few minutes and then gives up when she is slow to take it. At other times she is left to play on the floor.

> Jim is a three-year-old boy. He has been failing to thrive for two years. He was a normal sized baby but started to show problems with his weight when he was one-year-old. He lives with his mother and two sisters. His parents separated when he was six months old and his mother has found it difficult to cope with three young children on her own. She is frequently irritable, particularly with Jim who she finds the most difficult child. She has become overly strict with him and when he misbehaves at mealtimes she removes him from the table, sends him to his room and refuses to feed him until the next meal. Withdrawal of food has been used as a punishment and for some time he has not been receiving enough food for adequate growth.

The specific mechanism for these babies not receiving enough food varies from one family to another. In some families the mothers may not feed the child because they do not perceive them as being hungry or they may not have a very clear idea of how much the child needs to grow. The family may be particularly poor and not put the child's nutritional needs first. In other cases withdrawal of food may be used as a punishment.

Infants themselves also contribute to the situation. Some babies are more temperamentally difficult and are irregular in their habits and difficult to comfort. They may take a long time to feed or experience some discomfort on feeding which makes them more irritable. Relaxed, patient and confident mothers are likely to fare better in feeding these infants than mothers who are feeling depressed and tense.

CHILD-RELATED FACTORS IN NON-ORGANIC FAILURE TO THRIVE

Intrinsic food refusal

In our experience of treating children who are failing to thrive there are certainly some children in whom there is no evidence of neglectful parenting. Indeed, the parent is making every effort to feed the child but the child is steadfastly refusing to eat. In contrast to the children who are physically and emotionally deprived, these children do not improve in their feeding patterns and weight gain away from their parents. They are difficult for anyone to feed as described below.

Developmental factors

Some children have unrecognized problems with their mouths which make it intrinsically difficult for them to feed and thus their calorie intake is poor.

A detailed assessment of the functioning of the mouth, tongue, etc. is important in children who show a poor calorie intake. This can be made by a speech therapist. Functioning can be divided globally into normal (described earlier), delayed or immature (where the children are proceeding along appropriate lines but show delay for their chronological age) and dysfunction where the child is showing a deviant pattern in development.

The assessment includes taking an accurate history of feeding and the acquisition of feeding milestones including position during feeding, length of time feeding, texture of food, drooling, choking, vomiting, tongue thrusting, quality of sucking, chewing and swallowing. The history is followed by clinical observation of the oral reflexes interacting with one another. Movement of tongue, lips and jaw are analysed during bottle, breast, cup or spoon feeding as appropriate.

> Mary is a twelve-month-old child who is not putting on weight as well as she should. She takes a long time to feed. She was offered solids around four to five months old but did not seem to like them. Her parents persisted in trying to get her to take solids but have been unsuccessful and she is still on a largely liquid diet. When observed feeding it emerged that she had poor control of her lips and tongue. She had difficulty closing her lips over the food, and moving her tongue to transfer the food from the front to the back of her mouth. The speech therapist diagnosed mild oral motor problems and suggested a series of remedial exercises.

Food phobia

A child can become extremely frightened of food. These children will react by screaming or crying when they see food or anything that they associate with eating. If very distressed they start to retch or vomit. They may not be able to use their hands in touching or playing with food and are too frightened to have it touching their face.

The main factor in a child developing a fear of this kind is that at some point eating will have been a very uncomfortable or even painful experience. This may be the result of physical illness which made them feel ill when they ate, for example some food allergies can lead to abdominal pain or diarrhoea after eating certain foods. These children learn an association between food and pain and avoid eating to avoid discomfort or pain. Children who are force-fed can also react in a very frightened way towards food.

> David is an eighteen-month-old boy. He was admitted to hospital because his weight gain had been very poor over six months. At one year David had a gastric illness with vomiting and diarrhoea. He lost his appetite while he was ill but did not seem to regain it when his health improved. His parents initially coaxed him to eat but when this did not work they began to force-feed him. He was observed during a meal. He was playing happily with his mother before the meal began. A trolley with food was brought in and he started to scream. He became more and more distressed as he was seated and his food was placed in front of him. As his mother tried to feed him he turned his head away and tried to wriggle out of the chair, screaming. If any food got into his mouth he retched and spat it out. He did not swallow any food during the meal and stopped crying and retching only when the food was taken away.

Abnormal feeding experiences

Finally a small group of children fail to thrive following abnormal feeding experiences during infancy and seem not to develop normal appetites, taste preferences or the oral motor skills to break down foods efficiently. Some babies with severe illnesses are fed by nasogastric tube or intravenously for prolonged periods of time during a critical period of feeding development. The children miss normal experiences such as moving from sloppy to solid food, experiencing different tastes and textures and developing a preference for certain foods. There is not a great deal of research in this area but it may be that there is a critical period for children in developing feeding skills and tastes. If this period is missed the skills may be much more difficult to acquire later on.

BEHAVIOURAL FEEDING PROBLEMS

DEFINITION

Feeding problems are best viewed on a continuum of normal developmental difficulties. Most children have short periods of poor or finicky eating in their preschool years. In some children this becomes prolonged or particularly problematic for the family. Further along the continuum is failure to thrive where the child's feeding behaviour, or the parents' ability to feed the child, has become so deviant that the child does not get enough to grow and their health is compromised. Children with behavioural feeding problems are difficult to feed but the calorie intake is not inadequate and growth is normal. They are distinguished from children with failure to thrive because they continue to grow normally, and their problem is much less serious.

There are many more children with behavioural feeding problems than those who fail to thrive. The following descriptions are some examples of behavioural feeding problems.

> Anna is a six-year-old girl who has never eaten solid foods. She is, however, growing well in spite of this and her mother purées all her food. A number of physical investigations were done to see if she had any difficulty swallowing food but no physical problem was found. Anna's behaviour is difficult in other ways as she often refuses to do what her parents say. Her parents feel embarrassed and frustrated by her feeding problem but are frightened that if they stop giving her puréed food she will stop eating all together.

> Sara, aged three, is also growing satisfactorily but causing her family frustration and worry because of her eating. She takes several hours over her meals by eating very slowly or refusing to eat. Her mother follows her around the house with bowls of food. Her behaviour causes frequent quarrels between her parents as her father thinks that the mother is not being strict enough with her.

In a sample of three-year-old children representative of the general population, it has been found that 12 per cent were finicky about their food, taking only a limited range, and 16 per cent had poor appetites. Table 11.2 lists some of the causes of behavioural feeding problems.

Table 11.2   Some of the causes of behavioural feeding problems

Parental reinforcement of food refusal
The child's feeling of autonomy and control
Family tensions
Weaning

TYPES OF BEHAVIOURAL FEEDING PROBLEMS

Parental reinforcement of food refusal

Many children learn that refusing to eat is one way to get a parent to pay them a lot of attention. Some parents respond to a child not eating by sitting with them for a long time, preparing them special food, playing games during meals to distract them, cajoling, coaxing, etc. One view of this is that the child is being reinforced for the refusal to eat by a high level of attention. It will then be worth continuing to refuse food in order to maintain the high level of attention.

The child's feeling of autonomy and control

Through refusing food the child also finds an effective way of controlling the parent and feeling a sense of autonomy and power. Tracy a three-year-old girl would only eat food, and drink milk, warmed to a particular temperature. As soon as the food cooled down she would refuse to eat it and it had to be reheated. This would happen five or six times during a meal and her mother had bought a microwave oven to accommodate the child. This type of problem can arise as early as the end of the child's first year when children are beginning to experiment with separating from their parents and achieving mastery over their environment.

These behavioural patterns can range from mild to severe. However, it is much more common for them to result in family tensions and parental anxiety about the child than in failure to thrive. Most children will play their parents up and derive satisfaction from that but will not starve themselves. Only rarely does the battle become so entrenched that the child is severely at risk.

Finicky children

There are some children who are very fussy about what they eat. For example, some will refuse to eat vegetables, others will avoid all meat. Many, if given the chance, would stick only to eating sweet foods. Many food preferences are thought to be learned: some species of animals avoid new tastes and will eat only familiar foods. Tastes come through in breast milk so that some foods will be familiar before the children are eating the food themselves. It is thought that in some cases animals will eat only things that they have seen their mothers eating and the same may be true of young children; a lot of children's finicky eating may be learned by watching adults with peculiar food preferences. Finicky eating habits can at their worst result in nutritional deficiencies but more often they are just socially handicapping as parents are embarrassed that special arrangements have to be made for their children.

Family tensions

Many children, and adults, lose their appetite when they are feeling unhappy. Children may feel unhappy because there is a lot of quarrelling at home, or because one parent is depressed and unresponsive or perhaps because the parent is critical or uncaring towards them. When the difficulties in the family resolve and the child is feeling happier they will start to eat again.

Weaning

Moving from milk to puréed foods can often by quite difficult. Weaning is usually attempted between the fourth and sixth month. It is common for babies to gag a bit when first learning to swallow solid foods. It is also common for babies to resist new tastes. In these cases particularly anxious mothers find it difficult to be persistent because they fear there is something wrong with the babies' ability to cope with solids. However, quite quickly most babies will start to accept the new taste and learn how to swallow smoothly. If solids are not introduced around this time there may be more severe difficulties in getting children to accept them later. One of the difficulties of weaning a child can be that the breast or bottle has become a source of comfort and an alternative is needed. Depending on the age of the child it may be possible to substitute a blanket or teddy to provide a source of comfort.

Parental expectations

Parents may have very different expectations of mealtimes from their children's expectations. For many parents mealtimes are a sociable event with all members of the family spending time together. Meals often involve a lot of thought and preparation from at least one member of the family. Parents may feel that preparing food is a way of giving good things to their children and a way of expressing their love and concern. Preschool children are too young to grasp what mealtimes might mean to their parents. When they refuse food or make it clear that they do not like something, a parent can feel hurt and react as if the child is rejecting them. This mismatch of expectations can sometimes make mealtimes tense and uneasy. It is important for parents to remember that a young child's rejection of food is not a rejection of the parents' love and concern.

Parental fears

Parents often worry that their children are not eating enough. They see their children losing interest in food and refusing to eat even their favourite foods. They can become fearful that the children will become ill, or that a short-term fluctuation in interest will become a long-term problem. Fluctuations in appetite are very common. Usually an interest in food will reawaken after a few days. It is important for parents to remain calm at these times and not to make food into a source of conflict. Excessive worrying could turn what was a child's normal fluctuation in appetite, into a feeding problem.

Another common worry that parents have is that their children's diet is not sufficiently balanced. Some children will refuse to eat certain vegetables or will want to avoid meat altogether. In general most children eat a sufficiently balanced diet to remain healthy. Parents can make it more likely that children will eat a wide variety of foods by eating a wide variety of foods themselves. If children are reluctant to eat new foods it is best to present them with a very small amount and only gradually build this up to a normal size portion. A sensible balance needs to be struck by parents between insisting that children eat certain foods and allowing them their own preferences.

OBESITY

Overeating is also a problem in children. When children eat more food than they are expending in energy that start getting fat. It is difficult to know how common this is in early childhood because definitions of obesity vary. Probably between 2 and 15 per cent of young children are obese. There are several ways of assessing whether a child is too fat. Not surprisingly just looking at the child is one effective way. Weight and height charts are used to determine whether the child's weight is 20 per cent over what it is expected to be on the basis of their height and age. Sometimes skinfold thickness is measured as this too gives a good indication of whether a child is overweight.

Obesity is only very rarely caused by organic disease. It is much more commonly caused by poor feeding habits. It can start in infancy or early childhood. Bottle-fed infants are more likely than breast-fed babies to be overweight in their infancy. This is probably because breast-fed babies stop feeding when they have had enough, whereas bottle-fed babies may be encouraged to finish the amount of feed in a bottle. Most plump infants do not grow into fat toddlers, but overweight infants are more likely than normal infants to be overweight in adolescence and adult life. About 40 per cent of children who are obese in junior school will be obese in adult life, but most obese adults are generally not fat children.

Why do certain children get fat and others not? In some families the children are not taught to eat the right foods. They are given large quantities of carbohydrates such as sweets, crisps, bread, ice-cream, etc. and they do not develop a liking for lower calorie and more nutritious foods. Some parents give children food to comfort or calm them. The children then turn to food whenever they are feeling upset. Sometimes children eat out of boredom. Many parents of obese children may be fat themselves and do not find it easy to recognize their child's problem and restrict their diet.

Once a child is fat there are several factors which will serve to make it difficult to get slim. One of these is that obese children feel less inclined to exercise and consequently will be using up fewer calories. Fat children are also frequently teased at school which makes them feel miserable and lack confidence in themselves.

Obesity is a difficult condition to treat and preventing it is certainly more fruitful. This is done by encouraging children in good eating habits, and in taking regular exercise. If toddlers do start to look fat it is important to discourage further weight gain and allow the children to 'grow into' their height.

Peter was very overweight at three years old. He frequently ate sweets and crisps and often seemed to be eating because he had nothing else to do. His mother found it difficult to limit his food intake and he was brought into hospital in order to help him lose weight. In hospital his mother was encouraged to provide him with a more appropriate diet and different ways of keeping him occupied were discussed so that he would not eat out of boredom.

TREATMENT APPROACHES

A number of different therapeutic techniques have been used in the treatment of feeding problems. The choice of technique will depend on the underlying cause of the problem.

FAILURE TO THRIVE DUE TO EMOTIONAL AND SOCIAL DEPRIVATION

As there is considered to be a risk in terms of social, emotional and physical development, social work agencies and medical staff are primarily involved in the treatment of these children. Treatment aims focus on improving the parent–child relationship, the problem usually being tackled by social workers or other health care professionals on several levels at once. One focus of therapy is to help the parents cope with life stresses more effectively. Another focus is dealing with negative or ambivalent feelings that the parent has towards the child. The parents often need to be taught to play with the child as their level of positive interaction and thus stimulation is often low. Another central aim of therapy is to help the parents learn different methods to manage the child's difficult or demanding behaviour and cope with their own feelings of anger which the child's behaviour can precipitate.

The treatment of this problem is usually long-term and involves both parental counselling and intensive behavioural work with the parent and child, sometimes in a day nursery (see Chapter 9).

BEHAVIOURAL METHODS

A range of behavioural methods have been found to be successful in helping children with intrinsic food refusal to develop more appropriate eating habits (see also Chapter 11 for a fuller discussion of behavioural management).

Observation

The first step in planning a behavioural programme with a parent is to make a detailed observation of the child's behaviour during a mealtime. This allows the therapist to observe both the factors which lead up to the child's difficult behaviour and how people respond to it. By manipulating the precipitating factors and consequences of the child's difficult behaviour it is often possible to alter it.

Withdrawal of attention

The situation was described above in which a child learns to get attention from a parent by being difficult and controlling at mealtimes. This can be very effectively dealt with by advising a parent to ignore a child's refusal to eat. Instead of reacting by coaxing the child to eat, continuing a meal for several hours, feeding the child, etc. the food is given to the child and no notice is taken of any refusal. The child usually responds by being even more difficult for several days but after this there is usually a shift to more interest in satisfying hunger than in refusing food for attention.

Using rewards

For a difficult or finicky eater of four or five years it is useful to set up a reward scheme for introducing new foods, or for encouraging the development of more appropriate eating habits. This can be done by setting the child goals, of increasing difficulty and praising or rewarding the child each time a goal is achieved. Simple rewards can be used such as a chart, putting a star on it to mark success.

Food phobias

When children become frightened of food the focus of treatment is to demonstrate to them that eating does not cause them pain or discomfort. First all pressure to eat is taken off the children and for a short time their calories come from whatever source they will accept, for example milk only. Then food play is instituted where the children are simply encouraged to play with food, bowls, spoons, etc. As they become more relaxed in this play, there is a move on to messy play where the children are encouraged to touch the food with their hands, smear it on their face and near their mouths. Once their fear of eating has passed more normal habits are gradually adopted.

Encouraging children to accept a broader range of textured foods

For children who find it difficult to move from milk to liquidized food or from lumps to solid food one can make the changes so gradual that they are imperceptible to the child. So, for example, milk is thickened with foods such as cornflour or ice-cream, very small quantities being added each day to the acceptable food. If a child spits out all lumps one can begin on foods such as meringue or chocolate where the food is solid when it is taken but soft when it is swallowed. Cereals or puréed food can be used which are gradually thickened, until lumps are left in.

SPEECH THERAPY

If there is any concern that a child's feeding difficulty might be exacerbated by an inability to use the mouth properly a speech therapist should be consulted. They have developed a wide range of remedial methods.

OUTCOME FOR CHILDREN WITH FEEDING PROBLEMS

What is the outcome for children who have not had any medical or psychological intervention for their behavioural feeding problems? Substantial numbers of preschool children continue to have eating problems into their middle childhood years. In one study children were seen at three, four and eight years. Thirty-one per cent of the children whose parents reported that they had poor appetites at three years still had poor appetites at eight, and 26 per cent of children who were faddy eaters at three were still faddy eaters at eight.

There are no group studies which have evaluated behavioural treatments for children with these feeding problems. In our own clinical experience feeding problems do respond well to behavioural methods of treatment.

In terms of the outcome of non-organic failure to thrive, several studies suggest that children who can achieve a high enough calorie intake can regain a normal growth pattern. Then the question is whether the parent can manage to give the child an adequate calorie intake. Certainly some parents can be helped by counselling to manage to alter their child's diet so that the child is of normal height and weight at follow-up. However, there may be more negative outcomes in other areas. In many cases it appears that developmental delays, educational difficulties and behavioural problems remain. These negative outcomes are probably due to the children remaining in adverse social and emotional circumstances rather than to their nutritional status. In one follow-up study of 25 Australian children who initially presented with failure to thrive due to emotional and social deprivation two of the children were found to have died in suspicious circumstances on follow-up six years later.

In summary, the outcome for children with eating problems varies depending on the type of eating problem and its severity. Behavioural feeding problems which are mild, gradually show improvement. The outcome of children with failure to thrive who receive intervention may be satisfactory in terms of their growth, but may remain unsatisfactory in terms of their overall development and emotional well-being.

FURTHER READING

J.M. Wilson (1977) *Oral Motor Function and Dysfunction in Children*. Chapel Hill N.C.: University of North Carolina.

J.L. Woolston (1983) Eating Disorders in Infancy and Early Childhood. *Journal of the American Academy of Child Psychiatry*, **22**, 2:114–121.

S. Palmer, R.J. Thompson and T.R. Linscheid (1975) Applied behaviour analysis in the treatment of childhood feeding problems. *Developmental Medicine and Child Neurology*, **17**, 333–339.

Problems of Preschool Children
Edited by N. Richman and R. Lansdown
© 1988 John Wiley & Sons Ltd

CHAPTER 12

Gender Differences

JACQUELINE McGUIRE

INTRODUCTION

James, wearing a cape, dashes wildly about his nursery classroom, make believe shooting at his two friends Mark and Dean. James grabs Dean's truck, pushing Mark to the ground in the process. When the teacher demands that James return the truck he refuses and then throws it to the ground.

Sarah sits at a table and plays with fuzzy-felt figures. A younger child falls over near her and she jumps up to help. She then resumes her game and smiles when Charelle joins her. They start to lay out the picture together and the teacher joins them for a while. They obey quickly when told that it is tidy-up time.

These descriptions represent stereotypes of the typical preschool boy (slugs, snails and puppydog tails) and girls (sugar and spice and all things nice), but just how real are they? Are boys really wild aggressive and disobedient while girls are friendly, co-operative and helpful?

Certainly many teachers and parents, if asked, will say that boys and girls do behave differently and that boys are more of a problem to manage. But to what extent is this really so, and if it is the case, what explanations have been given for the differences? Since males and females differ in their genes and their hormones many people have looked for *biological* explanations of behaviour differences. Alternatively, the work and home roles which men and women usually take in our society (or most other societies in the world) differ so markedly that others have sought to explain gender differences in terms of the *environment*. This would include all the things that happen to children from the moment that they are born and particularly the way that parents behave with them. Generally it is now accepted that to follow either of these lines of explanation exclusively is insufficient; rather we must think about how the children's surroundings influence them and also how their biological characteristics

173

influence the way their surroundings operate. We must look throughout the life cycle at the ways in which 'nature' and 'nurture' combine. At some times of life, such as puberty, biological changes may have a greater influence on behaviour, while at other ages the behaviour of parents, friends or teachers may be more relevant to behaviour differences but at all ages there is an interaction between these two.

This chapter discusses differences between boys and girls in physical and intellectual development and in interests and activities during the preschool period. Behavioural and emotional difficulties are then compared. Finally there is a discussion of biological and environmental influences and the interaction between them.

PHYSICAL DIFFERENCES

PHYSICAL GROWTH AND DEVELOPMENT

Generally from birth and throughout the lifespan males are slightly heavier and taller than females though at birth and throughout the preschool period the actual differences are negligible. Newborn males have on average larger heads and faces and are more muscular. They have slightly less fat than girls and by nine months a lot less fat. They grow faster in length and weight until about seven months and then grow more slowly than girls. The central nervous system of females is more advanced at birth and matures more rapidly than that of males and girls also have a faster rate of bone hardening up to the age of about two years. From then up to the age of about eight the skeletal development of boys is ahead but there are no differences in the rate at which first or second teeth develop.

There is also more variability among males than females in terms of size. This means that both the heaviest and the lightest, the shortest and the tallest children are more likely to be boys. Physical milestones such as sitting, rolling, standing and walking are not overall very different for boys or girls but where there are differences boys do less well. For example, one national study found that more boys than girls were not walking by the age of eighteen months. Boys also take longer to achieve control of their sphincter and bowel muscles. In a study of three-year-olds, 23 per cent of boys wetted in the day at least once a week compared with 12 per cent of girls. In another nation-wide survey, 12 per cent of boys were bedwetting at five compared with 9 per cent of girls.

VULNERABILITY

Although boys are slightly larger during the newborn period, they are more fragile and vulnerable than girls, more prone to infection and less resistant to injury. More boys than girls are delivered but by the end of the first year of life these differences have evened out because more boys are stillborn, more die in the neonatal period and more die during the first year of life. Mortality of boys is greater than that of girls right through the preschool period, though not all deaths are related to 'natural causes'. Boys have more accidents in the home, are involved in more road accidents and have more head injuries involving loss of consciousness, perhaps related to their higher rates of activity and risk taking.

MENTAL ABILITIES

SPEECH AND LANGUAGE

There are wide variations in individual development for both boys and girls but on average young girls have more advanced verbal ability than boys and the development of speech is more stable and predictable for girls. From the age of about one onwards girls will be able to complete more items on a language assessment than a group of boys of the same age. By two on average girls have a larger vocabulary and link words more often to make phrases or sentences. At home with their mothers they will generally initiate more conversational exchanges than boys and will use speech more effectively to get help from adults. This early advantage shown by girls diminishes by about three years of age and increases again in later childhood.

Severe language delay is more common among preschool boys than girls. In a survey of three-year-olds severe language problems (e.g. not using prepositions, pronouns or adjectives, using sentences of one or two words) were identified in twice as many boys as girls. More preschool boys also have problems of articulation. Some rarer language disorders (e.g. developmental dysphasia, word deafness) are equally common for girls and boys (see Chapter 5).

Another difference is the greater stability of girls' language development. One can be more accurate for a girl than a boy in taking a language assessment at six months to predict the child's level of language ability at six years. Language is also more closely related to overall ability for girls than boys. If one wanted to predict a boy's intelligence test score at ten years, it would be better to base the prediction upon how well they did at age three with a form-board puzzle, sorting coloured buttons or some other task which did not involve language. For a girl prediction would be fairly accurate from information about how many pictures they could name, how many body parts they knew or how well they understood directions such as 'put the cup on the chair'.

INTELLECTUAL DEVELOPMENT

It has already been mentioned that there is more variability in the physical size of boys than girls; this is also true for intellectual development. More boys than girls have very high and very low levels of intelligence. Most standardized intelligence tests are constructed in such a way that gender differences are minimized but differences are sometimes found. Four-year-old girls were found to receive consistently higher scores on a recently developed intelligence test, the McCarthy scales of children's abilities, although the differences are not large. The girls were more likely to have a slightly larger vocabulary, complete simple puzzles a little more confidently and to draw slightly better. In drawing people and in the ability to make shapes (e.g. square, triangle) or letters, girls are better than boys throughout the preschool period. The test in which children are asked to draw a person gives a good example of differences in development. While a five-year-old girl usually includes a head, eyes, nose, mouth, body, legs and arms in her human figure, a five-year-old boy will be less likely to include arms.

Methods of assessing children by looking at the complexity of their play also show girls to be slightly ahead in certain areas.

> Martha, three years old is given a doll, spoon, cup, saucer and brush to play with. She holds the doll, walks it along the table, talks to it, sits it on a chair and pretends to feed it with some cereal. She then brushes its hair and pretends to put it to bed.

> Simon, also three years old, is given the same toys. He holds the doll, brushes its hair but does not talk to it. He seats it on a chair but does not offer it the cup or plate, then picks it up and takes off the clothes, pulls at the arms and legs and sees if they will come off.

Martha's play includes more fantasy and more correct use of the toys as if they were real while Simon's play is less advanced, with more exploration and no evidence that he is including any make-believe ideas. Although these particular toys may be more familiar to girls than boys, it is generally found that boys of two or three use toys in a less complex way than girls. However, by about four years these differences have diminished. In addition, boys' style of play may be viewed as more advanced in some respects. While girls are bound more by the 'correct' way to play with a toy, young boys are more likely to experiment, to create new ways of using a toy and they are also more curious about their surroundings. While this may be viewed as immature during the preschool period, it is thought by some that the greater flexibility and lack of conformity of boys will lead to more creativity and independence when older.

SOCIO-EMOTIONAL BEHAVIOUR

Differences occur in the normal social and emotional behaviour of children, and in their interests and play styles.

INDEPENDENCE

From about nine to eighteen months a child's dependence upon parents and feelings of closeness with them becomes more firmly established. Evidence of this 'attachment' is to be seen in behaviour such as fussing or crying when the mother or father suddenly leaves the room, staying close to the parent during situations which involve some stress or returning frequently to touch or talk to them during a play session. Generally girls show this kind of behaviour more markedly with their mothers than boys do and in particular they are likely to stay closer to mothers than boys do. There is no clear pattern of gender differences for relationships with fathers.

Girls are also more inclined to ask adults to help them with difficult tasks and their efforts to succeed are more related to encouragement and praise from adults, while boys seem to be more independently persistent.

As already mentioned boys are more exploratory and creative in their play, more likely to invent new uses for toys and more likely thoroughly to investigate their surroundings. But in some other ways preschool girls are more independent than boys. They are better able to look after themselves in terms of dressing, feeding and toileting and are more likely to be actively involved in choosing their own outfits.

AGGRESSION

During their games boys produce more make-believe aggression, making small dolls 'hurt' or 'kill' each other or by acting out hurtful and violent scenes themselves. The differences are carried over from fantasy to reality. In a typical nursery class or other group setting, the boys are more often to be found hitting and punching other children and throwing or breaking the toys. In particular when several boys play together it is quite likely that there will be some aggression, while they are less aggressive if playing with a girl and fighting is not so usual between two or three girls.

COPING WITH STRESS

Marie, who is 25 months old, is playing with some toys in an experimental playroom. A stranger comes in and blocks off the half of the room which contains the most exciting items. She runs to the barrier, rattles it and calls to her mother who is on the other side, asking her to undo it. When her mother fails to respond she starts to fiddle with the latch on the gate and eventually manages to get it open.

Dion, 27 months old, is placed in a situation similar to Marie's. He runs to the gate, screams, shakes it wildly and then wanders about on his side of the gate, whining and reaching out to his mother to lift him over.

Young boys on the whole cope less effectively with stressful situations than girls. The stress might be a short-lived one, such as failing to solve a puzzle or having a gate closed to restrict their play space, or an extended one such as family break-up or starting infant school. They are likely to show more frustration, for example in the way that Dion did, flinging to the ground a puzzle which he failed to solve, while girls more often seek help from adults or persist with a problem. After serious events like divorce, more boys than girls show emotional reactions and distress by behaviour such as becoming very clingy to one parent, fighting with brothers or sisters, doing less well at school or regressing in their behaviour (e.g. beginning to wet or soil again).

INTERESTS AND PLAY STYLES

TOY CHOICE

It has already been mentioned that boys indulge in more fighting, both play and real, than girls. There are many other ways in which the kinds of toys chosen and the sorts of games played differ for boys and girls from quite early on in life. Imagine a small playroom into which several thirteen to fourteen month-olds come in turn, accompanied by their mothers. The room contains a selection of toys including stuffed animals, bricks, a pushing lawn-mower, a ball and peg-boards. You will probably see that the boys play with the lawn-mower, ball and bricks more than the girls while the girls play with the stuffed toys more than the boys. However, in the first couple of years there are not very clearly marked gender differences in the toys children choose to play with, both girls and boys prefer building or active toys to dolls. By the third year this is changing.

Picture a typical nursery class in which several activities are laid out. There is a table with lego, a large garage with a box of small cars, a table with play dough and cutters and the teacher is sitting at another table doing a pasting and cutting activity. There are two easels with paints and on the carpet are large wooden construction bricks. The french doors are open and outside there are a water table, a rocking seat and four tricycles. For only one of these — the water table — would it be difficult to predict whether there would be more girls or boys playing. In numerous observations, dating from the 1930s to very recently, it has been shown that boys more often select small vehicles, construction activities with large or small bricks and riding toys, and they also choose rushing about and any outdoor play more than girls. Girls prefer art activities, quiet games, those with an adult (such as lotto) and domestic play in the 'home corner'. Outside they go to swings and see-saws or rocking toys more often than boys. These differences are repeated to some extent in the home, though of course the same choices might not be open to girls and boys at home since they are given markedly different toys from an early age.

ACTIVITY

Activity has been examined in children ranging from a few days old and throughout the preschool period. Male infants are slightly more restless, prone to startle and kick more when awake or asleep than females. This difference in activity continues to be found throughout the preschool years and for older children also. An important point to note is that activity varies according to the situation that the child is in. Differences are most marked when there are large numbers of children in a group and when outdoor play is an option.

The kind of play described as 'rough and tumble' is related to activity and aggression. It usually involves running, chasing, wrestling, jumping, threats of hitting, falling down and laughing. In Western societies such as Great Britain or the United States of America, this type of play is more typical of boys than girls. However, the influence of the environment is strongly suggested since such differences are not consistently found in other cultures.

Although there are consistent differences between boys and girls, activity levels for an individual child are quite variable over time. You cannot predict how active a child will be at three years from their activity as an infant.

HELPING AND CARING

Girls in groups such as nurseries are on the whole more attentive and caring to newcomers, showing them toys, soothing them if they seem distressed and reporting their difficulties to the adult in charge. They also play more co-operatively and helpfully, being particularly helpful to younger girls while boys are more competitive. When boys are helpful it will probably be with older rather than younger boys, possibly when trying to join in a game rather than actually looking after others.

DIFFERENCES IN DISTURBANCE

Studies looking at the amount of disturbed behaviour fall into two types. On the one hand information is collected from child guidance clinics and other centres where parents of young children go for help, and on the other surveys are carried out of a representative sample of all parents with preschool children, asking then what problems their children have.

CLINICAL STUDIES

In the first type of study, looking at young children whose parents have sought or been referred for help with serious problems, marked differences have been found throughout childhood from the preschool stage upwards. Parents are about twice as likely to attend clinics and other centres with boys than girls. The sorts of problems which parents of boys describe are also different from girls' problems.

> Brian has come to the child guidance clinic with his mother. He is three years old and she says that she finds it very difficult to manage him. He usually disobeys her, is often spiteful and aggressive to his young sister and to friends that he plays with. He is very excitable and active, rarely settling for more than a minute or two with any of his toys and his speech is not well developed. He does not usually use sentences, mainly two or three-word phrases.

> Julie is carried into the room crying bitterly and clinging to her mother. She is three-and-a-half and has come to see a psychologist to get some advice about starting nursery school. Previously her mother had tried a playgroup but she attended for only one week and would not let her mother leave. She refused to talk to the other children at the playgroup or to the helpers. For the past six months, since a dog barked at her loudly in the road, she has been very reluctant to go out to the shops or to parks. She is very small and pale and her mother says that she is extremely faddy, refusing most foods except biscuits, milkshakes or Weetabix.

These children illustrate the kinds of problems most typically presented by parents with young children who seek professional help. The kinds of problems more commonly described for boys are called 'conduct disorders' often linked with hyperactivity, while those more typical of girls are 'neurotic' or emotional difficulties. The behaviours associated with conduct problems are outwardly directed such as fighting, refusing to obey, being destructive, having violent temper outbursts and dashing about too wildly. In contrast girls are more likely to be timid and fearful. However, boys do also have emotional problems and girls conduct disorders.

Differences in clinic groups do not give the whole picture since there are many factors influencing why parents decide whether or not to seek help. Studies of a total population of children avoid this difficulty.

POPULATION STUDIES

Several large studies completed in Great Britain have found differences in the rates of behaviour problems in preschool girls and boys, although the differences are not as great as those in clinical groups. For example, in one study of three-year-olds 7.2 per cent were judged by a psychiatrist to have a moderate or severe problem; the percentages for girls and boys were 5.4 per cent and 9.3 per cent respectively. The rates of mild problems were almost identical for girls and boys, about 15 per cent for each group. Another study of children with ages ranging from two to four-and-a-half, found that almost twice as many boys as girls were causing their parents serious problems. It seems that boys may have slightly more severe problems but the differences are not great.

There are some symptoms which have consistent gender differences. High levels of activity, poor concentration, being difficult to control, wetting and soiling are more typical of boys than girls while faddiness over food and fearfulness are slightly more often found in girls.

SPECIFIC SYNDROMES

Some specific disorders are found more commonly in boys than girls. The rate of infantile autism is about 3–4 per 10,000 children but the gender difference is very marked. Out of every five autistic children four are likely to be boys, suggesting that genetic factors play an important role in its development. There is some disagreement about how common hyperactivity is, and how distinct it is from conduct problems for children of preschool age (see Chapter 4) but there is no dispute that throughout childhood hyperactive boys far outnumber girls.

Emotional disturbance in preschool children may also relate directly not just to what sex a child is biologically but to the sex that he or she identifies with. Thus children who insist that they are the opposite sex would be thought to have an emotional problem, particularly when the child will only wear clothes usually associated with the opposite sex. In Western societies it is considered abnormal when a young boy wears dresses but a preschool girl who wears trousers is quite acceptable. Consequently boys are more often referred to clinicians for gender identity confusion than girls.

PROBLEMS IN GROUP SETTINGS

Tom, three years and eleven months, attends a day nursery. He seeks adult attention very frequently, often crying and wanting to be held, but he generally ignores the other children unless they are playing with toys which he wants. He tends to be wild and destructive and often sweeps toys to the floor when others are playing with them. He swears a great deal at the staff and the children.

Chris, age four, attends a nursery class. He is bright and talkative and often initiates games. He is also very domineering, always wanting to decide on the rules and he frequently pushes or hits those who do not go along with his ideas. He likes rough wild games and whenever trikes are out he will always get the best one, charging about and knocking into things and people. He is defiant or sulky when told off and rarely obeys unless threatened with the loss of privileges.

Tom and Chris are typical of the sorts of behaviour problems reported in preschool groups, and more boys then girls are said to have these kinds of problems. In a recent British study which looked at children in day nurseries, school nursery classes and playgroups, difficult behaviours were more common in boys than girls. In the day nurseries, while the overall rate of children with problems was 35 per cent, the rate for boys was 41 per cent and for girls 24 per cent. In the nursery classes there were fewer children with problems (11 per cent) and the gender differences was smaller, 9 per cent of the girls and 12 per cent of the boys were identified as having definite problems. All the individual symptoms associated with 'conduct disorder' (fighting, destructiveness, teasing, overactivity, bothering other children) were more common in boys than girls. For example 9 per cent of the boys were said to be very destructive compared with 5 per cent of the girls and 14 per cent of the boys were frequently aggressive with other children, while only 3 per cent of the girls were. There were very few problems more common for girls than boys. Although more girls than boys who attend child guidance clinics have neurotic problems, this pattern was not evident in behaviour as described by nursery teachers or nursery nurses. Fearfulness, miserable or sensitive behaviour and isolation were as common for the boys as for girls.

EXPLANATIONS OF GENDER DIFFERENCES

BIOLOGICAL

It would be easy for anyone considering the physical differences between young children to assume that differences in behaviour are also biological in origin. This view is strengthened when one reflects that behavioural differences are evident so early in life.

But there are two reasons for doubting the view that all differences are the result of no more than inbuilt biological programming.

The first is that there are very few consistent differences between newborns and those that are evident, such as restlessness, are not stable throughout infancy. The second is that adults behave differently towards boys and girls from the moment they are born and so any influence of biology is combined with the way children are treated from the outset. This conclusion does not mean that biology plays no part, rather one must as always, look at the combination of factors.

A more precise biological origin of behaviour might be found in different levels of the secretion of several hormones. It is possible that these are related to some gender differences, particularly in aggression. Male infants have higher levels of male hormones (androgens) and in some animals these are associated with aggressive behaviour, but the results are not consistent for all the animals studied and a complication is that the male hormone testosterone also produces greater *physical* strength (in rats or mice) and this could explain the higher level of fighting between male rodents. It is also difficult to move from the simple 'social' situation used to study rat or monkey behaviour to humans and some would argue that it is not justified.

Experiments of course cannot be done to humans to alter their hormones but sometimes newborns have been influenced by drugs which their mothers took during pregnancy or are born with abnormal hormone levels. Girls who have been exposed to male hormones before birth or who have an imbalance of hormones in their own body are sometimes born with ambiguous or male-like genitals. This can be corrected surgically, but the girls with this sort of problem are often more tomboyish and active. However, they also receive treatment with cortisones, which increase activity in males and females. In addition, prior to the surgery parents or others may have responded to them as if they were boys. For these reasons it is hard to draw conclusions from this unusual group of children. It is generally held that in the preschool years hormones are not related in any clear way to gender differences in behaviour.

A third biological argument rests on the fact that girls' nervous systems mature more rapidly that boys'. One aspect of maturation is the gradual dividing of tasks between the two halves of the brain. In adults the left half or hemisphere is more involved with verbal and reasoning activities and the right hemisphere with visual and spatial thoughts. Since girls have slightly more advanced verbal skills it was thought that their brains might specialize sooner, but there is disagreement about this and at the moment it is not possible to say whether or not this is the case.

Overall, there are few indications that biological factors play a large part in explanations of behavioural differences, though this is not to say that biology is irrelevant. The slower rate of neurological maturation of boys is undoubtedly associated with their higher levels of bedwetting and soiling. These behaviours might in turn lead to differences in parental behaviour or, for example, to differences in the age that boys go to visit other families without parents. The slightly greater muscularity of boys may lead to perceptions that they are 'stronger' or more 'athletic' which in turn could influence parents to encourage rough and tumble games. Generally, biological influences are more difficult to demonstrate than environmental factors.

PSYCHOANALYTIC THEORY

Psychoanalytic thinking brings together biological differences and parent–child relationships to explain how children begin to understand that they are male or female and that males and females act in differing ways.

Boys, once they become aware that they have a penis but that girls do not are said then to fear castration. This anxiety is heightened by their increasing desire for their mother, bringing them into competition with the father (the Oedipal stage). In order to cope with their anxiety and since their father has a penis while their mother does not, they identify increasingly with their father and become more 'masculine' in their behaviour. From the time that the Oedipal anxiety is faced, boys will be predicted to value masculine attributes and reject femininity.

Girls on the other hand are thought to be motivated by envy, that boys have a penis and they do not. They may either think that they used to have a penis, which was taken away or that they could gain one in the future. They blame their mother for the perceived loss since she is in the same situation and turn to their father as a figure to identify with and love, hoping that he can provide the desired object. Once they realize that this is futile they resolve Oedipal anxiety by returning to their mother as the person they want to emulate, behaving in an increasingly 'feminine' way. From then on they will value femininity but may not reject masculine characteristics as completely as boys reject femininity, since the envy is still there.

An American sociologist, Nancy Chodorow, has rethought the psychoanalytic approach, taking into account the fact that most young children are brought up by women, usually their mothers. She suggests that girls develop their self-concept or identity as female and feminine through close intimate contact with their mother in the early years and that mothers contribute to the process by seeing themselves in their daughters. Thus girls are expected to become aware of their femininity, and all that implies, sooner than boys learn about masculinity. For boys the process is more negative, they learn that they are not the same as their mothers and that they need to negate femininity and identify with their fathers. Since fathers are not usually at home as much in the early years it is more difficult for boys to develop their 'gender identity' and knowledge about masculine behaviour. The fact that their learning involves negating their mother, upon what they should not be or do, is apparent in society's greater concern about femininity in boys (such as wanting to wear dresses) than masculinity in girls.

Of course the psychoanalytic approach, whether the more traditional Freudian theory or Chodorow's re-analysis, depend very much upon mothers and fathers behaving in traditionally feminine and masculine ways, which may not necessarily be the case in any particular family.

THE DEVELOPMENTAL THEORY OF CHILDREN'S UNDERSTANDING

A contrasting way of explaining gender differences in children's behaviour is to look at the development of their understanding of the fact that they are female or male, that this cannot change, and that different behaviours are associated with females and males.

Children want to make sense of the world and the gender division is one of the main ways in which children can categorize themselves (others may be tall/short, old/young, blonde hair/brown hair, etc.). It is argued that children begin to use gender as a category at aged three to four years and from then on they learn about the kinds of behaviour which are usually associated with each gender (gender stereotypes). It is argued that children remain unclear about the permanency of gender until they are six or seven years old. To make sense of this confusion they become quite rigidly stereotyped in their behaviour from about four years, rejecting attributes associated with the opposite sex. It is certainly clear in the play of four and five-year-olds, when children increasingly mix in single sex groups and talk disparagingly about 'girls' toys' or 'boys' games'. Once they are sure that gender does not change with altered clothing, hair styles or behaviour, they can then be more flexible in their behaviour.

One major problem with this theory is that children have been found in recent studies to have extensive knowledge of their own and others' gender at two to three years and some awareness of gender stereotypes. By asking questions in less roundabout ways than previous work, it has been possible to show that by four children show understanding of gender permanence and the relationship between physical genitalia and the social expectations for either sex. Thus a more likely explanation of their increasing conformity to stereotyped behaviour from school-age is that there are other influences in their environment such as parents, teachers, friends, siblings books and television, reinforcing their early learning.

DIFFERENT UPBRINGING

Gender stereotypes

Despite at least twenty years of protest from the Women's Movement for equal rights, in Western societies such as Great Britain there are still clear divisions in perceptions of the roles of men and women. Caring, nurturing and gentleness are seen by most to be feminine while activity, aggression, independence, bravery and ambition are thought of as masculine characteristics. Husbands and wives, if asked about ideas such as 'swapping roles' usually say that they would not seriously consider this, unless perhaps it was a short-term emergency. Since these expectations are so widespread, they are bound to have some influence upon the way parents or other adults respond to children. They will also influence what behaviour is perceived to be 'abnormal' or a problem. Since emotionality is not thought to be appropriate masculine behaviour, a fearful boy might not be accepted in the same way that a fearful girl would be. She might even receive some encouragement for showing fears or being timid if it is intepreted as 'feminine' or 'cute'. This could lead to a greater likelihood that girls would become very fearful. Similarly, if pugnaciousness is thought to be typical male behaviour, an aggressive boy might be checked less than an aggressive girl, leading to more boys with high levels of aggression.

Parent behaviour

A *girl* has been delivered to Mr and Mrs Marshall. The nurse suggests that Mr Marshall hold the infant. He looks anxious, takes her gingerly but keeps her wrapped in a shawl. After a minute he remarks to his wife, 'She's so tiny, she hardly weighs anything, here you take her, I don't want to have her getting too cold'.

A *boy* has just been born, the first child of Mr and Mrs Jones. Mr Jones asks if he may hold the infant. He gazes at him for several minutes, holds one finger, says 'He looks just like my Dad, he's really strong, just look at that little fist getting ready to punch me, he's super'. He then holds the baby for another four minutes, gazing at him and speaking softly.

Differences have been noticed in the way that parents think about and act towards girls and boys from almost the moment of delivery onwards. In fact there are differences even before birth. Parents who express a preference more often hope for a son than a daughter, particularly fathers, and if the first-born is a girl a second baby is likely to be born sooner than if it is a boy. Even when there are no actual physical differences, male babies are thought to be stronger and fitter looking, and females more delicate and soft. Fathers hold male babies for longer in the delivery room and talk to them more; this is particularly marked for first-born children. These kinds of different treatment continue at home, fathers holding and talking to boys more than girls and being more protective with girls. However, their child's gender does not appear to influence how much caretaking fathers do. When babies are very small and throughout the first year, fewer differences are noted in mothers' behaviour, except that they may breast-feed boys for longer, be less responsive to their crying and handle them in a more vigorous manner.

From the first year onwards, there are numerous differences in the behaviour of mothers and fathers with girls and boys. The toys which they provide for them or encourage them to use are generally very different and fathers in particular are very critical of boys who play with 'girls' ' toys such as dolls, cooking sets or push-chairs. Boys own more riding vehicles and other sport toys which involve active play, and parents are more likely to start up an active game with a boy than a girl.

These differences could, of course, relate primarily to the gender differences in activity levels already described. A girl who was not particularly energetic would probably not be encouraged to romp about while most boys will be. Similarly, parents may not calm a boy who tends to be very restless and active as much as a girl with the same sort of behaviour. Boys are also expected to be braver than girls, given less comfort when they hurt themselves and are more encouraged to take risks playing on slides or climbing frames. Boys' difficulties when placed in stressful circumstances could be linked to expectations that they will control their distress and not express anxiety or fear. If they have learnt to suppress feelings this could make it harder for them to cope when they are experiencing difficulties like their parents quarrelling.

Another difference shown by parents relates to achievement in boys and girls. Parents are often more helpful with daughters and more directive and concerned with success or achievement for sons. More caretaking and play from fathers has been associated with increased intellectual development, particularly for boys. However, it is not clear whether fathers prefer to play with more responsive children or whether their involvement helps to make the children brighter. As children enter school parents, especially fathers, are also more concerned about the academic achievement of boys than girls and when fathers are absent from the home, boys generally do less well academically. The expectation that boys should achieve might lead one to expect them to behave more quietly in school but generally this is not so. Possibly some of their behaviour problems are related to the difficulty in coping with competing demands: being a success at school work can be seen as cissy, 'real boys' are not teachers' pets.

Although preschool boys are more aggressive than girls, there is very little evidence that parents handle aggression any differently, when directed at themselves or other children. However, the toys given and the kinds of interests suggested for girls and boys are very likely to influence aggression and more wild behaviour with toys such as throwing, kicking or banging is tolerated from boys than girls. Few parents of a two-year-old would want her to have a toy tank, a police motor-cycle or even an action man doll, because of the implied aggressive play. However, most parents of boys the same age will tolerate these boys, with the expectation that 'boys will be boys'.

Generally, it is not clear whether parents are stricter with girls or boys. Some work has shown that boys are disciplined more, but in fact the boys were also naughtier. Other studies show the reverse, that girls are controlled more. Boys do receive more physical punishment than girls, which could provide them with a model of responding in an aggressive way to conflict.

So far parental behaviour has been discussed in terms of influences which will be different for boys and girls. It is equally possible, depending upon their own beliefs, that they may make a conscious effort to counteract biology, society or whatever other factors might be relevant to differences between girls and boys. Indeed, some parents who are trying to be 'non-sexist' have been interviewed. Generally they find that their task is not easy. Once children mix regularly with adults or children outside the home, external influences can powerfully counteract parents' attempts, for instance to persuade a son that it is OK to nurse a doll or to dress their daughter in sensible denim dungarees.

Young children like their ideas to be consistent and rule bound. For instance a child whose mother is a doctor may confidently assert that all doctors are men. While children are powerfully influenced by their parents, they are also keenly aware from a young age of the implicit and explicit rules of the society in which they live. The effects of non-sexist upbringing, of parents providing models which are non-traditional, may be observable in late childhood or when career choices have to be made, but during the preschool period they may be less easy to detect.

One final comment about the influence of families is that very little is known about the effect upon the parents of siblings. Do parents with an older son treat a younger daughter in a more feminizing way than those with three other girls, or do they treat her like a tomboy? Are only daughters treated more like a son? Do only sons get spoilt and overprotected by mothers? Generally it is very difficult to study large enough groups to compare all the different possible combinations of boys and girls within a family. The one consistent finding is that only daughters seem to achieve well in school and be more ambitious for careers than girls with older siblings. However, no other effects of the number or sex of siblings, or position in the family are clear-cut.

Other adults and peers

If a man or woman is presented with a baby that they do not know, they are likely to react in a different way to an infant which they think is a girl from one they believe to be a boy, even if the information they have been given about its sex is false. They are more active with boys and choose different toys for them, a doll for girls and a hammer or rattle for a boy.

Most preschool children have some group experiences away from home before they start school and here they are also treated differently. Teachers in preschool groups often reinforce 'stereotyped' play, introduce new toys or activities with cues suggesting they are more suitable for girls or boys, encourage girls to be passive and work orientated while letting boys rush around more. Boys also get more negative attention, they are more often told off than talked to about finishing some work or settling to an activity.

From three or four years children are increasingly critical of play which they see as 'cross-sex' such as boys playing with dolls or wanting to be a Mummy, but girls have more leeway to be boyish. Their play suggests that they are obeying rules about gender appropriateness, with boy to girl aggression happening much less than boy to boy. Older children are also important role models for fantasy play, which is usually strongly sex-typed, with older boys being superman or another TV hero and older girls a mother or teacher.

CONCLUSIONS

The higher rates of language delay of boys and their greater problems with sphincter control are most probabaly connected with their neurological immaturity, in comparison with girls. For most other behaviours there are no simple explanations of gender differences and there is no clear cut division between behaviour related to biology and that related to the environment. Throughout childhood they both influence behaviour to varying degrees.

Differences in children's behaviour have very close links with parent behaviour and social expectations. Boys have more behaviour problems than girls and these problems are more likely to persist to school age. This could be related to a number of factors. Their higher levels of language delay could contribute to problems in expressing frustration or in coping with other children. Boys are more physically vulnerable, they are under greater pressure to be tough and active and are discouraged from expressing upset or worry. Girls may be provided with better ways of coping as they are encouraged to be dependent on adults and to look to them for help. Throughout childhood the emotional and behavioural problems of girls and boys differ increasingly. The processes which take place during the preschool years show how this division starts to develop.

FURTHER READING

J. Archer and B. Lloyd (1982) *Sex and Gender*. Harmondsworth: Penguin.

D.J. Hargreaves and A.M. Colley (1986) *The Psychology of Sex Roles*. London: Harper & Row.

E.E. Maccoby and C.N. Jacklin (1974) *The Psychology of Sex Differences*. Stanford, CA.: Stanford University Press.

J. Nicholson (1979) *A Question of Sex*. London; Fontana.

E.G. Pitcher and L.H. Schultz (1983) *Boys and Girls at Play*. Brighton: The Harvester Press.

S. Sharpe (1976) *Just Like a Girl*. Harmondsworth: Penguin.

J. Statham (1986) *Daughters and Sons. Experiences of Non-sexist Childrearing*. Oxford: Basil Blackwell.

Problems of Preschool Children
Edited by N. Richman and R. Lansdown
© 1988 John Wiley & Sons Ltd

CHAPTER 13

Child Care Away from the Family

JACQUELINE MCGUIRE

Preschool provision varies enormously in different countries. For example, in Sweden children start school at seven years of age. Before then, starting at the age of three, they may attend a kindergarten with staff trained in education and child care. Or they may go to a group home (similar to child-minders in the United Kingdom), where a trained worker can take up to six children. Great Britain offers a great contrast. Compulsory school begins at five years, but many children now start when they are four, going into reception classes. In addition there are nursery classes or schools for some three to four-year-olds. A small percentage of children under five attend day care in day nurseries and a much larger percentage of three to four-year-olds are in voluntary playgroups. Many spend the day with child-minders or relatives while their parents work.

This chapter discusses the types of preschool provision available in Great Britain, the differences between them and what we know about the effects of attending. Unfortunately in Great Britain parents' choices are limited by cost and by what is available in their area; they may have very little choice, especially if they have a low income.

There are many reasons for needing group day care for a child; care might be sought because both parents are working, to provide a child with companions and group experience, for educational reasons, or because a child has a physical or developmental problem. Many children live rather isolated lives and parents increasingly seek preschool provision so their child can learn to mix and prepare for school.

The three children described below are likely to have quite different preschool experience.

Susan's mother is a doctor who works three days a week. She is two-and-a-half, an only child and is developmentally normal.

Nigel is three but has not started to talk. He is very active and restless, not able to

Table 13.1   Preschool setting in Great Britain and attendance

Setting	Who provides service?	Who attends?	Age range	Under fives (%)
Day Nursery	Social Services and probably a LEA teacher. Fee according to means	Mainly children with a variety of problems	0–4 in most nurseries depending on the facilities	1%
Private/ Workplace nursery	Social Services inspect and they are usually commercially run. Fee to parents	Children with working parents	0–4 in most	Less than 1%
Child-minder	Social Services authorize. Private individuals. Fee to parents unless organized by Social Services	Children with working parents. Some boroughs have specially trained minders for handicapped children	From babies to any age, but it depends on the minder	3–5%
Nursery class/ School	Local Education Authority. No fee	Any child who applies, though children with handicapping conditions may be given a day nursery place, depending on services	3–4	22% of 3–4-year-olds
Reception class	Local Education Authority. No fee	Any child who applies depending on the provision of nursery classes	4–5, i.e. 'rising fives'	18% of 3–4-year-olds
Playgroups	Social Services authorize. Usually run by parents, groups, charities, etc. Fee to parents	Any child who applies	2–4	13% upward depending on area

settle to any kind of simple puzzle or construction game, is not potty trained and cannot feed himself independently.

Liam, age three-and-a-half-years, is developing well and has a brother of one. His mother has no employment outside the home.

TYPES OF PROVISION

In Great Britain day care can be divided into three main types: all-day care for five days a week throughout the year (day nurseries), a service during the school terms (nursery schools or classes) and sessional group experience for a few sessions a week (playgroups).

ALL-DAY PROVISION

Day nurseries

Local authority day nurseries are run by social services departments and staffed by nursery nurses most of whom have the Nursery Nurse Examination Board (NNEB) certificate; their officers-in-charge also often have some kind of social work qualification. Day nurseries are open for very long hours, from about 8.00 a.m. until 6.00 p.m., all through the year. The places are kept for families with special needs and it is not possible to gain a place without going through a social services department. Criteria for admission include a parent with a chronic illness, a child with behaviour problems or a handicapping condition, lack of adequate stimulation at home, risk of child abuse, a young single parent badly needing to complete some training or take a job. Of the three children mentioned above, Nigel is the only one who is likely to be referred to a day nursery as his development is retarded. The nursery place could provide an assessment of his skills, stimulate his development and help his parents to understand his needs.

Family centres

The term family centres describes a wide variety of provisions. Some are simply day nurseries renamed, aiming to have more parent involvement. Some are combinations of a nursery class and a day nursery. Others include health, education and social services in the same building with a variety of provision. For example some children attend 'education' hours, others for the full day, there are mother and toddler groups for the youngest children and possibly a launderette on the premises. Child health checks are carried out by health visitors and contraceptive advice may also be available. Many activities are aimed at parent education, such as Open University courses on the preschool child and discussion groups on child management or diet. The parents often form a joint management committee with the staff and may be involved in hiring staff.

There is already an association of family centres in Scotland, where they are more common, but there are increasing numbers all over Britain attempting to avoid the artificial distinctions between health, education and social care which exist in more traditional services.

Private nurseries

A number of charitable organizations run institutions very similar to local authority day nurseries or family centres. They may be used by social services but are generally freer to offer places to families without a specific referral. They are often designed to have a therapeutic role, such as those organized by the National Society for the Prevention of Cruelty to Children (NSPCC), or to combat disadvantage.

There are also a small number of workplace nurseries and privately run day nurseries. These may be subsidized by employers and the majority are to be found attached to hospitals, universities or other very large organizations. They are primarily a service for the parent rather than the child and they would be unlikely to take a therapeutic role.

Susan, described above, might have been given a place in a workplace nursery if her mother had been working in a hospital, but for a GP the choices are probably limited to a nanny in the home, a child-minder, or a relative.

Child-minders

Child-minders are private individuals, usually mothers with a young child or grown-up children, who care for children in their own home. They are all supposed to be registered with Social Services Departments and abide by certain rules regarding safety and the numbers of children attending, but many child-minding arrangements are unofficial and not very satisfactory. There is no prerequisite for child-minders to have any training, though nowadays many do attend courses or support groups organized by social services. Continuing support or monitoring from social services is variable. Some local authorities use day foster care with child-minders as an alternative to day care in a nursery. This is helpful for children who are at risk and the foster mother often provides support and friendship to the child's parents.

PART-TIME PROVISION

Nursery and reception classes

A second possibility for three to four-year-olds is attendance at a nursery school or class, usually provided by the local education authority (LEA) although a few are private. Children usually attend daily for half-day sessions in the younger age groups. Nursery classes may be attached to an infant school or completely separate. The aims are to prepare for school, socially and educationally. Nursery groups will vary between 20 and 30 and are usually run by teachers trained for nursery work, together with at least one nursery nurse. Liam had been attending a playgroup and there is nothing to stop him from staying there until he is five, but probably he could have a half-day place in a nursery school if his parents wanted him to. Nigel could combine attendance in a day nursery with part-time nursery education but often children in day nurseries only start school when they are five.

Sessional provision

Playgroups

Playgroups fall into the third category of placement, usually children attend for a few sessions a week. Playgroups are a relatively new idea, started by a parent initiative in the 1960s. They aim to fill a need not met within either social services or educational provision. Many parents do not want all-day care but do want to have the chance of a few hours for themselves while their child mixes with others. The majority of playgroups (about 70 per cent are members of the Preschool Playgroup Association (PPA) and their philosophy is very much to involve parents (or at least mothers). Most of the people in charge of playgroups, as well as many of the assistants, will have done at least one PPA training coures.

Susan would probably attend a playgroup in addition to either having a nanny or going to a child-minder. At her age she would probably be going for two or three sessions a week, meeting similar aged children.

Therapeutic centres

Finally, there is a variety of special therapeutic centres for children with developmental delay, chronic handicap or behaviour problems. These may be nuture groups for the children or family centres where parents attend with their child. The staff usually include a variety of educational, health and social work professionals.

NUMBERS ATTENDING DIFFERENT SETTINGS

Local authorities in Britain vary widely in the provisions they offer. Some have few or no day nurseries at all, others have many. In some areas the majority of four-year-olds can attend nursery school if their parents want them to, in others school starts only at five years. It is difficult to compare information on numbers of places available between different areas but Table 13.1 summarizes the general picture.

Overall 1.3 per cent of under fives attend a local authority day nursery and less than 1 per cent attend a private day nursery. Registered child-minders cater for about 3–4 per cent under fives in England and Wales and fewer (2–3 per cent) in Scotland and Northern Ireland. Few under threes are attending school. Looking therefore at the three to fours, 22 per cent receive nursery education and a further 18 per cent are admitted to reception classes, mostly four-year-olds. The proportions of children attending playgroups are the most regionally variable, ranging from 13 per cent of under fives in England and Wales to nearly 50 per cent in Scotland and almost three-quarters in Northern Ireland.

DIFFERENCES IN POPULATIONS

As the aims and intake criteria of different settings vary so much it is not surprising to find that the characteristics of the children attending also differ.

Day nurseries are most likely to have children with handicapping conditions such as severe developmental delay, speech delay, growth retardation, deafness or physical disability. One study found that nearly a quarter of a sample of day nursery children had a chronic illness or handicap, compared with 4 per cent of children in nursery education. In addition a quarter of the day nursery children had speech delay compared with 2 per cent of the school children.

Many of the reasons for gaining a place in a day nursery relate to family disadvantage, discord or stress. Reflecting their stressful lives, a large proportion of the children are likely to show emotional or behavioural problems. Over 30 per cent of children in day nurseries have behaviour problems compared with 10 per cent of children in nursery education and 3 per cent in playgroups.

Although more children from ethnic minorities have no preschool experience at all, they are over-represented in the day nursery population. One large British survey found that in general, disadvantaged children are least likely to have any preschool experience. In addition, while about a quarter of children from European background had no preschool experience, this was true for a third of children with Afro-Caribbean parents and almost half the children with parents born in India or Pakistan.

THE EFFECTS OF DAY CARE

There are two main ways in which the effect of day care or preschool experience have been examined, firstly looking in possible harmful effects and secondly looking for advantages in either social or intellectual skills.

Mother–child relationships

Day care involves prolonged daily separation from the mother, one of the main reasons for concern about day care, especially with younger children. The effect of separation from mothers have been discussed in Chapter 3. Overall there is very little evidence that attending full-time day care, even when the care started before one year old, has any ill-effects upon the mother–child relationship. Generally children attending day care behave similarly to children being brought up at home. However, most conclusions about the effects of day care have been based upon American work, looking at children attending high quality, often University run, centres. In Britain there have been criticisms of the quality of day care available. There are very few high quality nursery places and the majority of women who work use private provision, mainly relatives or child-minders. There has been little work looking at the effect upon the father–child relationship of the child being cared for away from home, since until recently the father–child relationship was not thought relevant. There are indications that children with poor quality child-minding do suffer emotionally and developmentally.

Social behaviour

Social behaviour does seem to be influenced by attending day care in a number of ways.

> Lois and Charlene are both four years old, but only Lois has been attending a preschool group for some time. The two girls are taken to a playroom which is new to them, where there are three other children and one adult. Lois goes up to one of the other children, suggests that they use the dressing-up clothes and play at shops. She says that she will be the customer and helps the other child to get dressed. The play becomes rowdy but Lois refuses to follow the adult's suggestion that she should stop wheeling the shopping cart so fast. In contrast Charlene has been sitting at the table doing a puzzle by herself but moves away when another child joins her. She goes to the water table and agrees to wear an apron, but asks for help with getting it on.

Lois and Charlene react in contrasting ways to the unfamiliar surroundings. One is outgoing and full of ideas, while the other is less confident and less keen to mix. The contrast between them reflect partly differences in personality and partly the differences found between children who have spent most of their time in groups such as day nurseries and those who have spent most of their time at home. The social behaviour of children like Lois can be affected in both positive and negative ways. They tend to be relaxed in an unfamiliar place, assertive and talkative with unknown children, outgoing and cooperative and less timid and fearful. However, they may also be more active, boisterous, competitive and aggressive. They are likely to show greater ease and self-sufficiency with an unfamiliar adult, but be less concerned about adult approval or responsive to control. As a consequence of these sorts of difference they may not settle as quickly into more structured situations such as school.

It must be remembered, however, that these characteristics said to be typical of children who have been in group day care may be modified by several factors. It has already been mentioned that most of the research work has been done in the United States. When children in Swedish day-care centres were compared with those brought up at home, there were no differences in aggression. Cultural differences in attitudes towards aggression, the value placed upon assertiveness and competitiveness are likely to influence the effects of group care. The child's gender is another possible modifying factor. Some of the differences described are more typical of day care boys than girls, since overall boys generally are more aggressive, active and non-compliant (see Chapter 12). It is not clear that the amount of time spent in day care or the age of entry influence behaviour.

Parental behaviour is also likely to influence sociability. Mothers who go out to work may value independence more and might have made special efforts to introduce their child to many different children and adults *before* they even started day care. The mothers themselves may be more assertive. Most of the work comparing day care and 'home-reared' children does not take these kinds of influence into account.

Physical development

The provision of fresh air, exercise and a good diet were the prime aims of nurseries and day care centres when they were first started at the turn of the century. It was hoped that programmes for the more disadvantaged children would promote their physical development, and this proved to be true, particularly for children from poor families who have better motor and physical development than similar children brought up at home. However, for middle-class children these effects are not found and in fact those who go to a preschool group have a greater number of minor illnesses, presumably because they are more exposed to infection from other children.

Intellectual development

One aspect of President Johnson's 'War on Poverty' in the USA was to provide preschool experiences to make up for children's poor home experiences. The idea was to give them a 'Head Start' by boosting their intellectual development; it was then expected that they would do better in school as a result (see also Chapter 7).

It was clear from the assessment of many special preschool programmes that they were successful. Children who had attended had scores on intelligence tests often 10 or 20 points higher than comparable children with no preschool experience. They also did better at school work in the first year or two, with fewer being placed in special education classes. This led to great enthusiasm for preschools but further evaluations were not so encouraging. After two or three years in school it was not possible to distinguish the 'preschool' children from their controls, the ones who had not received the special help before school. Nevertheless, this is not to say that there are no benefits. The children have now been traced in their late teens and there are some differences between the groups. Those who had received preschool provision were less likely to be unemployed, to have received any convictions, to have repeated a year in school or to have been placed in special education. It is suggested that the crucial aspects of their experience may have been to give them a feeling of competence when they started school, to increase their desire to achieve and to give them a better opinion of themselves.

One key element of most of the special intervention programmes in the United States was parental involvement. Although the parents may not have continued to stimulate their children in the ways which had been taught, it is thought that they developed greater expectations of school success and subsequent employment for their children.

Most of the American interventions which have been evaluated were provided for extremely disadvantaged children, with initial measured intelligence usually much below normal. Positive benefits of attending preschool have also been identified in a broader cross-section of the population. In Britain several thousand children, all those born in one particular week in 1970 have been followed from birth. The experiences which they had were very varied but gains could be seen, apparently regardless of home background or parents' education, for those who had some preschool experience. At five and ten they scored higher on academic achievement tests and on intelligence tests.

There is some evidence, however, that attending *poor* quality day care may be detrimental, in comparison with being cared for in a home setting. Recent work has compared the language and speech of children either cared for at home, with a child-minder or in a nursery. Those in the nursery had less advanced language. Both workers in preschool and child-minders talk less to children than do parents at home and have fewer complex conversations so the children have less chance to extend their conversation skills.

There is no doubt that a preschool programme can produce gains in intellectual development: the more structured programme the greater are likely to be the gains, particularly when they encourage children to speak frequently to adults. But it is also recognized that advantaged, middle-class children often make the biggest gains. In other words preschool experiences do not minimize inequality but might even heighten it. Long-lasting benefits are more often socio-emotional than intellectual.

EXPLANATIONS FOR THE EFFECTS OF DAY CARE

When thinking about the possible effects of day care, either positive or

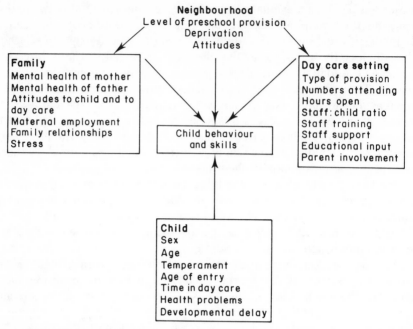

Figure 13.1   Understanding the effects of day care.

negative, interrelated aspects must be taken into account. First, effects upon development or behaviour will vary depending upon the child's sex, age, length of time in day care, age of entry, temperament, handicapping conditions or health problems. Second, family influence such as the emotional well-being of family members, maternal employment and family relationships are important. Finally, there is the day-care setting itself, its quality, the extent to which it fulfils the parents' and child's needs and the continuity of the staff. All these exist within a particular neighbourhood whose characteristics (e.g. level of preschool provision, amount of deprivation, opinions about employed mothers) are likely to influence the child, the family and the day-care facility (see Figure 13.1).

THERAPEUTIC USES OF DAY CARE

Clive is a four-year-old who has marked behaviour problems. He is defiant and disobedient at home, throwing frequent tempers, starting fights with his younger brother and racing about most of the day. His concentration is very poor and his speech is delayed. He has frequent colds and coughs and is small for his age. He lives with his mother and brother in a two-bedroomed high-rise flat which is dilapidated and damp. His mother visits the doctors often, complaining of tiredness, sleeplessness and general depression.

For Clive and his family, day care can be used therapeutically at a variety of levels, focusing upon the whole family, the parent(s) or the child, or all of these.

His attendance at a preschool centre might help his mother's depression by giving her some relief from the strain of his care, and her confidence could increase through support from other parents and staff, thus encouraging her efforts to get better housing. Clive's general health could also be improved, by removing him from the damp flat for part of the day and improving his meals. Indeed, in developing countries it is recognized that one of the prime benefits gained from preschools is stronger, healthier children who are then more likely to be enrolled in school by their parents, thus reducing the 'wastage' of children who do not become educated even to a minimal level. Staff in the centre can observe Clive's difficult behaviour, plan strategies for coping with them, try them out and possibly give advice to his mother on the best way to handle him. His understanding and language can be similarly observed and activities organized which will increase his concentration and develop his skills.

Some specialist centres aim to treat the whole family. Parents and children are seen together in play sessions to help them relate with less conflict and more enjoyment. The child may be seen individually by a teacher, speech therapist or psychologist in order to work on specific developmental and behaviour problems. The mother and/or father may also see someone separately and in parents' groups, to work on their own problems.

Within any sort of playgroup, nursery class or day nursery, behavioural methods can be used to reduce specific behaviour problems. A plan of help for isolated children could include:

(1) Rewarding children for all their approaches to other children or adults,
(2) Providing safe situations where they can be more comfortable about joining in, for example, encouraging a game or outing with just one child, then enlarging the group.
(3) Rewarding other children (or adults) for initiating contact with the withdrawn child, by using praise of special treats.

These strategies can also help children who are finding it hard to settle into a new placement. With these children it is important first to decide whether they are emotionally ready to start in a nursery setting and whether the settling-in period has been adequate. Ideally, close links are established between parents and centre staff (or home carers) before attendance starts, and the child is already familiar with the setting. Although some people recommend throwing a child in 'at the deep end' the majority of children settle best if they are allowed to acclimatize gradually and the length of daily attendance is slowly decreased. When parents are involved in the running of a centre and visit freely, this helps parents deal with their anxieties about leaving their children.

It is likely that the anxious or withdrawn child can be helped more effectively than the aggressive or overactive one. However approaches such as 'sit and watch' have proved very effective. Whenever unwanted behaviour occurs (e.g. grabbing toys, hitting) the child is put at the edge of the group and told to sit for a specific time and watch the others. They are then questioned about what they should do. This is likely to be more effective than merely telling them off which provides attention for bad behaviour and does not give the child constructive ideas about good behaviour.

Many factors will contribute to the potential for a centre to be therapeutic. These include the resources available, staff training and back-up from other professionals in the community. It is unrealistic to expect an overcrowded nursery, with high staff turnover and limited support, to be therapeutic, especially if 30 to 40 per cent of the children have marked problems.

TRANSITION TO SCHOOL

There are three major points which might influence transition to school: characteristics of the child, the kind of care experienced prior to starting school and the manner in which the transition takes place.

Child characteristics

One might expect that a child who was emotional and disobedient at home might also have trouble adjusting to school. In fact several investigations have shown that difficult behaviour at home does not usually predict coping poorly with school; only a very small number of children have difficult behaviour in both situations.

Boys tend to cope less well than girls with stress (see Chapter 12) and starting school is no exception to this. In one survey carried out in London, twice as many boys (18 per cent) as girls (9 per cent) were judged to be having difficulty after attending for half a term; the main problems were emotional disturbances such as unhappiness, anxiety or difficulty separating from parents. Part of this difference may be associated with the slower rate of maturation of boys, who were less skilled in fine motor control and physical co-ordination. Possibly parental treatment was also a factor as boys were less able to cope with activities such as dressing and toileting.

Most problems on starting school are short-lived. In one study few of the children with problems in nursery class still had these problems when in their first year of school.

The type of problem shown in the nursery has some relevance to whether they persist. Withdrawn behaviour is much less likely to continue than aggression, high levels of activity or non-compliance.

Other factors involve the home background. In contrast to children in nursery classes behaviour problems in children attending local authority day nurseries are very likely to continue into school. Continuing stresses in these children's families, usually a major reason for their placement in a day nursery in the first place, probably contribute to the continuity of their difficulties. Health and developmental problems (e.g. delayed language) also contribute to the persistence of problems into school in the day nursery children.

Experiences before school

One major investigation pinpointed children coming straight from home as the ones who would have the most problems adjusting in school. It was suggested that they were in danger of becoming withdrawn and nervous when faced with a large group, high noise levels, competition for adult attention and other aspects of group life such as waiting in a queue or being addressed communally about what to do

The physical characteristics of settings are important. Thus problems are likely for those transferring from compact settings with small rooms (such as homes and some day nurseries) to extended corridor plan schools, or for those coming from large halls with adult sized chairs (e.g. some playgroups) to congested classrooms. The disparity in aims of the staff between settings are also relevant. Minders and day nursery staff emphasize child-care and family support while playgroup leaders and teachers stress social experience and practice in basic skills. The amount of choice and structure to the timetable is also significant. Children with minders or parents probably have the most freedom of choice and the least structure to the daily timetable, followed by those who have been in day nurseries. Playgroups and nursery classes tend to provide less choice and more regular organization to the day. The adult : child ratio which the child has been used to will also be relevant to their ability to cope.

Method of transition

The age at which the child should begin school has generated more discussion than any other issue. Policies for starting school vary tremendously, both across the country and within local education authorities. The law in Great Britain requires that children should start school the term after they reach five but the age of new entrants can vary from barely four years old to five-and-a-half years old. Some schools stagger new entrants over the first half-term, starting a few a week; some take them all at once in September, irrespective of age; yet others take them in three times a year, in the term when they are 'rising five'.

Although the majority of the relevant research has not found that age of entry is associated with emotional problems or other difficulties, there is a great deal of support for the idea that four-year-olds should not be in reception classes. The main reasons given for this are that they need for choice and private space for the development of imaginative play and that emotionally they are not ready to be confined in a classroom or able to cope like a five-year-old. They are said to need more adult attention and the opportunity to ask questions, and talk to adults informally. This remains as yet an unresolved question.

Although age was not found to be related to emotional problems, some work shows that children who started school in January coped less well than those starting in the previous September. The relevant factors seemed to be that in January they were joining a larger group, and newcomers were in the minority. On the basis of this work one would be tempted to recommend that children all start at the beginning of the school year, but this needs fuller study.

It has been recommended that there should be more contact between parents and teachers both prior to starting school and during the first month or two. Policies on contact prior to starting vary considerably. Some parents will merely receive a letter saying that their child has a place, some will be invited to visit in the summer term, other families receive home visits from the teacher. Similarly the first few days may be very different, varying from parents being dismissed at the door, encouraged to come in briefly, or asked to stay for as long as they like. Since parents are usually very keen to contribute to their child's education and since their involvement is so important for educational progress, parents should be given as much information as possible and made to feel very welcome in their child's classroom. However, as yet there is not much systematic work looking at the effects upon the child of varying levels of parent involvement in transition to school.

SUMMARY

It must be remembered that day care is a rather misleading and confusing term. There is a wide variety of ways in which young children are cared for away from their own home, in group settings and any conclusions must be tempered by the knowledge that even within one category of child care, there may be wide variations in the service offered. Within those constraints it is clear that some aspects of care can contribute to behavioural or emotional problems, more usually to the kinds of behaviour seen in groups than to relationships with parents. Previous day care experience may also lead to problems in starting school, but the method of transition is also very important to outcome. On the other hand there are many potential benefits from preschool experience, boosting intellectual development in the short term, increasing confidence and competence in the long term, increasing sociability and the ability to cope in large groups. Specific problems such as speech delay or behaviour difficulties may also be ameliorated if adequate help is available.

The potential of a group-care setting depends on many factors. These include the specific qualities of the service, the setting in which it is provided, the family who are using it and the child who is being care for.

FURTHER READING

J. Bruner (1980) *Under Fives in Britain*. London: Grant McIntyre.
B. Mayall and P. Petrie (1983) *Childminding and Day Nurseries: what kind of care?* London: Heinemann Educational Books.
S. Scarr and J. Dunn (1987) *Mother Care/Other Care*. Harmondsworth: Penguin Books.

CHAPTER 14

Play

Naomi Richman and Helen Dawe

It is taken more or less for granted that children should be encouraged to play, but why do they devote so much energy to this activity and gain such intense pleasure from it? The first part of this chapter discusses the role of play in children's lives, and its importance in helping them to learn about the world and develop new skills.

A second important aspect of play is the information it gives about a child's level of development and functioning. Informal assessment provides a view of the child in action which cannot always be obtained from formal testing. The middle section of this chapter aims to provide a framework for understanding children through their play by looking at its features systematically.

Finally, play can be used as a form of communication between adults and children. Children find it difficult to communicate their feelings directly in words and can often express their concerns more easily in fantasy. Through play, relationships develop in a comfortable way which feels safe to a child. From an adult's point of view play allows them to convey information to a child in an acceptable and non-threatening manner.

DEFINITIONS OF PLAY

The characteristics of play are not easy to define but the following features are usually considered to be important. One striking aspect of play is that it has nothing to do with the ordinary activities necessary for survival like sleeping or eating and the *process* of play is an end in itself. There is no ultimate goal or achievement other than experiencing the play. In this way play differs from activities like trying to understand the mechanism of a toy or making a cake. The lack of a necessary end result means that play takes place outside the pressures of ordinary everyday life. It is voluntary and pleasurable, there is no anxiety about doing the right thing or behaving in a certain way. The child can experiment with ideas or materials without having to 'pay' for mistakes.

This is not to say that play is disorganized or does not have its own rules. There are structures and rules which constrain the players and these rules are part of what makes play interesting and important. Rules include turn-taking as in peek-a-boo. Here both adult and child follow a particular ritual, knowing exactly how the game has to be played and how it can be modified to add to the fun. Of course, the excitement of play sometimes lies in breaking the rules of the game deliberately. In normal children there is never any real doubt as to whether play is real or pretend. Most adults have experienced being told by a child 'its only pretend', when they intruded too far into the child's make believe. Play seems to be built up from pieces of behaviour which are tried out and linked together in various combinations, they become more elaborate as the child grows older. Becaue the constraints of real life are absent, the child is able to be innovative and experimental and to look at unusual combinations of ideas or behaviours.

THE FUNCTION OF PLAY

It has been suggested that this experimental process builds up a range of behaviours and a flexibility of response which will be useful in real life; it is a way of practising safely ways of solving real life problems.

Play is a behaviour typical of *young* animals. In kittens chasing a ball of wool can be seen as a forerunner of mice-hunting. This type of behaviour is relatively short-lived in animals like cats and dogs, but longer in some animals like chimpanzees. Their young have a childhood of about three years during which time play with materials like sticks and play with each other develops practical and social skills which are important for later survival.

Human beings have a very prolonged period of infancy compared with other mammals. This allows children a long time to practice all sorts of skills including social and language skills. They do not have to cope with independent living until these skills are mastered.

They can also use play to express safely frightening or worrying emotions, such as anger, without producing any actual consequences by their behaviour. When a mother and child swap roles and become respectively baby and mother, or a child acts a very 'naughty' role, the child's world of imagination is being expressed and possible outcomes of relationships explored. Children's interpretations of their world and their anxieties are often much more frightening than their actual experiences warrant, for instance many play at being extremely strict parents or harsh teachers though the reality is quite different. Through stylized play interactions they try to deal with anxieties about punishment and the power of adults, or with anxieties about illness and death.

These ideas suggest that play has an important role in learning and survival and could explain children's 'need' to play and why it is so important to them.

It could also explain why so much of young children's play is repetitive, for example a baby throws a ball down for retrieval again and again. The element of practice is marked in the way children play with language as described later in this chapter. The irritating repetitive 'why?' questions of the two to three-year-old are a case in point. Often the child is clearly not interested in the answer but only in the fascination of asking 'why' questions and how these elicit certain forms of response.

People continue to create throughout life: songs, dances, paintings, gardens, new recipes. Although the end result is important in these activities, the process of combining familiar elements to produce something new produces the same involvement and delight as in childhood play. Humour is another example of how both adults and children play with ideas and language. The joke is fun in itself and can also serve as a safe outlet for painful emotion.

STAGES OF PLAY

Play becomes more complex as children mature. There is a regular develop-mental process in play but it is not easy to divide this into clear stages by exact age. First, children vary in their development — one child is using symbolic play long before another. Second, as play becomes increasingly complex it involves many aspects of functioning which are difficult to separate out.

The following is a guide to the development of various aspects of play.

SOCIAL PLAY

As described in Chapter 3, social play begins in the earliest weeks through games of smiling and talking. The game of peek-a-boo illustrates the increasing complexity of play as understanding develops. The ability to play peek-a-boo depends on the child realizing that an object can disappear and come back again in more or less the same place. At first the mother (or other adult) initiates the game, covering her face, and then sometimes the baby's face. Soon a ritualized game develops involving disappearance and reappearance in a regular sequence; usually the mother keeps in touch by saying 'where are you?'. The length of time hiding may lengthen a little once the baby is used to the game. Sooner or later the children take charge and hide themselves. As with much play, the elements of turn-taking, repetition, and anticipation (in this case of being found or finding someone) are important and pleasurable, and provide the framework for the play. The introduction of new variations on the original theme allows the infant to test the limits of a situation without experiencing anxiety about separation.

Exploration of objects

In the early stages children's main interest is in their own body and that of their caretaker. They explore what their bodies can do and the properties of the immediate world around. For example, once they are able to move their hands into the main line they become fascinated by their hand movements, the play of their fingers and the patterns these make before their eyes. Soon they are playing with objects and enjoying their noise, feel or taste, making them move, dropping, banging or pulling them.

Gradually play with objects becomes more complicated, involving stacking, posting boxes, water play, finally leading on to constructional toys.

As they develop, infants progress from showing then giving an object, to sharing games like rolling a ball; other youngsters as well as adults will be welcomed as partners in these early social encounters. Initially much play will be side-by-side parallel play, and only gradually will sharing and turntaking appear.

Young children who receive few social responses and are not encouraged to interact with others become withdrawn and unresponsive. If they are deprived of the opportunity to explore and play they often resort to self-stimulatory habits like rocking, head-banging and later even biting or hitting themselves.

LANGUAGE PLAY

The beginning of language involves playing with sounds. Babies lie in their cots repeating sounds over and over, experimenting with the noises they can produce. They can make all the vocalizations occurring in any language. If this play with sounds is to develop, there must be a response from adults who repeat back what they hear and suggest variations. Gradually the infant stops using the sounds that are not responded to and retain only those in use in their parents' language.

Deaf children stop vocalizing completely because they cannot hear their own noises or their parents' responses. Neglected children may also become silent if their sounds are not reinforced.

Once words and then phrases have developed, children spend a great deal of time chanting to themselves. They enjoy repeating the same words and phrases over and over. Language play may consist of variations on an initial word like 'Dad . . . dad . . . bad . . . bad . . . had' from a two-year-old.

At other times language play involves changing one work in a particular sentence structure like:

I want jam
I want ham

Don't want jam
Don't want ham

In this way besides trying out the sounds of words, children experiment with grammatical structures like the use of negatives, questions, or pronouns. These experiments can take the form of a conversation in which the children ask a question and then give the answer themselves.

Language play is often heard from a child lying in bed in the early morning or before falling off to sleep. These experiments are playful because they are not being used for communication, and the child does not need to worry about whether they are getting their sentences right or whether they will be understood. To encourage language development it is necessary for early experiments or attempts in language to be accepted. Too much concentration on speaking 'properly' and on 'correct' grammar can lead to discouragement and restriction of speech. On the other hand, word games, rhymes and songs encourage a playful approach to communications and confidence in speaking.

With brothers and sisters and other children, verbal games are used to explore the meaning and limits of language. A common game is to take turns in a conversation which is a series of statements or a series of questions and answers with variations, e.g. Annie and Betty talking about a ball.

ANNIE

Its red

Its blue

BETTY

Its blue

Its green

After a time this verbal play may degenerate into nonsense words or a play on sounds as the children collapse in laughter. The joke for them is that because they *know* the rules of language they also know how to break the rules by speaking nonsense.

IMAGINATIVE PLAY

Representational and symbolic play

By ten to fourteen months children enjoy playing with real objects. They comb their own or someone else's hair with a real comb, feed a teddy with a real spoon.

Soon they can use toys which *represent* real objects like making pretend tea using a doll's tea-set, making car noises with a toy car, moo sounds to a toy cow or a picture of a cow. These toys *symbolize* a real car or cow. Finally, they no longer need miniature real objects for their play. A brick can be a car, a cake, a ship or a bed. The brick becomes a *symbol* for these objects.

The appearance of representational and symbolic play is an important stage in development. It is linked with the use of words to symbolize or stand for objects and if symbolic play is not developing, language will almost certainly be delayed.

The Symbolic Play Test was devised by Marianne Lowe and Anthony Costello to measure the stages of children's imaginative play. The child's ability to use and play with objects like little toy dolls, a bed, chair or table is assessed. The test was given to a large number of English children under five and provides norms for the development of symbolic play.

Even without formal testing it should be possible to assess imaginative play using a few toys. These could include a tea-set, a toy telephone, a few animals and a family of dolls. Delay in the development of imaginative play might be related to:

General developmental delay.
Lack of stimulation or of opportunity to play.
A disorder of development in which symbolic understanding is impaired as in autism.

Imaginative play in older children

Later imaginative play requires few props. The children are able to imagine any situation they wish and to play many roles. These roles might involve people from real life like mothers and fathers, animals, or imaginary characters derived from stories or invented by the children themselves. It is not uncommon for a child to have an imaginary friend or friends who participate(s) in family activities. In most cases this is not a cause for concern, although occasionally the involvement of an isolated, withdrawn child with an imaginary 'friend' is so all-consuming that further advice should be sought.

Although physical props are not necessary for children's play, once they are able to hold imagery in their head, they are often a great stimulus to imagination, and are particularly useful in therapeutic play (see later section). Imaginative play can be solitary or involve other children. It allows children to explore freely the implications of relationships looking at various eventualities, and play out fearful, unpleasant, or puzzling situations in a safe way.

Extensive imaginative play sequences are more likely to be seen in the home setting with a child alone, or perhaps with a well-known companion. Here the setting is most familiar, is quieter than in a preschool group, and there is more chance of carrying on a play sequence over a long period without interruption.

THE RELATIONSHIP BETWEEN PLAY AND UNDERSTANDING

In Chapter 3 it was mentioned that even very young babies enjoy making something happen, like moving a mobile. They experience similar pleasure when they find they can 'make' someone respond to their smiles and coos. In order to learn children need opportunities to experiment with their environment, to 'play around' with different possibilities in construction, language, social interaction, imaginative play. If these efforts are discouraged or ignored a child's lively wish to explore the social or physical world can be destroyed or diminished and learning impaired.

If children are encouraged to explore the functions and properties of equipment they are subsequently more efficient at solving problems with the material. This could explain why boys who are encouraged to play with mechanical and constructional toys more than girls in later childhood are more expert in certain practical tasks. Girls on the other hand are usually more confident about sewing and cooking.

In Western culture play often involves fantasy incorporating such characters as Spaceman. In other culture play activities seem to be more closely linked with everyday activities like farming and fishing. The use of fantasy play depends partly on whether it is encouraged and extended by adults; we do not know whether this particular aspect of make-believe play has special importance for intellectual development.

ASSESSMENT AND PLAY

Watching children playing can tell the observer a great deal about the way the child approaches the world, what skills have already been developed, and the areas that will need further help.

Observing the child playing alone, with other children, and with adults are all necessary to give a full picture of the child's capacities. Careful systematic observation can indicate:

(1) Children's concentration, how long they remain absorbed in a task, the level of activity and restlessness.
(2) The general level of understanding as shown by choice of materials and complexity of play.
(3) Use of imaginative and symbolic play.
(4) Whether play is creative and varied or very restricted and repetitive.
(5) The degree of organization of the play, which can range from chaotic, through well organized to over-organized and obsessional play.
(6) Level of social interaction with other children, ability to share and take turns.

(7) Use of language and communication.
(8) Whether play is approached joyfully and with enthusiasm or the child is constrained and worried.
(9) How easily the child is frustrated by other children or by play materials.

Generally children who are observed in quiet, familiar surroundings with familiar people are more likely to demonstrate their best level of language and of imaginative play.

PLAY AS A MEANS OF ASSESSING DEVELOPMENT

Not everyone wishing to assess the level of development of small children is going to have access to a fully equipped playroom or nursery classroom. However, there are some toys which because of their flexibility, provide the child with a great deal of fun, and the observer with the opportunities to see a variety of skills at work. As well as providing the means of demonstrating specific skills, toys and play are also indicators of the child's general approach to new situations and equipment.

The child's age obviously affects interpretation of what is seen. For example, Hannah, aged eighteen months, has a lift-out inset puzzle. She has removed the pieces by their knobs and is now trying to replace them. The piece selected does not fit. She does not reject it in favour of another but tries by force to ram it into the hole. Trial and error mark her approach to the task, and this is appropriate to her age.

In contrast, view two-and-a-half-year-old Nadim with the same puzzle. He looks carefully at each piece and then matches it to the correct shape. He is aware both of shape and picture, and has a strategy for selecting the right shape by scanning the pieces.

Usually one piece of equipment provides information about a range of functions. Lego/Duplo bricks can show children's ability to colour match, their fine finger skills and ability to manipulate small pieces of equipment, their patience and perseverance and their capabilities for imaginative play.

A push-up cone tree requires cones to be threaded on to a stick, the level depressed, and then a button pressed to release a spring and provide the surprise of all the cones springing up. The ability to solve this task demonstrates imitation skills or the ability to follow instructions, and capacity to complete a sequence.

A brief initial assessment can be carried out involving the activities described below.

(1) A *puzzle* appropriate to the child's age. This indicates the child's approach to solving the puzzle, e.g. trial and error or careful scanning of the pieces, concentration, whether the child is able to complete the puzzle, and if so whether interest lies in the picture produced or just the shape.

(2) *Constructional toys* involving stacking, seriation, posting, threading, building, for assessing visuo-spatial and motor abilities.

(3) Small figures, animals, cars for observing imaginative play.

(4) Drawing materials. Felt tips tend to be more popular than crayons and paint and easier to handle outside a well-equipped playroom. From the basics — does the child know a pen will produce a mark? How is the pen held? — through scribble and copying of simple shapes, to the production of a free drawn picture, fine motor skills and the child's approach to play are revealed.

(5) Looking at a book to assess interest in stories, recognition of pictures, ability to point at a picture on request, or to name pictures which are pointed to.

Observations need to be made in the context of what one would expect of a normal child. This is often easier for the teacher or adult who works with a range of children than for the specialist worker with handicapped or delayed children when it is all too easy to forget what is the norm.

It takes time to observe children at play. It is not enough just to watch a child briefly with one set of materials and from this hope to draw conclusions about development or emotional state. Careful observations over a period of time, watching a child in a number of different situations and with a range of materials can highlight problem areas. Having seen Rosie at three years wheeling a doll in a pram on one occasion it would have been easy to say that she had appropriate domestic play skills. It was only apparent through a series of observations that her approach to the dolls, the actions she used and indeed her language were limited and always remained exactly the same. Her ability to play with other materials was also that of a younger child and so it became obvious that she was overall developmentally delayed.

Observations over time also show how quickly new skills and interests are learnt and this can be important in deciding on a child's educational needs.

Limitations in the play of children with sensory or motor handicaps sometimes provide the first clue as to the presence of a specific difficulty. For instance in clumsy children who are unable to use certain materials or cannot use a paintbrush properly.

PROBLEMS OF PLAY

Neglected and abused children are often reluctant to involve themselves in play at all, perhaps spending long periods in rocking or head-banging and otherwise remaining withdrawn and apathetic. Others become violent and chaotic, unable to follow through any coherent sequence of action. The quality of their play is likely to be constricted and poorly organized.

The development of representative or imaginative play goes hand-in-hand with the development of understanding and should appear by the second year of life. Children who are slow in development, or have been understimulated or deprived will have delays in representative play. Lack of imaginative play is also typical of children with infantile autism. They characteristically play in a repetitive, rigid manner, and resent interference with their activities. For instance, one boy spent all his time lining up bricks or other objects in perfect rows, and became very agitated if an adult tried to introduce more variety into this routine. Another boy repetitively built a tent with blankets or sheets. His inability and unwillingness to elaborate this fantasy became apparent after a couple of observation periods but would not have been apparent after a single observation.

Similarly, Jamie (aged four-and-a-half) was able to paint a tractor with pedals, driver and appropriately sized wheels. However, a period of observation revealed that this was the only picture he was able to draw, and he always drew it exacty the same way, with the same features. Like his drawing, all of his activities were repetitive and in none of them did he show any creativity.

Handicapped children may need special materials and individual help in order to be able to express their ideas and imaginations freely. Computer games are increasingly used to assist learning in children with severe motor difficulties, and it could well be that these will also provide a means for assessing imaginative play.

PLAY IN THERAPY

The therapeutic possibilities of play are varied, some were discussed in Chapter 9. As with any form of therapy it is necessray to have a clear idea of the aims and methods of the therapy, and proper training and supervision in its use although the level of skill required will vary according to the setting. For example regular play sessions with one worker in a nursery enables a child to feel valued and to profit more from the group setting. Here the nursery worker must be prepared to cope with a child who challenges her by acting defiantly in the sessions or who becomes very attached or dependent on her.

Play therapy is increasingly used in different settings to help children deal with painful feelings as well as by trained child therapists. Thus it is used by social workers to explore children's understanding of the past and explain plans for the future; by hospital play specialists to help children in hospital; and by educational visitors in work with families at home.

PLAY FOR FAMILIES

Play is a useful tool in work with the family, especially where having a good time together is something which rarely happens and most interactions between parents and children are confrontations and arguments. Some parents have forgotten, or never learnt, how to relax and play, or are busy with work and have little time for small children. Others have unrealistic expectations that children will be quiet and do not see the necessity of guiding their play,or the importance of play activities as precursors of learning.

Norah was one of eight children, between the ages of one and thirteen, in a family composed of children from three relationships. Her parents were overwhelmed by the demands and chaotic activities of their children, they rarely did anything enjoyable together. The children were put to bed extremely early, when the parents' tolerance ran out. Play sessions were established on one evening a week at home for all the family by an educational home visitor. At first the parents were bemused observers, surprised at the children's abilities and amazed that they could play happily together, but they soon became absorbed and involved with the children and also enjoyed the opportunity to play themselves. These weekly sessions enabled the parents to have a time when they actually enjoyed being with the children rather than wanting to shut them away.

Many adults do not enjoy children's games and feel embarrassed about joining in with imaginative play. It is important not to overstress the need for parents and children to play in a certain way together. What the child needs is a parent to encourage them to play constructively and who *enjoys* their company. There are many ways parents and children enjoy being together — chatting, going for a walk, making a cake.

PLAY IN HOSPITAL

Increasingly efforts are made to prepare children for hospitalization through preparatory visits, books and 'hospital' play with dolls and dressing up clothes. This preparation is usually only possible for admissions planned in advance.

Once in hospital it is not always possible to protect children from unpleasant or frightening procedures. Hospital play specialists are trained to understand and help children cope with the many anxieties and fears they experience in hospital. Anxieties about separation from family, about their health, and about investigations and operations. The play specialist helps the child come to terms with their experience through play with dressing up clothes, hospital doll figures and equipment. At the same time she makes sure that as much practical information as possible is given to the child about what is going to happen to them. The role of the play specialist is particularly important for children who have prolonged stays in hospital or repeated admissions.

PLAY FOR CHILDREN WHO HAVE SUFFERED LOSS AND SEPARATION

It is difficult for young children to understand death. They cannot grasp the idea that someone has disappeared for ever and will never return, and even up to the age of about seven to eight years may find the idea confusing and not really believe that death is permanent. At the same time they have fears that other members of the family will die or disappear, or that something frightening will also happen to them.

Steven, aged four years, had lost his baby brother George, aged two years, after a long illness. His parents were very distressed and could not explain to Steven why George was no longer there. Steven became withdrawn, his speech regressed, he was reluctant to play and he was very afraid of being separated from his mother. In play sessions with his parents and a psychologist, Steven was initially very restricted in his play and then he began to make all the dolls 'disappear' one by one, repeating this many times. The therapist was able to link this play with Steven's worry about George and about his parents. The parents understood Steven's feelings more and began to explain to him about George's death in simple language and talk to him more freely.

Play with dolls is useful in helping children who have had many moves and changes of caretaker in their lives. Doll figures are used to represent the various people the child has known and they can recreate the situations and feelings they have lived through, trying to understand these. Through play they try to come to terms with the sadness and anger they experience about parents who cannot look after them, or their despair at the breakdown of a family placement.

One technique is to encourage the child to 'make a world' by creating their own world in a sand-tray, using miniature sets of objects and people. The play in itself may be therapeutic as the child imposes order on chaotic and painful feelings. The therapist can also use ideas expressed in the play to help the child organize their past experiences.

It is important to offer both boys and girls the opportunity to play with dolls and teddies. They can then use them to explore new or frightening situations.

CONCLUSIONS

We have seen that play is not merely a way of passing time for the child but an integral part of development, and an important precursor of more formal learning. Through play children are learning about the physical world, about their own capabilities and about social relationships.

It can be the means by which a bewildered child comes to terms with feelings such as anxiety, fear and anger; and an important tool for understanding children and helping those in distress.

FURTHER READING

B. Tizard and D. Harvey (1977) *Biology of Play*. London: Heinemann.

See also the Human Horizon series, published by Souvenir Press, London. This series includes several relevant titles, for example, *Let Me Play* by Dorothy Jeffree, Roy McConkey and Simon Hewson.

Problems of Preschool Children
Edited by N. Richman and R. Lansdown
© 1988 John Wiley & Sons Ltd

CHAPTER 15

The Law and the Young Child

KATHRYN BIEBER AND MARGOT TAYLOR

INTRODUCTION

Parents' freedom to make decisions about their children is restricted in a number of ways, for instance they are legally bound to see that their child has adequate education and medical care. The law has developed piecemeal over a long time, and is now very complex with many different types of court and legal proceedings. In this chapter we have tried to explain as simply as possible the law about (a) parents' duties to ensure the well-being of their children and (b) the involvement of statutory bodies to ensure that children's needs are met. In general it will be seen that when there is a conflict between children's needs and what the parents consider as their rights, the Courts will now tend to give precedence to the former.

PARENTS

In considering how the law regulates the lives of children it is important to bear in mind the role of the adults normally caring for children, namely parents. It can be helpful to think of the role of parent as split up into three parts.

(1) Birth parent, i.e. natural parents.
(2) Legal parent, e.g. adoptive parents.
(3) Caring parent, e.g. foster parents.

There are times when the law relating to children creates an overlap in responsibility between parents and the State which takes over some of the functions of parents.

SPECIAL EDUCATION AND THE PRESCHOOL CHILD

Under the Education Act (1981) Local Education Authorities have a general duty to identify children who have special educational needs. Statutory assessment procedures, making a statement of 'special educational needs' can be undertaken for any child of two years or older. In addition children under two years can be assessed if it is thought that they may have special educational needs. The Act gives parents rights to consultation in the assessment process; they also have access to the appeal committees set up under the Education Act, 1980.

MEDICAL TREATMENT — PARENTAL CONSENT

Parents have the duty to obtain essential medical treatment for their children. In addition their consent is always sought for medical treatment needed by their child. In certain circumstances a decision by parents to refuse consent to an operation for their child may be overridden by the court. For example, in 1981 the Court of Appeal ordered that an operation to save the life of a Down's syndrome baby should be carried out, after parents had refused permission.

When a child is a Ward of Court (see page 231) and the court is the child's legal parent the court's permission must be sought for medical or psychiatric treatment.

When a child is in the care of a local authority and the Social Services Committee (see page 228) is the 'legal parent' then the permission of that committee has to be obtained for treatment.

WHEN THERE IS A CONFLICT OF INTERESTS

The needs of children and parents can conflict at times, and the law has developed to deal with this over the years. It has developed rules to protect children, for example, when a child is thought to be at risk, there is a dispute between the parents themselves over custody or access, or parents and professionals with responsibility for the child disagree about plans for a child's future.

SUSPECTED CHILD ABUSE

A set of basic procedures is laid down within each local authority which must be followed, whenever there is concern that a child may have been abused or have sustained a non-accidental injury, e.g. a day-care worker is worried that a child is being beaten harshly. These procedures vary from borough to borough, but in general the guidelines will be as follows:

(1) The day-care worker informs the head of the day-care establishment of the concern.
(2) The head of the establishment contacts the local social services area office and informs the duty social worker.
(3) The social worker contacts the health visitor, GP, and other agencies who may have information about the child and the family. The social worker

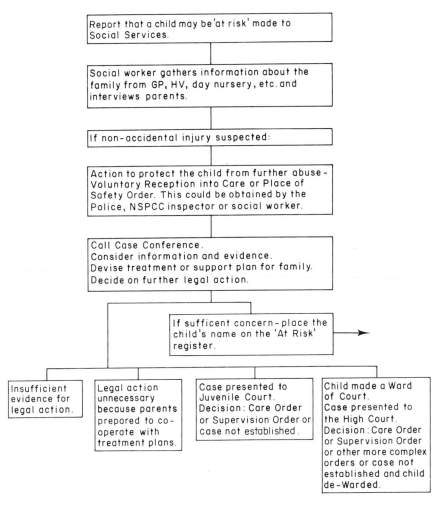

Figure 15.1   Case conference decisions about legal action.

also consults any records held in the department on the family or the child, including the 'At Risk' register (see page 224).

(4) The social worker interviews the parents and ensures that a medical examination is carried out that day, if this has not already been done. This must be done by a doctor (it may need to be a police surgeon in the case of child sexual abuse).

(5) The social worker may need to remove the child from home to protect the child from further abuse.

(6) The social worker convenes a case conference (see Figure 15.1).

(7) All workers involved need to keep a careful written record of any injuries seen, all action taken, and all discussions with the parents.

CASE CONFERENCES

The case conference is normally convened by the area team social worker or the hospital social worker. All the professional workers who know the child or family or who might need to become involved in work with them are invited. For a preschool child some or all of the following people would normally be invited to the case conference: social worker; GP; Health Visitor; senior nursing officer; day-care worker or officer in charge; teacher or head teacher, clinical medical officer from child health clinic; a representative from the juvenile bureau which is run by the police; lawyer from the local authority's legal division; non-accidental injury co-ordinator; a senior social worker from the local social services. If the child has been admitted to hospital or received treatment on an out-patient basis the relevant medical and nursing staff would be invited. In addition a representative from the Social Services fostering and adoption section may attend.

TASKS OF THE CASE CONFERENCE

To share information

The case conference begins with an account of the incident or recent events that gave rise to the case conference, then goes on to cover the background, family history and events since the abuse occurred. All available information is shared between the participants.

To consider evidence

Medical evidence from nurses, hospital doctors, community physicians and other professionals in contact with the child is considered. In the case of child sexual abuse a police surgeon's report or one from a specialist in this area of work is necessary.

Formulation

From the information available the case conference needs to make a 'diagnosis' of the problems of the family and to make an assessment of the position and the overall needs of the child.

Legal advice

The local authority lawyer present advises the case conference whether there is sufficient evidence for legal proceedings, if this is relevant. The social workers present the need to consider the child-care implications of any legal advice.

Action to safeguard the child

A Place of Safety Order may have previously been obtained by a social worker, the police or an NSPCC inspector, or the child may have been received into care on a voluntary basis. If the child still remains at home the case conference will decide whether the child has to be separated from either or both parents. If this is necessary to protect the child the social worker immediately obtains a Place of Safety Order from a magistrate either at a juvenile court or from the the magistrate at home if the court is not sitting.

Short-term placement

A preschool child is usually placed with short-term foster parents. If the child is already in hospital, the hospital becomes the Place of Safety. A copy of the Place of Safety Order must be left with the child's carer.

Treatment and management plans

In addition to practical and financial help for the family, the case conference considers what further assessment and what resources and treatment are needed to ensure that it is safe for the child to return home.

'At Risk' register (see page 224)

Should the child's name be placed on the 'At Risk' register? This may be done even though there is no clear evidence of abuse, because there are grounds for serious concern, e.g. a child lighting fires or running away and getting into dangerous situations.

Key worker

The key worker appointed by the case conference is usually the local authority social worker. This worker intiates or co-ordinates any action required arising from the case conference decisions.

Informing parents

Members of the case conference, usually the person who chaired the conference, and the key worker inform the parents of the decisions of the case conference as soon as possible.

Review

It is necessary to monitor the progress of the child and family and review plans regularly in the light of this progress. The case conference needs to set a date and venue for the next case conference.

PARENTS' ATTENDANCE AT CASE CONFERENCES

In some Social Services Departments it is policy that parents attend case conferences. This allows them to comment on information reported and to hear the decisions made, leading to greater clarity and a more constructive relationship between parents and social worker. The legal adviser may wish the parents to leave the case conference during the period in which the possibility of legal action is discussed.

'AT RISK' REGISTER

(This is sometimes referred to as the Child Abuse Register or the Non-Accidental Injury Register).

This is a list or central register containing the names of children who have been abused or who are considered to be at risk of this. It may also contain details about the family or of injuries sustained. The decision whether to place a child's name on the register is always taken at a case conference. After the initial referral, all subsequent incidents or injuries are also recorded. The register is kept in the central office of the Social Services Department and is usually the responsibility of a child abuse co-ordinator.

Social workers or medical staff in accident and emergency departments of hospitals can have access to the register to check if a particular child is listed. There are regular reviews of the names on this register to consider whether they should remain there.

There is no statutory responsibility to inform parents of the decision to include their child's name on the register, but it is good practice to do so as the basis of an open dialogue between parents and social worker. The decision does not affect the legal rights and responsibilities of carers. It is not a legal order, but a notification of a statement of concern.

CHILD ABUSE CO-ORDINATOR

Some local authorities have set up specialist teams of social workers to deal with child abuse, headed by a child abuse co-ordinator. A centrally based child abuse co-ordinator can offer expert advice and consultation based on wide experience and training in this field and is also able to offer independent comment at case conferences.

CHILD-CARE ISSUES

There are a number of child-care principles and policies which form a background to the discussion about a particular child at a case conference. Some are laid down in legislation or DHSS guidelines and some are the policies of individual Social Services Departments.

Prevention

Social Services Departments have a duty in law to prevent reception into care whenever possible.

The child

In law the interests of the child are paramount.

Parental participation

Parental participation is important. It is facilitated by parents' attendance at meetings such as case conferences, and being fully informed of the concerns of professionals, and of the aims and plan of treatment.

Planning

The DHSS guidelines specify that 'the local authority must reach a clear decision quickly on a short-term plan for the child and a longer-term plan where necessary'. Some Social Services Departments make a 'career plan' for all children in their care. This would include placement with a permanent substitute family if rehabilitation could not be achieved within a time scale appropriate to the child's needs.

Placement

Residential Children's Homes are rarely appropriate for preschool children. Foster parents could be members of the child's extended family or a family previously assessed by the Social Services Department. All such placements must be reviewed on a six-monthly basis. Recent emphasis on 'cultural matching' has stressed the importance for promoting a positive self-image in the child by being in a foster family from the same ethnic group.

Access

The DHSS code of practice on access of children in care to their parents states that local authorities 'have a positive responsibility to promote and sustain access'. The purpose of access must be clear and should be related to the overall plans for the child, e.g. to assist in the eventual return of the child home.

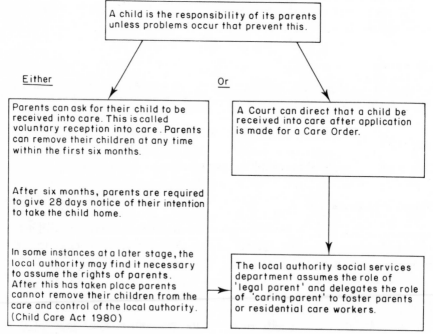

Figure 15.2   Being received into care.

PLACE OF SAFETY ORDER

A police officer has the power to remove a child to a place of safety for a maximum of eight days without a magistrate's order. Alternatively the local authority can make an application for a Place of Safety Order for up to 28 days without telling the parents first, to either the magistrates at a juvenile court or, when the court is not sitting to a single magistrate at home. The parents therefore do not have the opportunity to oppose it. The order gives the local authority the power to remove or maintain a child in a place of safety, e.g. foster home or hospital, but it does not give the local authority any parental rights. The parent must be told of the reason for the order.

CARE ORDERS AND SUPERVISION ORDERS

A local authority may apply to a juvenile court for an order to take a child into the care of the local authority, or for an order under which it may formally supervise the care of the child. It must prove that at least one of the conditions set out in the Children and Young Person's Act (1969) is satisfied. These conditions generally refer to the welfare of the child. Those relating to preschool children are that:

(1) The child's proper development is being avoidably prevented.
(2) The child's health is being avoidably impaired or neglected.
(3) The child is being ill-treated.
(4) The child is exposed to moral danger or is beyond the control of his or her parent or guardian.

In addition, the local authority must prove that the child is in need of care and control which will not be received unless an order is made.

A Care Order gives the local authority all the parental rights and duties except the rights to agree or refuse adoption applications or to change the child's name or religion. The order also enables the local authority to place the child with foster parents and to take other steps concerning the child's welfare. The parents may apply to the court for access to the child if this is denied by the local authority.

Alternatively a court may make a Supervision Order specifying certain conditions, such as the place the child will live. Usually, this results in the child living at home with their parents and a social worker supervising their care by visiting regularly.

Application can be made to the court by the local authority, child or parent to discharge a Care Order or a Supervision Order, if they feel the order is no longer necessary. The court only discharges the order if it considers it is appropriate to do so.

The next section explains how a child may be received into the care of a local authority.

VOLUNTARY CARE AND RESOLUTIONS

A local authority must receive children into care if they have no parents or have been abandoned. In addition parents themselves may ask the local authority to care for their children. The local authority cannot keep the children in care against the parents' wishes unless it 'passes a resolution' assuming parental rights and duties over the children. This is a formal procedure by the local authority involving senior officers and councillors. If the parents object to the local authority resolution its officers must apply to the juvenile court. The Court will listen to the parents and local authority and will then decide whether the resolution should be upheld or not. The 'resolution' procedure has been criticized for two reasons. It relies on the local authority proving that the parent is a bad parent; delays in court hearing may last for months during which time the parents have no right to remove the child even if in the end the resolution is not upheld.

CARE AND WARDSHIP PROCEEDINGS

Actions which local authorities can take to remove children from home include place of safety orders, and care and wardship proceedings.

CASE STUDY TO ILLUSTRATE A PLACE OF SAFETY ORDER AND A CARE ORDER

INTRODUCTION

This case study of Garry and his family shows how and why the Local Authority Social Services Department obtained a Place of Safety Order and then a Care Order through the Juvenile Court.

CASE STUDY

Jean (18 years) and Neil (19 years) had a son Garry aged 2 years. They had lived for three months in a two-bedroomed flat on an old estate, previously they had been living with an aunt of Jean's. Jean had been thrown out by her mother following a row. Jean called to see a Duty Officer at the Social Services office to request a day nursery place. She appeared stressed and agitated and said that she found Garry very difficult to manage, grizzling constantly and a poor eater. Jean and Neil rowed over managing Garry and over financial difficulties.

Jean had no doctor or health visitor in her new locality and so when an emergency occurred with Garry, she took him to hospital. When the doctor examined Garry, she found cuts, swelling and bruising and red marks on his back. Jean explained that Garry had fallen off his tricycle while Neil was looking after him.

The hospital doctor decided to admit Garry to the Children's Ward. The hospital social worker and the doctor interviewed Jean and later Neil and it emerged that Neil had beaten Garry with his belt.

The local Social Services Area Team was contacted immediately. Because there was concern that Garry's parents might remove him from hospital a Place of Safety Order was obtained. The area team social worker completed a form setting out the facts of the case and a form setting out the order sought (i.e. a Place of Safety Order or POS). During the daytime the social worker would have gone to the Juvenile Court to apply to the magistrate for the order. As it was evening the social worker went to the magistrate's home.

The next day a Case Conference was called. Information was collected from the previous health visitor, the duty officer who had seen Jean to complete a day nursery application, and the hospital doctor and medical social worker who saw the family. It was decided to apply for a Care Order at the juvenile court so that Garry should live with foster parents on his discharge from hospital. A plan of work was made to help Jean, Neil and Garry.

The local authority solicitor presented the case at the Juvenile Court. Witnesses including the hospital doctor and medical social worker were called to give evidence. The witnesses were also asked questions in cross-examination by a solicitor representing Garry. The magistrates asked some questions too. Other witnesses gave evidence on Garry's behalf. In addition Garry's parents were represented by a solicitor who asked some questions of the witnesses. The magistrates found the case proved and after reading a social enquiry report written by the area team social worker made a Care Order.

When work with Jean, Neil and Garry had continued for over a year, Garry was settled back with Jean and Neil. At a case conference it was decided to return to the juvenile court to ask the magistrates to change the Care Order to a Supervision Order. It was planned eventually to return to court again to rescind the Supervision Order when Garry was settled and progressing well with his parents.

CASE HISTORY TO ILLUSTRATE WARDSHIP PROCEEDINGS

INTRODUCTION

This case study of Jane and her family shows how and why the local authority social services department made Jane a Ward of the High Court and subsequently applied for a Care Order. It goes on to relate the plans made for Jane when the attempt to rehabilitate her home with her parents failed.

CASE STUDY

Jane was a three-year-old girl, whose parents sought help because they were very concerned about her not sleeping at night, not eating solid food and having difficulties with toilet training. In addition, the health visitor had noted that Jane's father was becoming increasingly involved in her physical care while her mother was becoming more and more distant and depressed. The health visitor became concerned about the father's physical contact with Jane that she had observed, and the issue of sexual abuse was considered. Jane was a 'frozen' child and had responded very little to a play visitor's work.

A case conference was called to consider how to deal with these concerns and the degree of risk to Jane. There was sufficient concern for Jane's name to be placed on the 'At Risk' register. The conference was told that Jane's parents were both urgently seeking professional help to cope with her. A treatment plan was made and offered to the parents. They agreed to Jane being received into care on a voluntary basis and she was placed with foster parents. The whole family agreed to attend a Social Services Department Young Family Centre on a daily basis, with specialist input from a psychologist and child psychiatrist and three months later Jane was made a Ward of Court.

Work with the family was not progressing well and Jane's parents were uncertain that they wanted Jane to remain away from them. However, the level of professional concerns remained high. A judge granted the local authority care and control while the work to rehabilitate Jane to her parents continued. The Court also appointed the Official Solicitor to act as an independent legal representative on Jane's behalf. (This meant that a representative from the Official Solicitor's office would interview all the people concerned and consider all written information such as case files and affidavits and then write a full report for the court making recommendations about Jane's future.) In spite of intensive work it did not prove possible for the parents to give Jane adequate care.

A further case conference was held and plans were made for Jane to remain with her present foster mother, and for the local authority to apply for full care and control and permission to place Jane with a new foster family with a view to her being adopted.

At the final hearing the judge considered all the evidence, including the Official Solicitor's report recommending that Jane should be placed with a foster family with a view to adoption, and decided to grant the local authority's application.

WARDSHIP PROCEEDINGS

Wardship proceedings are chosen by a local authority so that a wider range of evidence about the child's situation can be taken into account. This is particularly important when the evidence is not clear cut, e.g. when a child's emotional development is being affected.

It is important that the court has all the relevant information regarding the child's past and present progress and circumstances to help it decide what order to make in the best interest o the child. Each person's evidence, including that of the parents, is set out in written form and sworn by that person in front of a solicitor. The document is called an affidavit and is shown to all parties to the proceedings as well as to the judge.

In the case history just described, when the local authority made Jane a Ward of Court, and she thus became under the protection of the Family Division of the High Court, the Court in effect became Jane's parent and everything to do with Jane, including where she lived, who looked after her, what treatment she received, was subject to the Court's discretion. Special permission had to be given to the court for anything not routine, e.g. for her to go on holiday abroad or for her to see a child psychiatrist or have medical treatment (except in an emergency).

The judge can award care and control to the local authority or to the parents. In addition a number of conditions can be specified in the order, such as any treatment a child should receive, or where the child should live. The order may also state how often parents may see a child, if the child is not living at home. If a child is returned home to the parents the judge may make a Supervision Order specifying that a social worker must visit the child regularly to supervise progress.

The local authority can return to court to ask for a Care Order to be changed to a Supervision Order (see page 227) if the child and family are progressing well, or for a child to be de-Warded if the parents are able to take full responsibility for their child.

ADOPTION

Adoption is an order of the court through which a child acquires a new permanent legal family.

PLACEMENT AND ASSESSMENT

Children are placed with people with a view to adoption before the court makes an adoption order. The decision as to the placement is extremely important. Generally all placements for adoption and arrangements for adoption must be made by an adoption agency. In addition local authorities place children with foster parents with a view to them being adopted. The adoption agencies, including local authorities, interview and assess the applicants who wish to adopt.

APPLYING TO THE COURT

To adopt a child, the person wishing to adopt must apply to the court for an order. Before granting an order, the court must be satisfied that:

(a) It is in the child's interest.
(b) The child has already lived with the adopters for some time.
(c) The child's birth parents agree unconditionally to the adoption, or their permission can be dispensed.

APPLICATION TO FREE A CHILD FOR ADOPTION

This is a separate application to the court which can be made by the adoption agency (which can be the local authority social services department) not by the future adopters. This preliminary hearing deals only with the matter of the consent of the natural parents. The natural parents are asked to consent to the general principle that their child should be adopted, rather than being asked to consent to adoption by a particular family. The court has to be satisfied that the child is already placed or about to be placed with an adoptive family. The court must also be satisfied that the natural parents either give their consent or that their consent can be dispensed with. This procedure can diminish the uncertainty about the future both for the child and for the future adoptive family. It also allows the adoption agency to act as a buffer and reduce the possibility of conflict between natural and adoptive parents. For example, when an attempt to return the child to the natural family has failed, the child is then placed with an adoptive family.

PLACEMENT OF A CHILD WITH SUBSTITUTE CARERS

A child can be placed with: foster parents or adoptive parents or 'custodian' parents.

Adoption

An adoption order is permanent and this is the major difference between placement in an adoptive family and placement in a foster family. Once an adoption order has been made, the child remains a member of the adoptive family for life. Adoptive parents have full parental rights and duties just as with a natural child, for example an adopted child will take the adoptive family's name and will be treated as a natural child in respect of inheritance.

There is legal provision for some children who are adopted to maintain contact with their natural family. This does not affect the adoptive parents' full parental rights.

In some instances a few local authorities, who have placed a child for adoption, pay an allowance to adoptive parents. This can be helpful, for example, when there would be financial hardship for the family if 'boarding out' payment stopped, but where it is important for a child's position in the family should be made permanent and secure through adoption.

Foster placement

In ideal circumstances a foster placement should be a three-way partnership between the child's natural parents, the local authority and the foster parents. Foster parents and their families are assessed by the fostering section of the Social Services Department. Foster placements can be categorized as long-term or short-term. Foster parents receive a 'boarding out allowance', i.e. payment from the local authority for food, clothing, etc. for the child. They have no parental rights in respect of children placed with them. These remain with the natural parents or with the Social Services Department. For example, if a child in voluntary care needs medical care, permission must be sought from the natural parents. If a care order has been made the Social Services Department must give permission and if the child is a ward of court then the High Court's permission must be given. Foster placements differ from adoptive placements because the care can be terminated by the Social Services Department. For example when children are able to return home to their natural parents, or when they reach the age of eighteen, or if the placement is not satisfactory, either from the child's or the foster family's point of view.

Custodianship

This is a new provision introduced at the end of 1985 which provides an alternative to adoption, through which long-term stability can be provided for a child without the finality of adoption.

Generally anyone but a parent may apply to the Court for an order appointing them as custodian, usually this is a relative. The child must have lived with the applicant for a certain time prior to the application.

The local authority must be notified of the application and provides information to the court.

If an order is made the 'custodian' has a duty to look after the child until they are eighteen. Basically all decisions about the child's upbringing are taken by the custodian although the birth parents' consent must be obtained for certain things such as change of name, so it is not as final as adoption.

ORDERS IN DIVORCE PROCEEDINGS

In divorce or matrimonial proceedings the court may be sufficiently concerned about the welfare of the children that it orders them to be committed to the care or supervision of a local authority. These procedures are illustrated in the following case history.

CASE HISTORY — DIVORCE

INTRODUCTION

The case study describes the legal processes involved when parents are getting divorced and are not able to agree over custody and access arrangements for their children.

Elaine Green is seven and her brother Michael is nine. Their parents finally separated a year ago, and Mr Green went to live in a flat five miles away.

Mr and Mrs Green had had many bitter rows in the past and after Mr Green left the family home, they continued to quarrel about the children. Mr Green wanted to see the children and take them out every weekend. Sometimes he would not come to collect the children as he arranged because he had to work. When he did come there was often a difficult scene with Elaine crying and Michael being very awkward and refusing to do what he was told.

Michael began to be difficult at other times. His teacher reported to Mrs Green that he was disobedient at school and getting into fights. He was also difficult for his mother to manage at home and would sometimes be aggressive to her, kicking out at her when he did not want to do as he was told.

Mrs Green wanted Mr Green to deal with Michael while Mr Green felt that she should deal with these difficulties. He also felt that she was trying to set both children against him by telling them he had walked out on them and that his work was more important to him.

Mrs Green applied to the Divorce Court through her solicitor to divorce Mr Green. The judge asked the Court Welfare Officer to see each of the parents and both children and to write a report to help the Court make a decision about which parent should have custody, about contact with the other parent and about how this should be arranged. The CWO reported on the children's wishes about where they wanted to live.

At the divorce hearing Mrs Green was given custody of both children and Mr Green was granted access every Sunday, and one week in each of the Christmas, Easter and Summer school holidays. Because of the entrenched difficulties between the parents the Court referred them to a family mediation service, where the parents could receive professional help in negotiating a

Table of court orders

Order	Length of time applies	Which court obtained in	How the order is brought to an end
Place of Safety Order	Up to 28 days — usually less. Number of days stated on the order	Juvenile court or in emergency a magistrate at home	Runs out automatically after stated time
Care Order	Indefinite — can be until child is eighteen years	Juvenile court after 'care proceedings'	Child, parents or local authority can apply to court
		High court after 'wardship proceedings'	Parents or local authority can apply to the court
		'Matrimonial (County) court after 'divorce proceedings'	Parents or local authority can apply to the court
Supervision Order	Court can specify one or two years or indefinite until child is eighteen years	(As with Care Order), juvenile court, high court, matrimonial court	Application can be made by child, parent or local authority
Adoption Order	For ever	County court or high court	
		'Divorce' court after divorce or proceedings	High court, county court or magistrates' court in divorce or matrimonial proceedings

workable arrangement for access. If they could not resolve the difficulties and obey the court order, the court might then make a supervision order whereby the local authority would supervise the access arrangements.

THE COURTS

The case summaries have shown that there are several courts which have the power to make orders regarding the care and control of children.

The Juvenile Court, which is a type of magistrates' court, deals with charges against children and with care proceedings, applications to uphold resolution and access applications by parents.

Magistrates' courts may also deal with custody and access of children in certain circumstances.

The Family Division of the High Court deals with all family matters in contested divorces and wardship and adoption proceedings.

The County Court deals with uncontested divorce and adoption applications.

LEGAL ASSISTANCE

The complexity of the law and the increased awareness of children's and parents' rights means that parents and children need to be legally advised and represented in court cases. Legal Aid is available to people who have limited income. However, because of restrictions on legal aid, specialist agencies such as the Family Rights Group, and the Children's Legal Centre, have grown up to offer advice, assistance and representation to families when required. In addition most law centres have specialists who offer similar assistance.

Recent cases of child abuse have increased the concern about the state of the law and the need for lawyers who specialize in child care law. The Law Society has now established a panel of such specialists. To become a member of the panel a solicitor must show relevant experience and/or training.

NEW DEVELOPMENTS IN THE LAW

As can be seen the law relating to children is complicated. There are numerous Acts of Parliament and regulations. Some law is 'case law' arising from decisions in previous cases. Not all the law is clear. In addition there are a number of different courts which deal with cases relating to children.

Because of the widespread concern about child care and the state of the law relating to children, many legal and child care professionals have lobbied for changes in the law.

The DHSS have recently produced reviews which make recommendations for changes to clarify the law. In addition the recommendation that family courts be introduced, made by the Finer Committee Report in 1974, has recently been discussed in a legal review, but remains at present only a suggestion.

FURTHER READING

L. Feldman (1984) *Care Proceedings* (3rd edn). Oyez Longman.
J.G. Hall and D.S. Martin (1987) *Child Abuse: Procedure and Evidence in Juvenile Courts* (2nd edn). Barry Rose Books.
M. Hayes and V. Bevin *Child Care Law — A Practitioner's Guide*. Family Law.
J.S. Josling and A. Levy (1985) *Adoption of Children*. Longman.
T.G. Moore and T.P. Wilkinson (1984) *A Guide to the Law and Practice*. Barry Rose Books.
N. Pierce (1986) *Wardship*. Fourmat Publishing.

AUTHOR INDEX

SUBJECT INDEX